SQL Server Hardware

By Glenn Berry

First published by Simple Talk Publishing 2011

Technical Review by Denny Cherry

Cover Image by Andy Martin

Edited by Tony Davis

Typeset & Designed by Matthew Tye & Gower Associates

Copy Edited by Gower Associates

Table of Contents

Appendix B: Installing a SQL Server 2008 R2 Cumulative Update 307

Appendix C: Abbreviations 319

About the Author

Glenn Berry is a Database Architect at Avalara in Denver, Colorado.
He is a SQL Server MVP, and he has a whole collection of Microsoft certifications, including MCITP, MCDBA, MCSE, MCSD, MCAD, and MCTS, which proves that he likes to take tests. His expertise includes DMVs, high availability, hardware selection, full text search, and SQL Azure. He is also an Adjunct Faculty member at University College – University of Denver, where has been teaching since 2000. He has completed the Master Teacher Program at Denver University – University College. He is the author of two chapters in the book, *SQL Server MVP Deep Dives*, and he blogs regularly at HTTP://SQLSERVERPERFORMANCE.WORDPRESS.COM. Glenn is active on Twitter, where his handle is **@GlennAlanBerry**.

I want to thank my editor, Tony Davis, for his tireless efforts to help make this a much better book than it otherwise would have been. My technical editor, Denny Cherry, did a great job of keeping me honest from a technology and knowledge perspective. Of course, any remaining mistakes or omissions are my responsibility.

I also want to thank my employer at the time of writing, NewsGator Technologies. My managers and co-workers were very supportive as I labored to complete this book. My good friend, Alex DeBoe gave me valuable feedback on the early drafts of each chapter, and helped motivate me to keep making progress on the book. My friends in the SQL Server community, who are too numerous to mention, gave me lots of encouragement to finish the book. Finally, I want to apologize to my two miniature dachshunds, Ruby and Roxy, who were ignored far too often over the past year as I worked on this book. I owe you lots of belly rubs!

About the Technical Reviewer

Denny Cherry has over a decade of experience managing SQL Server, including some of the largest deployments in the world. Denny's areas of technical expertise include system architecture, performance tuning, replication and troubleshooting. Denny currently holds several of the Microsoft Certifications related to SQL Server for versions 2000 through 2008 including the Microsoft Certified Master, as well as having been a Microsoft MVP for several years. He is a long-time member of PASS and has written numerous technical articles on SQL Server management and how SQL Server integrates with various other technologies for SearchSQLServer.com, as well as several books including *Securing SQL Server*. Denny blogs regularly at HTTP://ITKE.TECHTARGET.COM/SQL-SERVER, as well as at HTTP://SQLEXCURSIONS.COM where information about boutique training events can be found.

Introduction

At its heart, this is (yet) another book about SQL Server Performance, but with the following crucial difference: rather than focus on tweaking queries, adding indexes, and all the tuning and monitoring that is necessary once a SQL Server database is deployed, we start right at the very beginning, with the bare metal server hardware on which SQL Server is installed.

This book provides a detailed review of current and upcoming hardware, including processors, chipsets, memory, and storage subsystems, and offers advice on how to make the right choice for your system and your requirements. It then moves on to consider the performance implications of the various options and configurations for SQL Server, and the Operating System on which it is installed, covering such issues as:

- strengths and weaknesses of the various versions and editions of Windows Server, and their suitability for use with different versions and editions of SQL Server

- how to install, patch, and configure the operating system for use with SQL Server

- SQL Server editions and licenses

- installing and configuring SQL Server, including how to acquire and install Service Packs, Cumulative Updates, and hot-fixes

- methods for quickly and easily upgrading to newer versions of the operating system and SQL Server with minimal down-time.

In short, this book focuses on all of the things you need to consider and complete *before* you even design or create your first SQL Server database.

Who is this book for?

The primary audience for this book is the Database Administrator, assigned the task of the design and subsequent maintenance of the SQL Server systems that support the day-to-day business operations of their organization.

I've often been surprised by how little some DBAs seem to know about the hardware that underpins their SQL Server installations. In some cases, this is because the DBA has other interests and responsibilities, or is just not interested in low-level hardware details. In other cases, especially at larger companies, there are bureaucratic and organizational roadblocks that discourage many DBAs from being knowledgeable and involved in the selection, configuration, and maintenance of their database server hardware.

Many medium to large companies have separate departments that are responsible for hardware selection, configuration, and maintenance, and the DBA is often completely at their mercy, with no access or control over anything besides SQL Server itself. Conversely, in many smaller companies, the DBA's responsibilities extend beyond SQL Server, to the hardware and operating system, whether they like it or not. Some such DBAs may often find themselves overwhelmed, and wishing that they had a dedicated department to take care of the low-level details, so that they can concentrate on SQL Server.

If you're one of the DBAs who is responsible for everything, this book will help you be more self-sufficient, by giving you the fundamental knowledge and resources you need to make intelligent choices about the selection, configuration, and installation of hardware, the operating system, and SQL Server. If you're at a larger company, it will help put you in a better and stronger position to work effectively with other team members or departments in your organization in choosing the appropriate hardware for your system.

In either case, this book will help you ensure that your SQL Server instances can handle gracefully the CPU, memory, and I/O workload generated by your applications, and that the operating system and SQL Server itself are installed, patched, and configured for maximum performance and reliability.

How is the book structured?

Chapter 1 covers **hardware fundamentals** from a SQL Server perspective, focusing on processors, motherboards, chipsets, and memory. Once you know how to evaluate hardware for use with different types of SQL Server workloads, you will be in a much better position to choose the best hardware for your available budget.

Chapter 2 delves into the **storage subsystem**, including consideration of storage configuration (DAS or SAN), drive types (magnetic or solid-state), drive sizing, RAID configuration and more. Most high-volume SQL Server workloads ultimately run into I/O bottlenecks that can be very expensive to alleviate. Selecting, sizing, and configuring your storage subsystem properly will reduce the chances that you will suffer from I/O performance problems.

Chapter 3 provides a detailed examination of the **database and application bench-marking tools**, such as Geekbench and SQLIO, which will allow the DBA to verify that the system should perform adequately for the predicted workload. Never just hope for the best! The only way to know for sure is to test.

Chapter 4 covers a number of useful **hardware investigation** tools, including CPU-Z and Task Manager, which can identify precisely what kind of hardware is being used in an existing system, from the motherboard to the processor(s), to the memory and storage subsystem, and how that hardware is configured.

Chapter 5 is a deep dive into the different versions and editions of the **Windows Server Operating System**. Once you have acquired the hardware for your database server and racked it, someone needs to select, install, and configure the operating system. Starting at Windows Server 2003, this chapter discusses some of the strengths and weaknesses of the various versions and editions of Windows Server, and their suitability for use with different versions and editions of SQL Server. It covers how to install, patch, and configure the operating system for use with SQL Server. Again, depending on your organization and policies, you may be doing this yourself, or you may have to convince someone else to do something in a specific way for the benefit of SQL Server.

Chapter 6 is an exploration of the various **SQL Server versions and editions**. Once the operating system is installed, patched, and configured, someone needs to install, patch, and configure SQL Server itself. Before you can do this, you need to know how to choose the version and edition of SQL Server that is most appropriate for your business requirements and budget. Each new version of SQL Server has added new editions that have different capabilities, and make this choice more complicated. Do you need to use Enterprise Edition, or will a lower edition serve your business needs?

Chapter 7 will cover how to properly **install, patch, and configure SQL Server** for maximum performance, scalability, security and reliability. After you have acquired your SQL Server licenses, you are finally ready to install, patch, and configure SQL Server itself. Unfortunately, the setup programs for SQL Server 2005, 2008, and 2008 R2 do not always make the best default choices for this area. This chapter will demonstrate how to create slipstream installation media, and how to acquire and install Service Packs, Cumulative Updates, and hot-fixes. We will also discuss different methods for quickly and easily upgrading to newer versions of the operating system and SQL Server with minimal down-time.

Appendix A supplements *Chapter 1* and provides lower-level details on a range of recent Intel and AMD processors and chipsets.

Appendix B supplements *Chapter 7* and provides a full walk-through of the installation of a SQL Server 2008 R2 Cumulative Update.

Appendix C contains a list of many of the abbreviations and acronyms used in this book, with their definitions.

Code examples

Throughout this book are scripts demonstrating various ways to gather data concerning the configuration of your hardware, operating system, and SQL Server instances. All examples should run on all versions of SQL Server from SQL Server 2005 upwards, unless specified otherwise.

To download all code samples presented in this book, visit the following URL: WWW.SIMPLE-TALK.COM/RedGateBooks/GlennBerry/SQLServerHardware_Code.zip.

Other sources of hardware information

Enthusiast hardware review websites are extremely valuable resources in helping the DBA stay abreast of new and upcoming hardware and technology. It is not unusual for both Intel and AMD to introduce new CPUs and chipsets in the desktop and enthusiast space before they are rolled out to the server space. The better hardware review sites provide very deep and extensive background papers, reviews, and benchmarks of new products, often weeks or months before the server version is available. The two sites I frequent most regularly are:

- **AnandTech** (WWW.ANANDTECH.COM/) – a valuable hardware enthusiast website, started by Anand Lal Shimpi in 1997, and including coverage of desktop-oriented hardware. Over time, a specific section of AnandTech, called AnandTech IT (HTTP://WWW.ANANDTECH.COM/TAG/IT), has become an extremely useful resource for IT related reviews and benchmarks.

- **Tom's Hardware** (WWW.TOMSHARDWARE.COM) – a useful hardware review site that was started in 1996 by Dr. Thomas Pabst and is available in several different languages. Not quite as focused on server hardware as AnandTech IT.

In addition, there are several bloggers in the SQL Server community who regularly cover hardware-related topics:

- **Joe Chang** (HTTP://SQLBLOG.COM/BLOGS/JOE_CHANG/DEFAULT.ASPX) – a well-known SQL Server consultant who specializes in performance and hardware evaluation.

- **Linchi Shea** (HTTP://SQLBLOG.COM/BLOGS/LINCHI_SHEA/DEFAULT.ASPX) – a SQL Server MVP since 2002, Linchi writes frequently about server hardware, performance, and benchmarking.

- **Glenn Berry** (HTTP://SQLSERVERPERFORMANCE.WORDPRESS.COM) – yes, that's me! I write quite often about server hardware from a SQL Server perspective.

Chapter 1: Processors and Associated Hardware

Relational databases place heavy demands on their underlying hardware. Many databases are mission-critical resources for multiple applications, where performance bottlenecks are immediately noticeable and often very costly to the business. Despite this, many database administrators are not very knowledgeable about server hardware.

Part of the problem is that, when evaluating a processor for a SQL Server installation, the DBA faces an initially intimidating array of choices and considerations including, but not limited to:

- number of sockets
- processor CPU clock speed and cache size
- processor architecture, including number of cores, hyper-threading options
- choice of associated motherboard and chipsets
- choice of controllers, network interfaces, and so on.

In the face of such an overwhelming number of options, it's easy, and relatively common, for less experienced DBAs to make poor choices, and/or to hamstring a potentially powerful system by overlooking a crucial detail. I've had direct experience with expensive, high-performance database servers equipped with fast multi-core processors and abundant RAM that are performing very poorly because of insufficient disk I/O capacity to handle the requirements of a busy SQL Server workload. I have also seen many instances where a production database server with multiple, modern, multi-core processors was hobbled by only having 8 GB of RAM, thereby causing extreme memory and I/O pressure on the system and very poor performance.

This chapter will examine each of the critical aspects of evaluating and selecting a processor and associated hardware, for your database server. It will explain the options available in each case, offer advice regarding how to choose the most appropriate choice of processor and chipset for SQL Server, given the nature of the workload, and discuss other factors that will influence your choices.

SQL Server Workload Types

The type of workload that must be supported will have a huge impact on your choice of hardware, including processors, memory, and the disk I/O subsystem, as well as on sizing and configuration of that hardware. It will also affect your database design and indexing decisions, as well as your maintenance strategy.

There are two primary relational workload types that SQL Server commonly has to deal with, the first being Online Transaction Processing (OLTP) and the second being Decision Support System / Data Warehouse (DSS/DW). OLTP workloads are characterized by numerous short transactions, where the data is much more volatile than in a DSS/DW workload. There is usually much higher write activity in an OLTP workload than in a DSS workload and most OLTP systems generate more input/output (I/O) operations per second (IOPS) than an equivalent-sized DSS system.

A DSS or DW system usually has longer-running queries than a similar size OLTP system, with much higher read activity than write activity, and the data is usually more static. In such a system, it is much more important to be able to be able to process a large amount of data quickly, than it is to support a high number of I/O operations per second.

You really should try to determine what type of workload your server will be supporting, as soon as possible in the system design process. You should also strive to segregate OLTP and DSS/DW workloads onto different servers and I/O subsystems whenever you can. Of course, this is not always possible, as some workloads are mixed in nature, with characteristics of both types of workloads.

Throughout the process of selecting, sizing and configuring the various pieces of necessary hardware, we'll discuss, in each case, how the type of workload will affect your choices.

Evaluating Processors

The heart of any database server is the central processing unit (CPU). The CPU executes instructions and temporarily stores small amounts of data in its internal data caches. The CPU provides four basic services: **fetch**, **decode**, **execute**, and **store**. The CPU carries out each instruction of the executing program in sequence, performing the lowest level operations as quickly as possible.

Most people, when evaluating CPUs, focus on CPU capacity, i.e. the **rated clock speed**, measured in cycles/second (Gigahertz, GHz), and on **cache size**, in megabytes (MB). These are certainly important factors, but don't make the common mistake of *only* focusing on these properties when comparing the expected performance of processors from different manufacturers, or different processor families. Instead, you need to consider the overall architecture and technology used in the processors under comparison. As you become more familiar with how to identify and characterize a processor based on its model number (explained later in the chapter), so it will become easier to understand the architectural and performance differences between different models and generations of processors.

It is also very useful to consider standardized synthetic and application-level benchmark scores when evaluating processor performance. For example, you may want to estimate how much more CPU capacity a new six-core processor will offer compared to an old single-core processor. This will allow you to make a more realistic assessment of whether, for example, a proposed server consolidation effort is feasible. These techniques are discussed in much more detail in *Chapter 3*, but suffice to say here that, using them, I was recently able to successfully consolidate the workload from four older, (2007 vintage) four-socket database servers into a single, new two-socket server, saving about $90K in hardware costs and $350K in SQL Server license costs.

Cache size and the importance of the L2 and L3 caches

All server-class, Intel-compatible CPUs have multiple levels of cache. The Level 1 (**L1**) cache has the lowest latency (i.e. the shortest delays associated with accessing the data), but the least amount of storage space, while the Level 2 (**L2**) cache has higher latency, but is significantly larger than the L1 cache. Finally, the Level 3 (**L3**) cache has the highest latency, but is even larger than the L2 cache. In many cases, the L3 cache is shared among multiple processor cores. In older processors, the L3 cache was sometimes external to the processor itself, located on the motherboard.

Whenever a processor has to execute instructions or process data, it searches for the data that it needs to complete the request in the following order:

1. internal registers on the CPU

2. L1 cache (which could contain instructions or data)

3. L2 cache

4. L3 cache

5. main memory (RAM) on the server

6. any cache that may exist in the disk subsystem

7. actual disk subsystem.

The further the processor has to follow this data retrieval hierarchy, depicted in Figure 1.1, the longer it takes to satisfy the request, which is one reason why cache sizes on processors have gotten much larger in recent years.

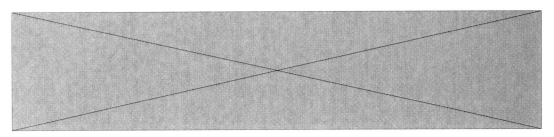

Figure 1.1: A typical data retrieval hierarchy.

For example, on a newer server using a 45 nm Intel Nehalem-EP processor, you might see an L1 cache latency of around 2 nanoseconds (ns), L2 cache latency of 4 ns, L3 cache latency of 6 ns, and main memory latency of 50 ns. When using traditional magnetic hard drives, going out to the disk subsystem will have an average latency measured in milliseconds. A flash-based storage product (like a Fusion-io card) would have an average latency of around 25 microseconds. A nanosecond is a billionth of a second; a microsecond is a millionth of a second, while a millisecond is a thousandth of a second. Hopefully, this makes it obvious why it is so important for system performance that the data is located as short a distance down the chain as possible.

The performance of SQL Server, like most other relational database engines, is hugely dependent on the size of the L2 and L3 caches. Most processor families will offer processor models with a range of different L2 and L3 cache sizes, with the cheaper processors having smaller caches and I advise you, where possible, to favor processors with larger L2 and L3 caches. Given the business importance of many SQL Server workloads, economizing on the L2 and L3 cache sizes is *not* usually a good choice.

If the hardware budget limit for your database server dictates some form of compromise, then I suggest you opt to economize on RAM in order to get the processor(s) you want. My experience as a DBA suggests that it's often easier to get approval for additional RAM at a later date, than it is to get approval to upgrade a processor. Most of the time, you will be "stuck" with the original processor(s) for the life of the database server, so it makes sense to get the one you need.

Clock speed

Gordon Moore, one of the founders of Intel, first articulated what is known as "Moore's Law" in 1965. Moore's Law states that microprocessor performance doubles roughly every 18–24 months. For the 20–30 years up until about 2003, both Intel and AMD were able to keep up with Moore's Law, with processor performance approximately doubling about every eighteen months. Both manufacturers increased microprocessor performance primarily by increasing the clock speed of the processor, so that single-threaded operations completed more quickly.

One problem encountered as clock speeds increase, however, is that the processor uses more electrical energy and dissipates more heat. Around 2003, both Intel and AMD began to run into reliability problems, as processor speeds approached 4GHz (with air cooling). In addition, each stick of memory in a server uses additional electrical power, and requires additional cooling capacity. Modern 1U servers support two CPU sockets, and often have 12 or 18 memory slots, so they can require a significant amount of electrical and cooling capacity.

The ever-increasing processor and memory density of 1U rack-mounted or blade servers meant that many datacenters began to have issues as they found that use of a large number of fully-populated racks often exceeded the power and cooling capacity of the datacenter. As a result, both manufacturers got to the point where they could not always allow customers to have fully-populated 42U racks of servers.

These factors, along with significant cost advantages due to the way in which SQL Server is licensed, have led to the increasing popularity of **multi-core processors** for server usage.

Multi-core processors and hyper-threading

The problems regarding excessive power consumption and heat generation at very high clock speeds has led to the continued and increasing popularity of **multi-core processors** which, along with multi-threaded applications, can break larger tasks into smaller slices that can be run in parallel. This means that the tasks complete quicker, and with lower maximum power consumption.

Sockets, cores, and SQL Server licensing

I recently followed a rather confused conversation on Twitter where someone stated that he tended to "use the terms, sockets and cores, interchangeably, since everyone else does." Back in prehistoric days (around 2001), you could probably get away with this, since all Intel and AMD processors had but a single core, and so one socket meant one physical processor and one physical core.

However, with the advent of multi-core processors and hyper-threading, it is simply incorrect to equate sockets to cores. The hierarchy works like this:

- **physical socket** – this is the slot on a motherboard where a physical processor fits

- **physical core** – in a multi-core processor, each physical processor unit contains multiple individual processing cores, enabling parallel processing of tasks

- **logical core** – with the hyper-threading technology, a physical core can be split into two logical cores (logical processors), again facilitating parallel execution of tasks.

In the days of single-core processors, if you wanted multiple threads of execution, your only option was to add physical sockets and processors. In 2002, however, Intel introduced the first processor with hyper-threading (covered in more detail shortly). Within each physical processor core, hyper-threading creates two logical processors that are visible to the operating system.

23

By splitting the workload across two logical cores, hyper-threading can improve performance by anywhere from 5–30%, depending on the application.

In 2005, AMD introduced the first dual-core processor, the Athlon 64 X2, which presented two discrete physical processor cores to the Windows operating system, and provided better multi-threaded performance than hyper-threading. In late 2006, Intel introduced the first Core2 Quad, which was a processor with four physical cores (but no hyper-threading). Since then, both AMD and Intel have been rapidly increasing the physical core counts of their processors. AMD has a processor called the Opteron 61xx, Magny Cours, which has 12 physical cores in a single physical processor. Intel has the Xeon 75xx, Nehalem-EX, which has eight physical cores, plus second-generation hyper-threading. This means that you have a total of 16 cores visible to Windows and SQL Server for each physical processor.

The critical point to bear in mind here is that, unlike for other database products, such as Oracle or DB2, SQL Server licensing (for "bare metal" servers) is only concerned with **physical processor sockets**, not physical cores, or logical cores. This means that the industry trend toward multiple core processors, with increasing numbers of cores, will continue to benefit SQL Server installations, since you will get more processing power without having to pay for additional processor licenses. Knowing this, you should always buy processors with as many cores as possible (regardless of your workload type) in order to maximize your CPU performance per processor license. For example, it would make sense, in most cases, to have one quad-core processor instead of two dual-core processors. Having additional processor cores helps increase your server workload capacity for OLTP workloads, while it increases both your workload capacity *and* performance for DSS/DW workloads.

Of course, there are some restrictions. Both SQL Server 2005 and SQL Server 2008 are limited to 64 logical processors. In order to use more, you must be running SQL Server 2008 R2 on top of Windows Server 2008 R2, which will raise your limit to 256 logical processors. SQL Server 2008 R2 Enterprise Edition has a license limit of eight physical processor sockets. If you need more than eight physical processors, you will need to run SQL Server 2008 R2 Datacenter Edition.

Nevertheless, within these restrictions, and given the rapid advancement in processor architecture, the sky is more or less the limit in terms of available processing power. In mid-2011, AMD will release the Bulldozer processor, which will have 16 physical cores per physical processor, while Intel has recently released the Xeon E7, Westmere-EX family, which has 10 physical cores, plus second-generation hyper-threading, which means that you will have a total of 20 logical cores visible to Windows per physical processor. So, with eight SQL Server 2008 R2 Enterprise Edition licenses, and eight Intel E7-8870 processors, you can get up to 160 logical processors!

As a result of such advancements in processor technology, it is becoming more and more common to utilize excess processing power to relieve the pressure on other parts of the system.

Making use of excess CPU capacity: data and backup compression

While processor power has increased rapidly, the performance of the main memory and the disk subsystem has not improved nearly as quickly, so there is now a very large disparity between processor performance and the performance of other components of the hardware system. As such, it is becoming increasingly common to use surplus CPU capacity to perform tasks such as data compression, backup compression, and log stream compression, in order to help relieve pressure on other parts of the system.

In particular, the idea of using excess processor capacity to compress and decompress data as it is written to, and read from, the disk subsystem, has become much more prevalent. SQL Server 2008 and 2008 R2 provide both **data compression** (Page or Row) as well as SQL Server native **backup compression**. In SQL Server 2008, these are all Enterprise Edition-only features. In SQL Server 2008 R2, backup compression is included in Standard Edition. SQL Server 2008 R2 also adds Unicode data compression for nvarchar and nchar data types, which makes data compression even more useful in many cases. A good example of this would be if you are using Unicode data types to store mostly Western European language characters, which Unicode data compression does an excellent job of compressing, often being able to reduce the required storage space by up to 50%. Data compression is explained in more detail in *Chapter 7*.

Both of these features can be very effective in reducing stress on your I/O subsystem, since data is compressed and decompressed by the CPU before it is written to, or read from, the disk subsystem. This reduces I/O activity and saves disk space, at the cost of extra CPU pressure. In many cases, you will see a significant net performance gain from this tradeoff from I/O to CPU, especially if you were previously I/O bound. SQL Server data compression can also reduce memory pressure, since the compressed data stays compressed in memory after it is read in off the disk subsystem, only being decompressed if the data is changed while it is in the buffer pool. Keep in mind that you need to be more selective about using data compression on individual indexes with OLTP workloads than you do with DSS/DW workloads. This is because the CPU cost of compressing and decompressing highly volatile data goes up quickly with more volatile tables and indexes in an OLTP system.

Another new feature in SQL Server 2008 is log stream compression for database mirroring, which is enabled by default. This feature uses the CPU to compress the log stream on the Principal instance before it is sent over the network to the Mirror instance. This can dramatically reduce the network bandwidth required for database mirroring, at the cost, again, of some extra CPU activity. Generally, this also gives better overall database mirroring performance.

Bearing the increasing importance of various forms of compression in mind, you may want to purposely overprovision your CPU capacity realizing that you may be devoting some of this extra capacity to compression activity. It is not unusual to see CPU utilization go up by 10–15% during a database backup that uses SQL Server native backup compression, while heavy use of data compression can also cause increased CPU utilization. Compared to the cost of additional I/O capacity and storage space, having the best available CPU and using its excess capacity for compression can be a very cost-effective solution.

Hyper-threading

Another processor feature to consider (or perhaps reconsider) is Intel hyper-threading. Hyper-threading (HT) is Intel's marketing term for its simultaneous multi-threading architecture where each physical processor core is split into two logical cores. Note that "simultaneous" doesn't mean that you can have two threads running simultaneously on two logical cores; the threads run alternately, one working while the other is idle.

Unlike physical cores, completely separate logical cores have to share some resources, such as the L2 cache, but they do offer a noticeable performance benefit under some circumstances, with some types of workloads.

Hyper-threading was originally implemented in 2002, as part of the NetBurst architecture in the Northwood-based Pentium 4 processors, and equivalent Xeon family. Intel had noticed that, quite often, the processor was waiting on data from main memory. Rather than waste processor cycles during this wait time, the idea was to have a second logical processor inside the physical core that could work on something different whenever the first logical processor was stalled waiting on data from main memory.

Many server and workstation applications lend themselves to parallel, multi-threaded execution. Intel hyper-threading technology enables simultaneous multi-threading within each processor core, up to two threads per core. Hyper-threading reduces computational latency, making better use of every clock cycle. For example, while one thread is waiting for a result or event, another thread is executing in that core, to maximize the work from each clock cycle. This idea works pretty well for desktop applications. The classic example is doing an anti-virus scan in the background, while in the foreground the user is working on a document in another application. One logical processor handles the virus scan, while the other logical processor handles the foreground activity. This allows the foreground application to remain more responsive to the user while the virus scan is in progress, which is a much better situation than with a single non-hyper-threaded processor.

Unfortunately, the initial implementation of hyper-threading on the Pentium 4 Netburst architecture did not work very well on many server workloads (such as SQL Server). The L2 data cache was shared between both logical processors, which caused performance issues as the L2 cache had to be constantly reloaded as application context switched between each logical processor. This behavior was commonly known as cache thrashing, which often led to an overall performance decrease for server applications such as Microsoft Exchange and Microsoft SQL Server.

As such, it was pretty common for database administrators to disable hyper-threading for all SQL Server workloads. However, the newer (second-generation) implementation of hyper-threading (as used in the Intel Nehalem or Westmere based Xeon 5500, 5600, 6500, and 7500 families) seems to work much better for many server workloads, and especially with OLTP workloads. It is also interesting that every TPC-E benchmark submission that I have seen on Nehalem-EP, Nehalem-EX, and Westmere-EP based platforms has had hyper-threading enabled.

My rule-of-thumb advice for the use of hyper-threading is to enable it for workloads with a high OLTP character, and disable it for OLAP/DW workloads. This may initially seem counter-intuitive, so let me explain in a little more detail. For an OLAP workload, query execution performance *will* generally benefit from allowing the query optimizer to "parallelize" individual queries. This is the process where it breaks down a query, spreads its execution across multiple CPUs and threads, and then re-assembles the result. For an ideal OLAP workload, it would be typical to leave the Max Degree of Parallelism (`MAXDOP`) setting at its default value of zero (unbounded), allowing the optimizer to spread the query execution across as many cores as are available (see the *Max degree of parallelism* section in *Chapter 7* for full details).

Unfortunately, it turns out that this only works well when you have a high number of true **physical cores** (such as those offered by some of the newer AMD Opteron 6100 series Magny Cours processors). Complex, long-running queries simply *do not* run as well on logical cores, so enabling HT tends to have a detrimental impact on performance.

In contrast, an OLTP workload is, or should be, characterized by a large number of short transactions, which the optimizer will not parallelize as there would be no performance benefit; in fact, for an ideal OLTP workload, it would be common to restrict any single query to using one processor core, by setting MAXDOP to 1. However, this doesn't mean that OLTP workloads won't benefit from HT! The performance of a typical, short OLTP query is not significantly affected by running on a logical core, as opposed to a physical core so, by enabling HT for an OLTP workload, we can benefit from "parallelization" in the sense that more cores are available to process more separate queries in a given time. This improves capacity and scalability, without negatively impacting the performance of individual queries.

Of course, no real workload is perfectly OLTP, or perfectly OLAP; the only way to know the impact of HT is to run some tests with your workload. Even if you are still using the older, first generation implementation of hyper-threading, it is a mistake to always disable it without first investigating its impact in your test environment, under your workload.

A final, important point to remember is that Windows and SQL Server cannot tell the difference between hyper-threaded logical processors and true dual-core or multi-core processors. One easy way to get some hardware information, including the number of logical cores, is via the T-SQL DMV query shown in Listing 1.1 (requires VIEW SERVER STATE permission). It returns the logical CPU count, which is the total number of CPUs visible to the operating system, the hyper-thread ratio (which can be a combination of actual multiple cores and hyper-threaded cores), the number of physical CPUs in the system and, finally, the amount of physical RAM installed in a system.

```
-- Hardware information from SQL Server 2005/2008/2008R2
-- (Cannot distinguish between HT and multi-core)
SELECT   cpu_count AS [Logical CPU Count] ,
         hyperthread_ratio AS [Hyperthread Ratio] ,
         cpu_count / hyperthread_ratio AS [Physical CPU Count] ,
         physical_memory_in_bytes / 1048576 AS [Physical Memory (MB)]
FROM     sys.dm_os_sys_info ;
```

Listing 1.1:   CPU configuration.

The `hyperthread_ratio` column treats both multi-core and hyper-threading the same (which they are, as far as the logical processor count goes), so it cannot tell the difference between a quad-core processor and a dual-core processor with hyper-threading enabled. In each case, these queries would report a `hyperthread_ratio` of 4.

Processor Makes and Models

In this section, we'll review details of recent, current, and upcoming processors from both Intel and AMD, with a focus on factors that are important for SQL Server workloads. These include the following items:

- specific model number
- manufacturing process technology
- rated clock speed
- number of cores and threads
- cache sizes and types
- supported instruction sets.

This will help you evaluate the processors in your existing database servers and it will help you when the time comes to buy a new database server. Additional reference information for each processor series can be found in *Appendix A*.

Since SQL Server only runs on the Microsoft Windows operating system, we only have to worry about Intel-compatible processors for this discussion. All modern Intel-compatible x86 and x64 processors are Complex Instruction Set Computer (CISC) processors, as opposed to Reduced Instruction Set Computer (RISC) processors. Intel also has the EPIC-based Itanium and Itanium2 IA64 processors, which are popular with some larger companies.

My overall philosophy is that, for each physical socket in a SQL Server database server, you should buy and use the very best individual processor. This is a somewhat different strategy from the one I use when it comes to normal laptop or workstation hardware selection but, to summarize what we've discussed to this point, my reasoning is outlined below.

- SQL Server is licensed by physical processor socket, so you *really* want to get as much performance and capacity as you can for each processor license that you purchase.

- The incremental cost of getting the top-of-the-line processor for each socket is quite small compared to the overall system cost (especially when you factor in SQL Server license costs).

- You can use excess processor performance and capacity to perform data compression or backup compression, which will relieve pressure on your storage subsystem at a lower cost than many other solutions.

- By selecting the best available processor, you may be able to run your workload on a two-socket machine instead of a four-socket machine. If you can do this, the savings in SQL Server license costs can more than pay for your hardware (for the server itself). The reduced SQL Server license costs would effectively make your two-socket server free, from a hardware-cost perspective.

Intel is currently pretty dominant in the server arena, both in terms of performance and market share. AMD is Intel's main competitor here, but they have been struggling to keep up with Intel in terms of performance since about 2007. However, AMD does offer processors that are very competitive from a cost perspective.

Intel Xeon processors

In the x86/x64 server space, Intel has various incarnations of the Xeon family. The first generation of the Xeon (which replaced the Pentium Pro), released back in 1998, was based on the Pentium II processor.

The main current branches of the family are:

- Xeon 3000 series – for single-socket motherboards

- Xeon 5000 series – for dual-socket motherboards

- Xeon 6000 series – for dual- or quad-socket motherboards

- Xeon 7000 series – for multi-socket motherboards.

The Intel Itanium family, discussed later in the chapter, uses the 9000 numerical sequence for its processor numbers.

It's much easier to understand some of the differences between the models if you know how to decode the model numbers, as shown in Figure 1.2, that Intel uses for their processors.

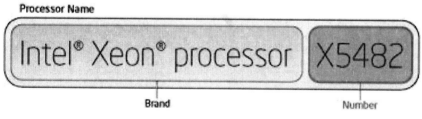

Figure 1.2: 2010 Intel Xeon Processor numbering.

Both Intel Xeon and Intel Itanium processor numbers are categorized in four-digit numerical sequences, and may have an alpha prefix to indicate electrical power usage and performance. The alpha prefixes are as follows:

- **Xxxxx** meaning Performance

- **Exxxx** meaning Mainstream

- **Lxxxx** meaning Power-Optimized.

So, for example, a Xeon X7460 is a high-end Performance processor for multi-processor systems, an Intel Xeon E5540 is a Mainstream dual-processor, while an Intel Xeon L5530 is a Power-Optimized dual-processor. The final three digits denote the generation and performance of the processor; for example, an X7460 processor would be newer and probably more capable than an X7350 processor. Higher numbers for the last three digits of the model number mean a newer generation in the family, i.e. 460 is a newer generation than 350, in this example.

Got all that? Good because, just to confuse everyone, Intel has now (as of April 2011) rolled out a new processor numbering scheme for its processors! All very recent or future processors with be identified by a **Product Line** (E3, E5, or E7), followed by a dash, then a four-digit numerical sequence, an optional alpha suffix (L, used only to denote low-power models) to denote the **Product Family**, and then a version number (v2, v3, and so on), as shown in Figure 1.3.

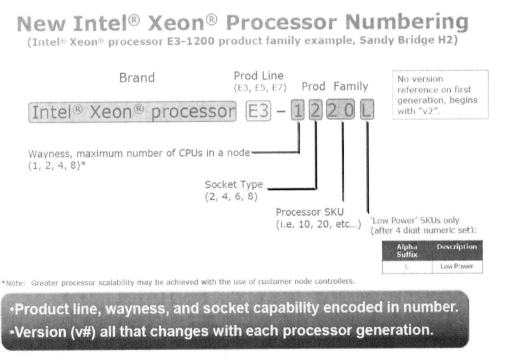

Figure 1.3:   2011 Intel Xeon Processor numbering.

The four-digit sequence describing the product family breaks down as follows. The first number after the dash denotes the CPU "wayness," which means the maximum number of CPUs allowed in a node (which is generally an entire machine). System vendors can combine multiple nodes with special interconnects to build a server with 16 or 32 processors, for example. The second number denotes the Socket Type of the CPU, which can be 2, 4, 6, or 8. This refers to the physical and electrical socket design into which the processor plugs. The third and further digits are the Processor Stock Keeping Unit (SKU). Higher numbers for the SKU mean higher-performance parts (so a 70 SKU would be a higher-performance model than a 20 SKU).

Finally, an "L" suffix, if present, will denote a Low-Power model (i.e. a model optimized to reduce electrical power usage). First-generation releases of a given processor will have no version number, but subsequent generations of the same processor will be denoted by v2, v3, and so on. Intel has already released the first E3- and E7- processors, while the E5- product line will be released later in 2011.

In my opinion, for SQL Server usage you should *always* choose the Performance models with the **X** model prefix (or higher SKU numbers, in the new naming system). The additional cost of an X series Xeon processor, compared to an E series, is minimal compared to the overall hardware and SQL Server license cost of a database server system.

You should also avoid the power-optimized L series, since they can reduce processor performance by 20–30% while only saving 20–30 watts of power per processor, which is pretty insignificant compared to the overall electrical power usage of a typical database server.

Disabling power management features

On mission-critical database servers, it is extremely important to disable power management features in the system BIOS or set it to OS Control. This is discussed in much more detail in Chapter 5.

Figures 1.4 and 1.5 display the CPU information for a couple of different processors, using the CPU-Z tool (see *Chapter 4* for more detail). Figure 1.4 shows the information for an Intel Xeon X5550 processor.

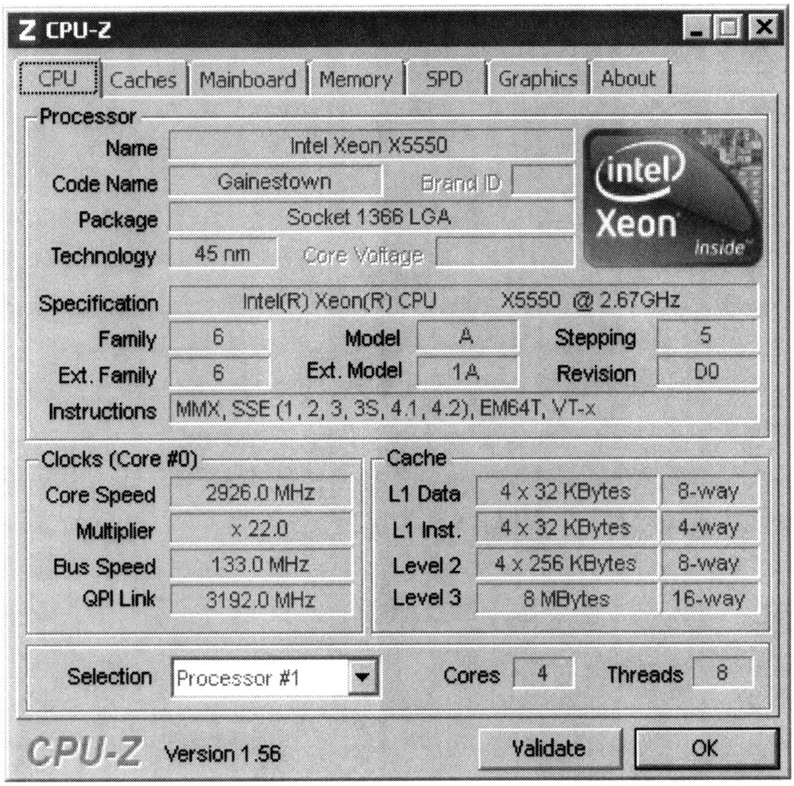

Figure 1.4:   Intel Xeon X5550 information displayed in CPU-Z.

The newer Xeon X5550 is a much more capable processor than the older Xeon E5440, shown in Figure 1.5. Even though the former runs at a slightly slower clock speed (2.67 GHz vs. 2.83 GHz), it uses a newer micro-architecture and has nearly double the performance of the E5440 on most processor and memory performance component benchmarks.

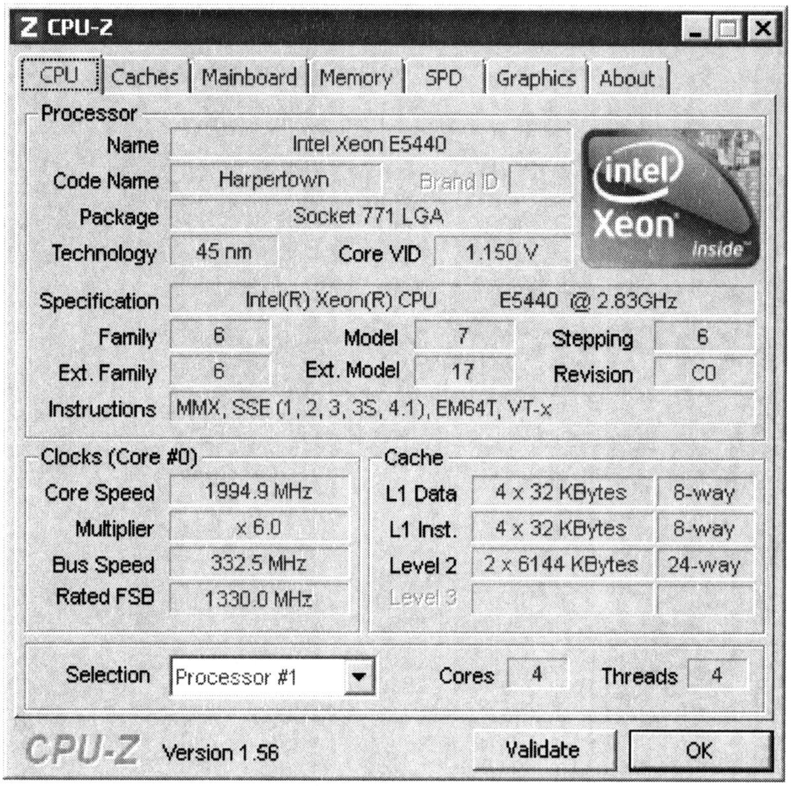

Figure 1.5:   Intel Xeon E5440 information displayed in CPU-Z.

Intel Tick-Tock release strategy

Since 2006, Intel has adopted a **Tick-Tock** strategy for developing and releasing new processor models. Every two years, they introduce a new processor family, incorporating a new microarchitecture; this is the **Tock** release. One year after the Tock release, they introduce a new processor family that uses the same microarchitecture as the previous year's Tock release, but using a smaller manufacturing process technology and usually incorporating other improvements such as larger cache sizes or improved memory controllers. This is the **Tick** release.

This Tick-Tock release strategy benefits the DBA in a number of ways. It offers better predictability regarding when major (Tock) and minor (Tick) releases will be available. This helps the DBA plan upgrades.

Tick releases are usually socket-compatible with the previous year's Tock release, which makes it easier for the system manufacturer to make the latest Tick release processor available in existing server models quickly, without completely redesigning the system. In most cases, only a BIOS update is required to allow an existing system to use a newer Tick release processor. This makes it easier for the DBA to maintain servers that are using the same model number (such as a Dell PowerEdge R710 server), since the server model will have a longer manufacturing lifespan.

As a DBA, you need to know where a particular processor falls in Intel's processor family tree if you want to be able to meaningfully compare the relative performance of two different processors. Historically, processor performance has nearly doubled with each new Tock release, while performance usually goes up by 20–25% with a Tick release.

Some of the recent Tick-Tock releases are shown in Figure 1.6.

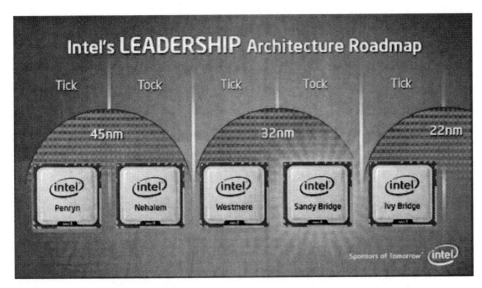

Figure 1.6:   Intel's Tick-Tock release strategy.

The manufacturing process technology refers to the size of the individual circuits and transistors on the chip. The Intel 4004 (released in 1971) series used a 10-micron process; the smallest feature on the processor was 10 millionths of a meter across. By contrast, the Intel Xeon Westmere 56xx series (released in 2010) uses a 32 nm process. For comparison, a nanometer is one billionth of a meter, so 10-microns would be 10,000 nanometers! This ever-shrinking manufacturing process is important for two main reasons:

- **increased performance and lower power usage** – even at the speed of light, distance matters, so having smaller components that are closer together on a processor means better performance and lower power usage

- **lower manufacturing costs** – since you can produce more processors from a standard silicon wafer; this helps make more powerful and more power-efficient processors available at a lower cost, which is beneficial to everyone, but especially to the database administrator.

The first Tock release was the Intel Core microarchitecture, which was introduced as the Woodcrest (for servers) in 2006, with a 65 nm process technology. This was followed up by a shrink to 45 nm process technology in the dual-core Wolfdale and quad-core Harpertown processors in late 2007, both of which were Tick releases.

The next Tock release was the Intel Nehalem microarchitecture, which used a 45 nm process technology, introduced in late 2008. In 2010, Intel released a Tick release, code-named Westmere, that shrank to 32 nm process technology in the server space. In 2011, the Sandy Bridge Tock release debuted with the E3-1200 series.

These Tick and Tock releases, plus planned releases, are summarized in Figure 1.7.

Type	Year	Process	Model Families	Code Name
Tock	2006	65nm	3000, 3200, 5100, 5300, 7300	Core 2 Woodcrest, Clovertown
Tick	2007	45nm	3100, 3300, 5200, 5400, 7400	Core 2 Wolfdale, Harpertown
Tock	2008	45nm	3400, 3500, 5500, 6500, 7500	Nehalem-EP, Nehalem-EX (2010)
Tick	2010	32nm	3600, 5600, E7-8800/4800	Westmere-EP, Westmere-EX (2011)
Tock	2011	32nm	E3-1200, E5, E8 ?	Sandy Bridge-EP, Sandy Bridge-EX
Tick	2012?	22nm		Ivy Bridge
Tock	2013?	22nm		Haswell

Figure 1.7:   Intel's Tick-Tock milestones.

Future Intel Xeon releases

The next Tick release after the Xeon 7500 series was the ten-core Xeon E7-8800/4800/2800 series, Westmere-EX, which has a process shrink to 32nm, a larger L3 cache, an improved memory controller, and other minor improvements. The Xeon E7-8800/4800/2800 Westmere-EX is a Tick release that became available in April 2011, which supports 32 GB DDR3 DIMMs, giving you the ability to have 2 TB of RAM in a four-socket server (if you have deep enough pockets).

The next Tock release after the Xeon 5600 series will be the eight-core, Xeon E5, Sandy Bridge-EP series, meant for two-socket servers. It is scheduled for production during the second half of 2011. It will also have hyper-threading, and an improved version of Turbo Boost that will be more aggressive about increasing the clock speed of additional cores in the physical processor based on the overall system temperature. This will help single-threaded application performance (such as OLTP database workloads).

The subsequent Ivy Bridge Tick release will be a 22 nm process technology die shrink of Sandy Bridge with some other minor improvements. A Tock release called Haswell is due sometime in 2013 and Intel is planning to get to 15 nm process technology by late 2013, 11 nm process technology by 2015, and 8 nm process technology by 2017.

Current recommended Intel Xeon processors

Complete details of the current Intel Xeon family can be found at HTTP://ARK.INTEL.COM/PRODUCTCOLLECTION.ASPX?FAMILYID=594, while *Appendix A* of this book provides further details of each of the processor series.

Generally, speaking any Intel processor based on the Nehalem microarchitecture and later, can be considered a modern processor and will give very competitive performance. Older models that relied on the SMP memory architecture and a shared front-side bus (see the *Memory Architecture* section, later in this chapter) offer considerably lower performance, as is borne out by TPC-E benchmark tests results (see *Chapter 3*).

My current recommendations for Intel processors are below.

One-socket server (OLTP)

Xeon E3-1280 (32 nm Sandy Bridge)

- 3.50 GHz, 8 MB L3 Cache, 5.0 GT/s Intel QPI

- Four cores, Turbo Boost 2.0 (3.90 GHz), hyper-threading

- Two memory channels.

One-socket server (DW/DSS)

Xeon W3690 (32 nm Westmere)

- 3.46 GHz, 12 MB L3 Cache, 6.40 GT/s Intel QPI
- Six cores, Turbo Boost (3.73 GHz), hyper-threading
- Three memory channels.

Two-socket server (OLTP)

Xeon X5690 (32 nm Westmere-EP)

- 3.46 GHz, 12 MB L3 Cache, 6.40 GT/s Intel QPI
- Six cores, Turbo Boost (3.73 GHz), hyper-threading
- Three memory channels.

Two-socket server (DW/DSS)

Xeon E7-2870 (32 nm Westmere-EX)

- 2.40 GHz, 30 MB L3 Cache, 6.40 GT/s Intel QPI
- Ten cores, Turbo Boost 2.0 (2.8 GHz), hyper-threading
- Four memory channels.

Four-socket server (any workload type)

Xeon E7-4870 (32 nm Westmere-EX)

- 2.40 GHz, 30 MB L3 Cache, 6.40 GT/s Intel QPI
- Ten-cores, Turbo Boost 2.0 (2.8 GHz), hyper-threading
- Four memory channels.

Eight-socket server (any workload type)

Xeon E7-8870 (32 nm Westmere-EX)

- 2.40 GHz, 30 MB L3 Cache, 6.40 GT/s Intel QPI
- Ten-cores, Turbo Boost 2.0 (2.8 GHz), hyper-threading
- Four memory channels.

Intel Itanium and Itanium 2

In the IA64 arena, Intel has the Itanium family. The Intel Itanium architecture is based on the Explicitly Parallel Instruction Computing (EPIC) model, which was specifically designed to enable very high Instruction Level Parallelism (ILP). The processor provides a wide and short pipeline (eight instructions wide and six instructions deep). The original Merced Itanium was released in 2001, but was quickly replaced by the first McKinley Itanium2 in 2002. The original Itanium used an 180 nm manufacturing process, and its performance was simply not competitive with contemporary x86 processors. Since then, subsequent Itanium2 processors have moved from a 180 nm process all the way to a 65 nm process, while clock speeds have gone from 900 MHz to 1.73 GHz, and L3 cache sizes have grown from 1.5 MB to 30 MB. Even so, the Itanium2 family remains a relatively specialized, low-volume part for Intel.

The Intel Xeon 9000 series is Intel's "big iron;" specialized high-end server processors, designed for maximum performance and scalability, for RISC replacement usage with 2- to 512-processor server motherboards. RISC is a rival processor technology to the more widespread CISC processor technology. RISC became popular with the SUN SPARC workstation line of computers.

I have heard one SQL Server hardware expert describe Itanium as a big semi-trailer truck compared to the Xeon, which is more like a Formula 1 race car, and certainly they are intended for use in cases where extremely high RAM and I/O capacity is required, along with the highest levels of Reliability, Availability and Serviceability (RAS). Itanium-based machines have many more expansion slots for RAID controllers or host bus adapters, and many more memory slots, which allow them to have the I/O capacity to handle the very largest SQL Server workloads.

Further details about the recent generations of the 9000 sequence are listed in *Appendix A*. Of future releases, the Intel Itanium Poulson will use the 32 nm manufacturing process and will have eight cores. It is scheduled for release in 2012. This will presumably be the Itanium 9400 series. The Intel Itanium Kittridge is the follow-on to the Poulson, due to be released in 2014. Intel has not yet released any specific details about Kittridge and, in light of the fact that Microsoft announced in April in 2010 that Windows Server 2008 R2, Visual Studio 2010, and SQL Server 2008 R2 will be the last releases of those products that will support the Itanium architecture, it remains to be seen whether Kittridge will actually be released.

Given that SQL Server Denali will not support the Itanium processor family, it makes it difficult to recommend the use of an Itanium processor for any new SQL Server installations. Mainstream support for Windows Server 2008 R2 for Itanium-based systems will end on July 9, 2013, while extended support will end on July 10, 2018.

AMD Opteron processors

In the x86/x64 space, AMD has various versions of the Opteron family. When assessing AMD processors, it is very helpful, once again, to understand what the model numbers mean. Recent AMD Opteron processors are identified by a four-digit model number in the format ZYXX, where Z indicates the product series:

- 1000 Series = 1-socket servers

- 2000 Series = up to 2-socket servers and workstations

- 4000 Series = up to 2-socket servers

- 6000 Series = high-performance 2 and 4-socket servers

- 8000 Series = up to 8-socket servers and workstations.

The Y digit differentiates products within a series. For example:

- Z2XX = dual-core

- Z3XX = quad-core

- Z4XX = six-core

- First-generation AMD Opteron 6000 series processors are denoted by 61XX.

The XX digits indicate a change in product features within the series (for example, in the 8200 series of dual-core processors, we have models 8214, 8216, 8218, and so on), and are not a measure of performance. It is also possible to have a two-digit product suffix after the XX model number, as below.

- No suffix – indicates a standard power AMD Opteron processor.

- SE – performance optimized, high-powered.

- HE – low power.

- EE – lowest power AMD Opteron processor.

For example, an Opteron 6176 SE would be a 6000 series, twelve-core, performance optimized processor; an Opteron 8439 SE would be an 8000 series, six-core, performance optimized processor, while an Opteron 2419 EE would be a 2000 series, six-core, energy efficient processor. For mission-critical database servers, I would recommend that you select the SE suffix processor, if it is available for your server model. The reason that it is not always available in every server model is due to its higher electrical power requirements.

Recent Opteron AMD releases, plus planned releases, are summarized in Figure 1.8. Since 2010, the Magny Cours processor has been AMD's best-performing model.

Year	Process	Model Families	Code Name
2006	90nm	1200, 2200, 8200	Santa Ana, Santa Rosa
2007-8	65nm	1300, 2300, 8300	Budapest, Barcelona
2009	45nm	1300, 2300, 2400, 8300, 8400	Suzuka, Shanghai, Istanbul
2010	45nm	4100, 6100	Lisbon, Magny Cours
2011	32nm	??	Interlagos, Valencia

Figure 1.8: AMD Opteron milestones.

Future Opteron AMD releases

In 2011, AMD will have the Interlagos and Valencia platforms, which will both use the next-generation Bulldozer-based processors. The Bulldozer will have technology similar to Intel hyper-threading, where integer operations will be able to run in separate logical cores, (from the operating system's perspective). The Interlagos will be a Socket G34 platform that will support 12- and 16-core 32 nm processors. The Valencia will be a Socket C32 platform that will use 6- and 8-core 32 nm processors. Interlagos and Valencia will first begin production in Q2 2011, and AMD is scheduled to launch them in Q3 2011. In each module, the two integer cores (used only for integer, as opposed to floating point, operations) will share a 2 MB L2 cache, and there will be an 8 MB L3 cache shared over the entire physical processor (16 MB on the 16-core Interlagos processor).

AMD is going to include AMD Turbo CORE technology in the Bulldozer processor. This Turbo CORE technology will boost clock speeds by up to 500 MHz, with all cores fully utilized. The current Intel implementation of Turbo Boost technology will increase the clock speed of a few cores, when the others are idle, but with the upcoming AMD Turbo CORE the processors will see full core boost, meaning an extra 500 MHz across all 16 threads for most workloads. This means that all 16 cores will be able to have their clock speed increased by 500 MHz for short periods of time, limited by the total power draw of the processor, not the ambient temperature of the system itself.

AMD has also announced greater memory throughput for the newly redesigned memory controller. AMD claims about a 50% increase in memory throughput with the new Bulldozer integrated memory controller. About 30% of that increase is from enhancements to the basic design of the memory controller, while the other 20% is from support of higher speed memory.

Current recommended AMD Opteron processors

Complete current details of the current AMD Opteron family can be found at WWW.AMD.COM/US/PRODUCTS/SERVER/PROCESSORS/PAGES/SERVER-PROCESSORS.ASPX, and *Appendix A* of this book provides further details of each of the processor series. However, my current recommendations are as follows.

One-socket or budget two-socket server

- Opteron 4184 (45 nm Lisbon), six cores

- 2.8 GHz, 6 MB L3 cache, 6.4 GT/s.

Two-socket server

- Opteron 6180 SE (45 nm Magny Cours), twelve cores

- 2.5 GHz, 12 MB L3 Cache, 6.4 GT/s.

Four-socket server

- Opteron 6180 SE (45 nm Magny Cours), twelve cores

- 2.5 GHz, 12 MB L3 Cache, 6.4 GT/s.

Server Motherboards: how to evaluate motherboards and chipsets

For any given processor, a server vendor may make available a number of different motherboards, and associated chipsets that support it. When you are evaluating and selecting a motherboard, you will want to consider such factors as:

- number of sockets

- supported chipsets, including number and type of expansion slots and reliability, availability, and serviceability (RAS) features

- memory requirements, including number of memory slots and supported memory architecture

- type and number of other integrated components, such as Network Interface Cards (NICs).

Number of sockets

Until recently, it was standard practice to choose a four-socket system for most database server applications, simply because two-socket systems usually did not have enough processor cores, memory sockets or expansion slots to support a normal database server workload.

This prescription has changed dramatically since late 2008. Prior to that time, a typical two-socket system was limited to 4–8 processor cores and 4–8 memory slots. Now, we see two-socket systems with up to 24 processor cores, and 18–24 memory slots.

The number and type of expansion slots has also improved in two-socket systems. Finally, with the widespread acceptance of 2.5" SAS (Serial Attached SCSI) drives (see *Chapter 2*), it is possible to have many more internal drives in a 1U or 2U system than you could have with 3.5" drives. All of these factors allow you to build a very powerful system, while only requiring two SQL Server processor licenses.

The technology of four-socket Intel systems (in terms of processors and chipsets) usually lags about one year behind two-socket server systems. For example, the processor technology available in the two-socket 45 nm Intel Xeon 5500 systems, launched in early 2009, was not available in four-socket systems until early 2010. By mid-2010, the latest two-socket Intel systems were based on 32 nm Intel Westmere-EP architecture processors and the latest 4-socket systems were still based on the older 45 nm Intel Nehalem-EX architecture processors. The 4-socket-capable 32 nm Intel Xeon E7-4800 Westmere-EX was not introduced until April 5, 2011.

Another factor to consider in this discussion is **hardware scaling**. You might assume that a 4-socket system will have twice as much overall load capacity or scalability as the equivalent 2-socket system, but this assumption would be incorrect. Depending on the exact processor and chipsets involved, rather than the theoretical maximum of 2.0 you typically see a hardware scaling factor of anywhere from 1.5 to 1.8 as you double the number of sockets.

This, taken with the fact that the latest 2-socket Intel processors use newer technology and have faster clock speeds than the latest 4-socket Intel processors, means that you may be better off with two 2-socket servers instead of one 4-socket server, depending on your overall workload and your application architecture. You will often see better single-threaded performance with a brand new 2-socket system compared to a brand new 4-socket system, especially with OLTP workloads. Single-threaded performance is especially relevant to OLTP workloads, where queries are usually relatively simple and low in average elapsed time, normally running on a single processor core.

In general, the latest 2-socket systems from both Intel and AMD are extremely capable, and should have more than enough capacity to handle all but the very largest database server workloads.

Server chipsets

When you are evaluating server models from a particular server vendor (such as a Dell PowerEdge R710), you should always find out which chipset is being used in that server. Intel processors are designed to use Intel chipsets. For each processor sequence (3000, 5000, 6000, 7000, or 9000), several different chipsets will be compatible with a given processor. Intel usually has at least two different chipsets available for any processor, with each chipset offering different levels of functionality and performance.

What you want to focus on as a SQL Server DBA are the number and types of expansion slots and the number of memory slots supported by the chipset. This affects how many RAID controllers or Host Bus Adapters you can install in a server, which ultimately limits your total available I/O capacity and performance.

Also important are RAS features. The goal is to have a system that is always available, never corrupts data and delivers consistent performance, while allowing maintenance during normal operation. Examples of RAS features include, for example, hot-swappable components for memory, processors, fans, and power supplies. You also want to see redundant components that eliminate common single points of failure, such as a power supply, RAID controller, or a network interface card (NIC).

Details of most recent and current Intel chipsets are available in *Appendix A*. Based on the above advice, I recommend you choose a server that uses either the Intel 3420, 5520, or 7500 series chipsets for one-, two-, and four-socket servers respectively.

BIOS

The Basic Input Output System (BIOS) software, built into the motherboard, contains the first code run by a server when it is turned on. It is used to identify and configure hardware components, and it is stored in upgradeable firmware. Your hardware system vendor (such as Dell, HP, or IBM) will periodically release updated BIOS firmware for your server model to correct problems that were identified and corrected after your server was initially manufactured. Other items in your server (such as your system backplane and RAID controllers) will also have upgradeable firmware that needs to be periodically updated. Upgradeable firmware is increasingly common in everyday consumer electronic devices such as Blu-ray players, AV Receivers, Smart Phones, and Kindle Readers.

Memory requirements

The basic rule of thumb for SQL Server is that you can never have too much RAM. Server RAM is relatively inexpensive, especially compared to SQL Server licenses, and having as much RAM as possible is extremely beneficial for SQL Server performance in many ways.

- It will help reduce read I/O pressure, since it increases the likelihood that SQL Server will find in the buffer pool any data requested by queries.

- It can reduce write I/O pressure, since it will enable SQL Server to reduce the frequency of checkpoint operations.

- It is cheap insurance against I/O sizing miscalculations or spikes in your I/O workload.

In order to take the best advantage of your available RAM, you should make sure that you are running a 64-bit version of SQL Server, which requires a 64-bit version of Windows Server (Windows Server 2008 R2 is only available in a 64-bit version). This will allow SQL Server to fully utilize all installed RAM, rather than being restricted to 2 GB (out of the 4 GB of virtual address space to which each 32-bit process has access). To be clear, 32-bit SQL Server is limited to using 2 GB of RAM, unless you use the **/PAE** and/or the **/3GB** switches (see *Chapter 5* for full details).

However, keep in mind that SQL Server 2008 R2 Standard Edition has a memory limit of 64 GB, so there is little point in buying more memory than that if you will be using that edition.

Memory types

Any relatively new database servers should be using DIMMs (Dual In-line Memory Modules) with one of the modern DRAM (Dynamic Random Access Memory) implementations, specifically either DDR2 SDRAM or DDR3 SDRAM memory.

DDR2 SDRAM is a double-data-rate, synchronous, dynamic, random access memory interface. It replaces the original DDR SDRAM specification (and the two are not compatible) and offers higher bus speed with lower power consumption.

DDR3 SDRAM is a double-data-rate *type three*, synchronous, dynamic, random access, memory interface. It supersedes DDR2, offers more bandwidth and is required by most of the latest processors.

ECC, or registered, memory (RDIMM) is required by most server chipsets. It is pretty likely that you will need DDR3 ECC SDRAM for nearly any new server that you buy in 2010/2011.

DIMMS can contain multiple ranks, where a rank is "two or more independent sets of DRAM chips connected to the same address and data buses." Memory performance can vary considerably, depending on exactly how the memory is configured in terms of the number of memory modules and the number of ranks per module (single-rank, dual-rank, and so on). This is discussed in more detail in *Chapter 3*, on benchmarking.

An older memory type that you may run into with some older servers is Fully Buffered Dual In-line Memory Modules (FB-DIMM), which is memory that uses an Advanced Memory Buffer (AMB) between the memory controller and the memory module. Unlike the parallel bus architecture of traditional DRAM, an FB-DIMM has a serial interface between the memory controller and the AMB. Compared to conventional, registered DIMMs, the AMB dissipates extra heat and requires extra power. FB-DIMMs are also more expensive than conventional DIMMs, and they have not been widely adopted in the industry.

Memory slots

One very important consideration with regard to the server motherboard and its suitability for use in a SQL Server installation, is the **total number of memory slots**. This, along with the limitations of the memory controller in the chipset or the CPU itself, ultimately determines how much RAM you can install in a database server. Obviously, the more slots the better. For example, many server vendors currently offer 1U, two-socket servers that have a total of twelve memory slots, while they also offer nearly identical 2U servers that have a total of eighteen memory slots. In most cases, I would prefer the server that had eighteen memory slots, since that would allow me to ultimately have more memory in the database server. This assumes that the memory controller (whether in the chipset or the integrated memory controller in the processor) will support enough memory to fill all of those available memory slots.

A related consideration is **memory density**, by which I mean the memory capacity of each memory stick. One tactic that hardware vendors used quite often with standard configurations in the past was to fill all of the available memory slots with relatively low capacity sticks of memory. This is less expensive initially, but leads to additional cost and waste when it is time to add additional RAM to the server, since you will have a number of smaller capacity DIMMs that must be replaced, and which you may have no use for after the upgrade. You can avoid this situation by specifying larger memory stick sizes when you pick the server components.

Be careful to choose the most cost-effective size; at the time of writing (April 2011), 8 GB sticks of RAM represented the sweet spot in the Price-Performance curve, because of the prohibitive cost of 16 GB sticks of RAM. Violating this sweet spot rule might cause you to spend far more on memory for the server than the rest of the server combined. However, once 32 GB sticks of RAM are available in 2011, the price-performance sweet spot will shift pretty quickly towards 16 GB sticks of RAM.

Many older processors and chipsets will not be able to use that capacity offered by the forthcoming 32 GB sticks. One known exception will be the 32 nm Intel E7 (Westmere-EX) processor series that is meant for use in 4-socket, or larger, systems. This opens up the possibility, sometime in 2011, of a 4-socket system with 4 processors x 16 DIMMS per processor x 32 GB per DIMM = 2 TB of RAM. You'll have to have very deep pockets though; 32 GB SDRAM DIMMs will be very, very expensive when they are first available.

Memory architecture: SMP versus NUMA

Another important consideration, when evaluating a server motherboard, is whether it uses Symmetric Multiprocessing (SMP) or Non-Uniform Memory Architecture (NUMA).

SMP refers to a multiprocessor computer hardware architecture where two or more identical processors are connected to a single shared main memory, and are controlled by a single operating system. Many earlier Intel multiprocessor systems use SMP architecture. In the case of multi-core processors, the SMP architecture applies to the logical cores, treating them as separate processors.

The bottleneck in SMP scalability is the bandwidth of the front-side bus, connecting the various processors with the memory and the disk arrays; as the speed and number of processors increase, the competition between CPUs for access to memory creates bus contention and limits the ability of a system to scale. Consequently, system throughput does not grow linearly with the number of processors; for example, doubling the number of processors in an SMP computer does not double its performance or capacity. This makes it harder to design high-performance SMP-based systems with more than four processor sockets. All Intel x64 processors that were released before the Nehalem family use SMP architecture, since they rely on a front-side bus.

A newer alternative, especially useful for systems with more than four processor sockets, is NUMA, which dedicates different memory banks, called NUMA nodes, to different processors. Nodes are connected to each other via an external bus that transports cross-node data traffic. In NUMA, processors may access local memory quickly but remote memory access is much more expensive and slower. NUMA can dramatically improve memory throughput, as long as the data is localized to specific processes.

The NUMA node arrangement addresses the front-side bus contention and, therefore, scalability issue by limiting the number of CPUs competing for access to memory; processors will access memory within their own node faster than the memory of other NUMA nodes. You can get much closer to linear scaling with NUMA architecture.

Having NUMA architecture is more important with systems that have four or more processor sockets, and not as important with two-socket systems.

AMD server systems have supported NUMA architecture for several years, while Intel server systems have only supported NUMA since the introduction of the Nehalem micro-architecture (Xeon 5500) in 2008. One new development for SQL Server 2008 R2 is the concept of NUMA Groups, which are logical collections of up to 64 logical processors. This makes it easier to make NUMA configuration changes for SQL Server.

Network Interface Cards

A Gigabit Ethernet NIC is seldom the bottleneck with most OLTP work-loads. A common exception is if you are doing backups over the network, and the destination for the backup files has lots of I/O capacity. In this situation, you may be able to completely saturate a single Gigabit Ethernet NIC. Most recent-vintage server motherboards have at least two, and sometimes four, Gigabit Ethernet NICs embedded on the motherboard. This allows you to combine your available NICs using NIC Teaming, or to segregate your network traffic using multiple IP addresses for your various NICs.

Fast Ethernet was introduced in 1995, and has a nominal bandwidth of 100 Mb/sec. Any database server that has Fast Ethernet NICs embedded on the motherboard will be quite ancient, (at least 8–10 years old), and I would really not recommend you use it if you have any other option available. You should also make sure that you don't have any Fast Ethernet switches that are used by your database servers, since they will restrict your bandwidth to that level. Gigabit Ethernet (which is rated at 1 Gb/sec) has completely replaced Fast Ethernet in servers (and workstations) built in the last four to five years. 10-Gigabit Ethernet, although still quite expensive, is starting to be used more often in mission-critical servers. It is rated at 10 Gb/sec, and is especially useful for iSCSI SAN applications (see the *Storage Area Networks (SAN)* section of *Chapter 2* for more details). The next standard on the horizon is 40 Gb/sec.

Choosing a Processor and Motherboard for Use with SQL Server

As discussed previously, I'm a strong proponent of getting the very best processor that your budget will allow, over-provisioning if possible, and using spare CPU capacity (and memory) to remove load from the disk I/O sub-system. High-performance CPUs are much more affordable than additional I/O capacity, so it makes financial sense to get the best CPU available for a given server model.

When provisioning CPU, remember that your server not only has to cope smoothly with your normal workload, but also deal with inevitable spikes in CPU usage, for example, during:

- performing database backups

- index rebuilds and reorganization; the actual process of rebuilding or reorganizing an index is CPU-intensive

- periods of concurrent, CPU-intensive queries, especially Full Text Search queries.

Layered on top of my general advice to get the best-in-class processor, with as many cores as possible, in order to maximize CPU capacity per SQL Server license, comes consideration of the nature of the workload.

OLTP workloads, characterized by a high number of short-duration transactions, tend to benefit least from parallelization. If I knew that I was going to have a primarily OLTP workload, I would lean very heavily towards getting a two-socket system that used Intel Xeon X5690 Westmere-EP six-core processors, because of their excellent single-threaded performance. The Intel Xeon X5690 currently has the absolute best single-threaded performance of any server-class processor. Once the upcoming Intel Sandy Bridge-EP processors become available, later in 2011, they should have even better single-threaded performance than the Xeon X5690.

Of course, this assumes that the two-socket system that you choose has enough memory capacity and expansion slot capacity to support your entire OLTP workload. The number of expansion slots ultimately limits how many RAID controllers or Host Bus Adaptors (HBAs) you can use in a system (see *Chapter 2*). If you are convinced that a single two-socket system cannot handle your workload, my advice would be to partition, or shard, the workload in such a way that you could use multiple two-socket systems.

There are several benefits to this strategy. Firstly, even if you could use identical Intel processors in two-socket and four-socket systems (which you cannot do right now, since Intel uses different processors for two- and four-socket systems), CPU performance and load capacity do not scale at 100% when you move from two sockets to four sockets. In other words, a four-socket system does not have twice as much CPU capacity as a two-socket system. Secondly, two-socket Intel systems are usually one release ahead of their four-socket counterparts. The current example is the 32 nm 3.46 GHz Intel Xeon X5690 for two-socket systems vs. the 45 nm 2.26 GHz Xeon X7560 for four-socket (and above) systems. The Xeon X5690 is much faster than the Xeon X7560 for single-threaded OLTP performance. Finally, going through the architectural and engineering work required to partition or shard your database is a good long-term strategy, since it will allow you to scale out at the database level, whether it is with on-premises SQL Server or with SQL Azure.

Another factor to consider is the number of Intel-based systems that have been submitted and approved for the TPC-E OLTP benchmark, compared to how few AMD-based systems have been submitted and accepted (see *Chapter 3* for further details on benchmarking). As of January 2011, there are 37 Intel-based TPC-E results compared to four AMD-based TPC-E results. I don't think this is an accident. Lest you think I am simply an Intel cheerleader, I am actually rooting for AMD to become more competitive for OLTP workloads with the upcoming Bulldozer family of CPUs. If AMD cannot compete with Intel for raw performance, I am afraid that Intel will get lazy and slow down their pace of innovation, which is bad for the DBA community.

By contrast, if I were managing a primarily DSS/DW workload, characterized by large, long-running queries, I would tend to favor using the AMD Opteron 6180 SE Magny

Cours 12-core processors, or the AMD Bulldozer processors (when they are available later in 2011) because they have high core counts and they tend to perform quite well with multi-threaded applications.

If you use a modern Intel processor (such as a Xeon X5690 or Xeon X7560) with a DSS/DW workload, you should strongly consider disabling hyper-threading, since long-running queries often do not perform as well on hyper-threaded cores in a processor.

Summary

In this chapter, we have discussed some of the basics of processors and related hardware, from a database server perspective.

The latest processors – Nehalem and later from Intel, and Magny Cours and later from AMD – will allow you to run many SQL Server workloads on a much less expensive two-socket database server instead of a more traditional four-socket database server. This can save you an enormous amount of money in both hardware costs and SQL Server license costs. I strongly advocate getting the best available processor for a given server model, since the price delta compared to a less expensive processor is quite small compared to the overall hardware cost (not to mention the SQL Server license costs). Having extra processor capacity will allow you to use SQL Server features like backup compression and data compression, which can dramatically reduce I/O pressure, usually at a much lower cost than adding I/O capacity.

Maximizing the amount of installed RAM in a database server is another relatively inexpensive tactic to reduce pressure on your I/O subsystem and improve overall database performance. You need to make sure that you select the size of individual sticks of RAM that gives you the best price/performance ratio in order to make sure you don't spend an inordinate amount of money on RAM.

Ultimately, having appropriate and modern hardware can save you lots of money in SQL Server licensing costs, and can help you avoid future performance and scalability issues with your database servers. As you begin to understand some of the differences between different types of hardware, and how to evaluate hardware for use with different types of SQL Server workloads, you will be in a much better position to actually select appropriate hardware for SQL Server yourself, or to make an intelligent argument for proper hardware with another part of your organization. In the next chapter, we move on to discuss the storage subsystem, the correct provisioning of which is also critical for SQL Server performance.

Chapter 2: The Storage Subsystem

There are many factors to consider when choosing an appropriate processor and associated chipsets, and there are just as many considerations when sizing and configuring the storage subsystem. It is very easy to hamstring an otherwise powerful system with poor storage choices. Important factors discussed in this chapter include:

- disk seek time and rotational latency limitations
- type of disk drive used:
  - traditional magnetic drive – SATA, SCSI, SAS, and so on
  - solid-state drives (SSDs)
- storage array type: Storage Area Network (SAN) vs. Direct Attached Storage (DAS)
- redundant Array of Independent disk (RAID) configuration of your disks.

Having reviewed each component of the disk subsystem, we'll discuss how the size and nature of the workload will influence the way in which the subsystem is provisioned and configured.

Disk I/O

RAM capacity has increased constantly over the years and its cost has decreased enough to allow us to be lavish in its use for SQL Server, to help minimize disk I/O. Also, CPU speed has increased to the point where many systems have substantial spare capacity that can often be used to implement data compression and backup compression, again, to help reduce I/O pressure. The common factor here is helping to reduce disk I/O. While disk capacity has improved greatly, disk speed has not, and this poses a serious problem; most large, busy OLTP systems end up running into I/O bottlenecks.

The main factor limiting how quickly data is returned from a single traditional magnetic disk is the overall disk latency, which breaks down into **seek time** and **rotational latency**.

- **Seek time** is the time it takes the head to physically move across the disk to find the data. This will be a limiting factor in the number of I/O operations a single disk can perform per second (IOPS) that your system can support.

- **Rotational latency** is the time it takes for the disk to spin to read the data off the disk. This is a limiting factor in the amount of data a single disk can read per second (usually measured in MB/s), in other words the I/O throughput of that disk.

Typically, you will have multiple magnetic disks working together in some level of RAID to increase both performance and redundancy. Having more disk spindles (i.e. more physical disks) in a RAID array increases both throughput performance and IOPS performance.

However, a complicating factor here is the performance limitations of your RAID controllers, for direct attached storage, or Host Bus Adaptors (HBAs), for a storage area network. The throughput of such controllers, usually measured in gigabits per second, e.g. 3 Gbps, will dictate the upper limit for how much data can be written to or read from a disk per second. This can have a huge effect on your overall IOPS and disk throughput capacity for each logical drive that is presented to your host server in Windows.

The relative importance of each of these factors depends on the type of workload being supported; OLTP or DSS/DW. This, in turn, will determine how you provision the disk storage subsystem.

As discussed in *Chapter 1*, OLTP workloads are characterized by a high number of short transactions, where the data tends to be rather volatile (modified frequently). There is usually much higher write activity in an OLTP workload than in a DSS workload. As such, most OLTP systems generate more IOPS than an equivalent-sized DSS system.

Furthermore, in most OLTP databases, the read/write activity is largely random, meaning that each transaction will likely require data from a different part of the disk. All of this means that, in most OLTP applications, the hard disks will spend most of their time seeking data, and so the **seek time** of the disk is a crucial bottleneck for an OLTP workload. The seek time for any given disk is determined by how far away from the required data the disk heads are at the time of the read/write request.

A DSS or DW system is usually characterized by longer-running queries than a similar size OLTP system. The data in a DSS system is usually more static, with much higher read activity than write activity. The disk activity with a DSS workload also tends to be more sequential and less random than with an OLTP workload. Therefore, for a DSS type of workload, sequential I/O throughput is usually more important than IOPS performance. Adding more disks will increase your sequential throughput until you run into the throughput limitations of your RAID controller or HBA. This is especially true when a DSS/DW system is being loaded with data, and when certain types of complex, long-running queries are executed.

Generally speaking, while OLTP systems are characterized by lots of fast disks, to maximize IOPS to overcome disk latency issues with high numbers of random reads and writes, DW/DSS systems require lots of I/O channels, in order to handle peak sequential throughput demands. An I/O channel is an individual RAID controller or an individual HBA; either of these gives you a dedicated, separate path to either a DAS array or a SAN. The more I/O channels you have, the better.

With all of this general advice in mind, let's now consider each of the major hardware and architectural choices that must be made when provisioning the storage subsystem, including the type of disks used, the type of storage array, and the RAID configuration of the disks that make up the array.

Drive Types

Database servers have traditionally used magnetic hard drive storage. Seek times for traditional magnetic hard disks have not improved appreciably in recent years, and are unlikely to improve much in the future, since they are electro-mechanical in nature. Typical seek times for modern hard drives are in the 5–10 ms range.

The rotational latency for magnetic hard disks is directly related to the rotation speed of the drive. The current upper limit for rotational speed is 15,000 rpm, and this limit has not changed in many years. Typical rotational latency times for 15,000 rpm drives are in the 3–4 ms range.

This disk latency limitation led to the proliferation of vast SAN-based (or DAS-based) storage arrays, allowing data to be striped across numerous magnetic disks, and leading to greatly enhanced I/O throughput. However, in trying to fix the latency problem, SANs have become costly, complex, and sometimes fault-prone. These SANs are generally shared by many databases, which adds even more complexity and often results in a disappointing performance, for the cost.

Newer solid-state storage technology has the potential to displace traditional magnetic drives and even SANs altogether, and allow for much simpler storage systems. The seek times for SSDs and other flash-based storage are much, much lower than for traditional magnetic hard disks, since there are no electro-mechanical moving parts to wait on. With an SSD, there is no delay for an electro-mechanical drive head to move to the correct portion of the disk to start reading or writing data. With an SSD, there is no delay waiting for the spinning disk to rotate past the drive head to start reading or writing data, and the latency involved in reading data off an SSD is much lower than it is for magnetic drives, especially for random reads and writes. SSD drives also have the additional advantage of lower electrical power usage, especially compared to large numbers of traditional magnetic hard drives.

Magnetic disk drives

Disks are categorized according to the type of interface they use. Two of the oldest types of interface, which you still occasionally see in older workstations, are Integrated Drive Electronics (IDE) or Parallel Advanced Technology Attachment (PATA) drives. Of course, it is not unusual for old, "retired" workstations, with PATA disk controllers, to be pressed into service as development or test database servers. However, I want to stress that you should *not* be using PATA drives for any serious database server use.

PATA and IDE drives are limited to two drives per controller, one of which is the Master and the other is the Slave. The individual drive needed to have a Jumper Setting to designate whether the drive was acting as a Master or a Slave drive. PATA 133 was limited to a transfer speed of 133 MB/sec, although virtually no PATA drives could sustain that level of throughput.

Starting in 2003, Serial Advanced Technology Attachment (SATA) drives began replacing PATA drives in workstations and entry-level servers. They offer throughput capacities of 1.5, 3, or 6 Gbps (also commonly known as SATA 1.0, SATA 2.0, and SATA 3.0), along with hot-swap capability. Most magnetic SATA drives have a 7,200 rpm rotational speed, although a few can reach 10,000 rpm. Magnetic SATA drives are often used for low-cost backup purposes in servers, since their performance and reliability typically do not match that of enterprise-level SAS drives.

Both traditional magnetic drives and newer SSDs can use the SATA interface. With an SSD, it is much more important to make sure you are using a 6 Gbps SATA port, since the latest generation SSDs can completely saturate an older 3 Gbps SATA port.

External SATA (eSATA) drives are also available. They require a special eSATA port, along with an eSATA interface to the drive itself. An eSATA external drive will have much better data transfer throughput than the more common external drives that use the much slower USB 2.0 interface. The new USB 3.0 interface is actually faster than eSATA, but your throughput will be limited by the throughput limit of the external drive itself, not the interface.

Small Computer System Interface (SCSI) drives have been popular in server applications since the mid 1980s. SCSI drives were much more expensive than PATA drives, but offered better performance and reliability. The original parallel SCSI interface is now being rapidly replaced by the newer Serial Attached SCSI (SAS) interface. Most enterprise-level database servers will use either parallel SCSI or SAS internal drives, depending on their age. Any new or recent-vintage database server will probably have SAS internal drives instead of SCSI internal drives.

Server-class magnetic hard drives have rotation speeds ranging from 7,200 rpm (for SATA) to either 10,000 rpm or 15,000 rpm (for SCSI and SAS). Higher rotation speeds reduce data access time by reducing the rotational latency. Drives with higher rotation speed are more expensive, and often have lower capacity sizes compared to slower rotation speed drives. Over the last several years, disk buffer cache sizes have grown from 2 MB all the way to 64 MB. Larger disk buffers usually improve the performance of individual magnetic hard drives, but often are not as important when the drive is used by a RAID array or is part of a SAN, since the RAID controller or SAN will have its own, much larger, cache that is used to cache data from multiple drives in the array.

Solid-state drives

Solid-State Drives (SSD), or Enterprise Flash Disks (EFD), are different from traditional magnetic drives in that they have no spinning platter, drive actuator, or any other moving parts. Instead, they use flash memory, along with a storage processor, controller, and some cache memory, to store information.

The lack of moving parts eliminates the rotational latency and seek-time delay that is inherent in a traditional magnetic hard drive. Depending on the type of flash memory, and the technology and implementation of the controller, SSDs can offer dramatically better performance compared to even the fastest enterprise-class magnetic hard drives. This performance does come at a much higher cost per gigabyte, and it is still somewhat unusual for database servers, direct attached storage or SANs, to exclusively use SSD storage, but this will change as SSD costs continue to decrease.

SSDs perform particularly well for random access reads and writes, and for sequential access reads. Some earlier SSDs do not perform as well for sequential access writes, and they also have had issues where write performance declines over time, particularly as the drive fills up. Newer SSD drives, with better controllers and improved firmware, have mitigated these earlier problems.

There are two main types of flash memory currently used in SSDs: Single Level Cell (SLC) and Multi Level Cell (MLC). Enterprise-level SSDs almost always use SLC flash memory since MLC flash memory does not perform as well and is not as durable as the more expensive SLC flash memory.

Fusion-IO drives

Fusion-IO is a company that makes several interesting, SSD-like products that are getting a lot of visibility in the SQL Server community. The term, SSD-like, refers to Fusion-IO cards that use flash memory, just like SSDs do, but are connected to your server through a PCI-E slot, instead of a SAS or SATA controller.

The Fusion-IO products are relatively expensive, but offer extremely high performance. Their three current server-related products are the **ioDrive**, **ioDrive Duo** and the new **ioDrive Octal**. All three of these products are PCI-E cards, with anywhere from 80 GB to 5.12 TB of SLC or MLC flash on a single card. Using a PCI-E expansion slot gives one of these cards much more bandwidth than a traditional SATA or SAS connection. The typical way to use Fusion-IO cards is to have at least two of the cards, and then to use software RAID in Windows to get additional redundancy. This way, you avoid having a pretty important single point of failure in the card itself and the PCI-E slot it was using (but you incur the accompanying increase in hardware expenditure).

Fusion-IO drives offer excellent read and write performance, albeit at a relatively high hardware cost. As long as you have enough space, it is possible and feasible to locate all of your database components on Fusion-IO drives, and get extremely good I/O performance, without the need for a SAN. One big advantage of using Fusion-IO, instead of a traditional SAN, is the reduced electrical power usage and reduced cooling requirements, which are big issues in many datacenters.

Since Fusion-IO drives are housed in internal PCI-E slots in a database server, you cannot use them with traditional Windows fail-over clustering (which requires shared external storage for the cluster), but you can use them with database mirroring or the upcoming AlwaysOn technology in SQL Server Denali, which allows you to create a Windows Cluster with no shared storage.

SSDs and SQL Server

I'm often asked which components of a SQL Server database should be moved to SSD storage as they become more affordable. Unfortunately, the answer is that it depends on your workload, and on where (if anywhere) you are experiencing I/O bottlenecks in your system (data files, `TempDB` files, or transaction log file).

Depending on your database size and your budget, it may make sense to move the entire database to solid-state storage, especially with a heavy OLTP workload. For example, if your database(s) are relatively small, and your budget is relatively large, it may be feasible to have your data files, your log files, and your TempDB files all running on SSD storage.

If your database is very large, and your hardware budget is relatively small, you may have to be more selective about which components can be moved to SSD storage. For example, it may make sense to move your `TempDB` files to SSD storage if your `TempDB` is experiencing I/O bottlenecks. Another possibility would be to move some of your most heavily accessed tables and indexes to a new data file, in a separate file group, that would be located on your SSD storage.

Internal Storage

All blade and rack-mounted database servers have some internal drive bays. Blade servers usually have two to four internal drive bays, while rack servers have higher numbers of drive bays, depending on their vertical size. For example, a 2U server will have more internal drive bays than an equivalent 1U server (from the same manufacturer and model line). For standalone SQL Server instances, it is common to use at least two 15 K drives in RAID 1 for the operating system and SQL Server binaries. This provides a very basic level of redundancy for the operating system and the SQL Server binaries, meaning that the loss of a single internal drive will not bring down the entire database server.

Modern servers often use 2.5" drives, in place of the 3.5" drives that were common a few years ago. This allows more physical drives to fit in the same size chassis, and it reduces the electrical and cooling requirements. The latest 2.5" drives also tend to out-perform older 3.5" drives. Despite these improvements, however, for all but very lightest database workloads, you simply **won't have enough internal drive bays to completely support your I/O requirements**.

Ignoring this reality is a very common mistake that I see made by many DBAs and companies. They buy a new, high-performance database server with fast multi-core processors and lots of RAM and then try to run an OLTP workload on six internal drives. This is like a body-builder who only works his upper body, but completely neglects his legs, ending up completely out of balance, and ultimately not very strong. Most production SQL Server workloads will require much more I/O capacity than is obtainable from the available internal drives. In order to provide sufficient storage capacity, and acceptable I/O performance, additional redundant storage is required, and there are several ways to provide it.

Attached Storage

The two most common form of storage array used for SQL Server installations are DAS and the SAN.

Direct Attached Storage

One option is to use Direct Attached Storage (DAS), which is also sometimes called "locally attached storage." DAS drives are directly attached to a server with an eSATA, SAS, or SCSI cable. Typically, you have an external enclosure, containing anywhere from 8 to 24 drives, attached to a RAID controller in single database server. Since DAS enclosures are relatively affordable compared to a Storage Area Network, it is becoming more common to use DAS storage, with multiple enclosures and multiple RAID controllers, to achieve very high throughput numbers for DW and Reporting workloads.

However, with relative simplicity and low cost, you do give up some flexibility. It is relatively hard to add capacity and change RAID levels when using DAS, compared to SAN.

The diagram in Figure 2.1 shows a somewhat simplified view of a server that is using DAS.

You have a server with one or more PCI-e RAID controller cards that are connected (via a SAS or SCSI cable) to one or more external storage enclosures that usually have between 14 and 24 SAS or SCSI hard drives. The RAID controller(s) in the server are used to create and manage any RAID arrays that you decide to create and present to Windows as logical drives (that show up with a drive letter in Windows Explorer). This lets you build a storage subsystem with very good performance, relatively inexpensively.

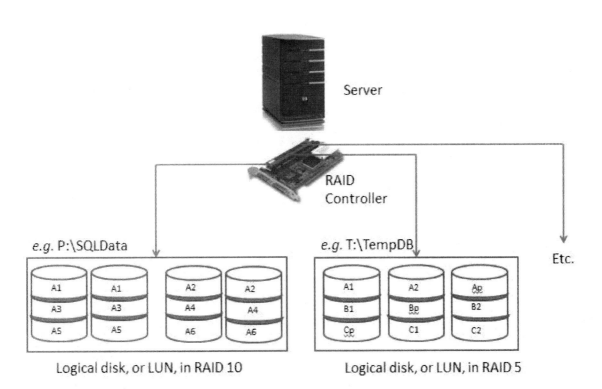

Figure 2.1: Direct Attached Storage.

Storage Area Network

If you have a bigger budget, the next level of storage is a Storage Area Network (SAN). A SAN is a dedicated network that has multiple hard drives (anywhere from dozens to hundreds of drives) with multiple storage processors, caches, and other redundant components.

With the additional expense of the SAN, you do get a lot more flexibility. Multiple database servers can share a single, large SAN (as long as you don't exceed the overall capacity of the SAN), and most SANs offer features that are not available with DAS, such as SAN snapshots. There are two main types of SANs available today: Fiber Channel and iSCSI.

A **Fiber Channel SAN** has multiple components, including large numbers of magnetic hard drives or solid-state drives, a storage controller, and an enclosure to hold the drives and controller. Some SAN vendors are starting to use what they call tiered storage, where they have some SSDs, some fast 15,000 rpm Fiber Channel drives, and some slower 7,200 rpm SATA drives in a single SAN. This allows you to prioritize your storage, based on the required performance. For example, you could have your SQL Server transaction log files on SSD storage, your SQL Server data files on Fiber Channel storage, and your SQL Server backup files on slower SATA storage.

Multiple fiber channel switches, and Host Bus Adapters (HBAs) connect the whole infrastructure together in what is referred to as a **fabric**. Each component in the fabric has a bandwidth capacity, which is typically 1, 2, 4 or 8 Gbits/sec. When evaluating a SAN, be aware of the entire SAN path (HBA, switches, caches, storage processor, disks, and so on), since a lower bandwidth component (such as a switch) mixed in with higher capacity components will restrict the effective bandwidth that is available to the entire fabric.

An **iSCSI SAN** is similar to a Fiber Channel SAN except that it uses a TCP/IP network, connected with standard Ethernet network cabling and components, instead of fiber optics. The supported Ethernet wire speeds that can be used for iSCSI include 100 Mb, 1 Gb, and 10 Gb/sec. Since iSCSI SANs can use standard Ethernet components, they are usually much less expensive than Fiber Channel SANs. Early iSCSI SANs did not perform as well as contemporary Fiber Channel SANs, but that gap has closed in recent years.

One good option for an iSCSI SAN is to use a TCP Offload Engine, also known as a TOE Card instead of a full iSCSI HBA. A TOE offloads the TCP/IP operations for that card from the main CPU, which can improve overall performance (for a slightly higher hardware cost).

Regardless of which type of SAN you evaluate or use, it is very important to consider multi-path I/O (MPIO) issues. Basically, this means designing and implementing a SAN to eliminate any single point of failure. For example, you would start with at least two HBAs (preferably with multiple channels), connected to multiple switches, which are connected to multiple ports on the SAN enclosure. This gives you redundancy and potentially better performance (at a greater cost).

If you want to see what a real-life SAN looks like, Figure 2.2 shows a 3PAR S400 SAN with (216) 146 GB 10,000 rpm Fiber Channel drives and (24) 500 GB 7,200 rpm SATA drives in a single, 42U rack enclosure. This SAN cost roughly $500,000 when it was purchased in 2006.

Figure 2.2:   NewsGator's 3PAR S400 SAN.

RAID Configurations

Redundant array of independent disks (RAID) is a technology that allows the use of multiple hard drives, combined in various ways, to improve redundancy, availability and performance, depending on the RAID level used. When a RAID array is presented to a host in Windows, it is called a logical drive.

Using RAID, the data is distributed across multiple disks in order to:

- overcome the I/O bottleneck of a single disk, as described previously

- get protection from data loss through the redundant storage of data on multiple disks

- avoid any one hard drive being a single point of failure

- manage multiple drives more effectively.

Regardless of whether you are using traditional magnetic hard-drive storage or newer solid-state storage technology, most database servers will employ RAID technology. RAID improves redundancy, improves performance, and makes it possible to have larger logical drives. RAID is used for both OLTP and DW workloads. Having more spindles in a RAID array helps both IOPS and throughput, although ultimately throughput can be limited by a RAID controller or HBA.

Please note that, while RAID does provide redundancy in your data storage, it is not a substitute for an effective backup strategy or a High Availability / Disaster Recovery (HA/DR) strategy. Regardless of what level of RAID you use in your storage subsystem, you still need to run SQL Server full and log backups as necessary to meet your recovery point objectives (RPO) and recovery time objectives (RTO).

There are a number of commercially available RAID configurations, which we'll review over the coming sections, and each has associated costs and benefits. When considering which level of RAID to use for different SQL Server components, you have to carefully consider your workload characteristics, keeping in mind your hardware budget. If cost is no object, I am going to want RAID 10 for everything, i.e. data files, log file, and `TempDB`. If my data is relatively static, I may be able to use RAID 5 for my data files.

During the discussion, I will assume that you have a basic knowledge of how RAID works, and of the basic concepts of striping, mirroring, and parity.

RAID 0 (disk striping with no parity)

RAID 0 simply stripes data across multiple physical disks. This allows reads and writes to happen simultaneously across all of the striped disks, so offering improved read and write performance compared to a single disk. However, it actually provides no redundancy whatsoever. If any disk in a RAID 0 array fails, the array is offline and all the data in the array is lost. This is actually more likely to happen than if you only have a single disk, since the probability of failure for any single disk goes up as you add more disks. There is no disk space loss for storing parity data (since there is no parity data with RAID 0), but I don't recommend that you use RAID 0 for database use, unless you enjoy updating your resumé. RAID 0 is often used by serious computer gaming enthusiasts to reduce the time it takes to load portions of their favorite games. They do not keep any important data on their gaming rigs, so they are not that concerned about losing one of their drives.

RAID 1 (disk mirroring or duplexing)

You need at least two physical disks for RAID 1. Your data is mirrored between the two disks, *i.e.* the data on one disk is an exact mirror of that on the other disk. This provides redundancy, since you can lose one side of the mirror without the array going offline and without any data loss, but at the cost of losing 50% of your space to the mirroring overhead. RAID 1 can improve read performance, but can hurt write performance in some cases, since the data has to be written twice.

On a database server, it is very common to install the Windows Server operating system on two (at least) of the internal drives, configured in a RAID 1 array, and using an embedded internal RAID controller on the motherboard. In the case of a non-clustered database server, it is also common to install the SQL Server binaries on the same two-drive RAID 1 array as the operating system. This provides basic redundancy for both the operating system and the SQL Server binaries. If one of the drives in the RAID 1 array fails, you will not have any data loss or down-time. You will need to replace the failed drive and rebuild the mirror, but this is a pretty painless operation, especially compared to reinstalling the operating system and SQL Server!

RAID 5 (striping with parity)

RAID 5 is probably the most commonly-used RAID level, both for general file server systems and for SQL Server. RAID 5 requires at least three physical disks. The data, and calculated parity information, is striped across the physical disks by the RAID controller. This provides redundancy because, if one of the disks goes down, then the missing data from that disk can be reconstructed from the parity information on the other disks. Also, rather than losing 50% of your storage in order to achieve redundancy, as for disk mirroring, you only lose 1/N of your disk space (where N equals the number of disks in the RAID 5 array) for storing the parity information. For example, if you had six disks in a RAID 5 array, you would lose ⅙ of your space for the parity information.

However, you will notice a very significant decrease in performance while you are missing a disk in a RAID 5 array, since the RAID controller has to work pretty hard to reconstruct the missing data. Furthermore, if you lose a second drive in your RAID 5 array, the array will go offline, and all of the data will be lost. As such, if you lose one drive, you need to make sure to replace the failed drive as soon as possible. RAID 6 stores more parity information than RAID 5, at the cost of an additional disk devoted to parity information, so you can survive losing a second disk in a RAID 6 array.

Finally, there is a write performance penalty with RAID 5, since there is overhead to write the data, and then to calculate and write the parity information. As such, RAID 5 is usually not a good choice for transaction log drives, where we need very high write performance. I would also not want to use RAID 5 for data files where I am changing more than 10% of the data each day. One good candidate for RAID 5 is your SQL Server backup files. You can still get pretty good backup performance with RAID 5 volumes, especially if you use backup compression.

RAID 10 and RAID 0+1

When you need the best possible write performance, you should consider either RAID 0+1 or, preferably, RAID 10. These two RAID levels both involve mirroring (so there is a 50% mirroring overhead) and striping, but they differ in the details of how it is done in each case.

In RAID 10 (striped set of mirrors), the data is first mirrored and then striped. In this configuration, it is possible to survive the loss of multiple drives in the array (one from each side of the mirror), while still leaving the system operational. Since RAID 10 is more fault tolerant than RAID 0+1, it is preferred for database usage.

In RAID 0+1 (mirrored pair of stripes) the data is first striped, and then mirrored. This configuration cannot handle the loss of more than one drive in each side of the array.

RAID 10 and RAID 0+1 offer the highest read/write performance, but incur a roughly 100% storage cost penalty, which is why they are sometimes called rich man's RAID. These RAID levels are most often used for OLTP workloads, for both data files and transaction log files. As a SQL Server database professional, you should always try to use RAID 10 if you have the hardware and budget to support it. On the other hand, if your data is less volatile, you may be able to get perfectly acceptable performance using RAID 5 for your data files. By "less volatile," I mean if less than 10% of your data changes per day, then you may still get acceptable performance from RAID 5 for your data files(s).

RAID Controllers

There are two common types of hardware RAID controllers used in database servers. The first is an integrated hardware RAID controller, embedded on the server motherboard. This type of RAID controller is usually used to control internal drives in the server. The second is a hardware RAID controller on a PCI-E expansion card that slots into one of the available (and compatible) PCI-E expansion slots in your database server. This is most often used to control one or more DAS enclosures, which are full of SAS, SATA, or SCSI hard drives.

It is also possible to use the software RAID capabilities built into the Windows Server operating system, but I don't recommend this for production database use with traditional magnetic drives, since it places extra overhead on the operating system, is less flexible, has no dedicated cache, and increases the load on the processors and memory in a server. For both internal drives and direct attached storage, dedicated hardware RAID controllers are much preferable to software RAID. One exception to this guidance is if you are going to use multiple Fusion-IO drives in a single database server, in which case it is acceptable, and common, to use software RAID.

Hardware-based RAID uses a dedicated RAID controller to manage the physical disks that are part of any RAID arrays that have been created. A server-class hardware RAID controller will have a dedicated, specialized processor that is used to calculate parity information; this will perform much better than using one of your CPUs for that purpose. Besides, your CPUs have more important work to do, so it is much better to offload that work to a dedicated RAID controller.

A server-class hardware RAID controller will also have a dedicated memory cache, usually around 512 MB in size. The cache in a RAID controller can be used for either reads or writes, or split between the two purposes. This cache stores data temporarily, so that whatever wrote that data to the cache can return to another task without having to wait to write the actual physical disk(s).

Especially for database server use, it is extremely important that this cache is backed up by a battery, in case the server ever crashes or loses power before the contents of the RAID controller cache are actually written to disk. Most RAID controllers allow you to control how the cache is configured, in terms of whether it is used for reads or writes or a combination of the two. Whenever possible, you should disable the read cache (or reduce it to a much smaller size) for OLTP workloads, as they will make little or no use of it. By reducing the read cache you can devote more space, or often the entire cache, to write activity, which will greatly improve write performance. You can also usually control whether the cache is acting as a write-back cache or a write-through cache. In a **write-through** cache, every write to the cache causes a synchronous write to the backing store, which is safer, but reduces the write performance of the cache. A **write-back** cache improves write performance, because a write to the high-speed cache is faster than to the actual disk(s). As enough of the data in the write-back cache becomes "dirty," it will eventually have to actually be written to the disk subsystem. The fact that data that has been marked as committed by the database is still just in the write-back cache is why it is so critical to have a battery backing the cache.

For both performance and redundancy reasons, you should always try to use multiple HBAs or RAID controllers whenever possible. While most direct attached storage enclosures will allow you to daisy-chain multiple enclosures on a single RAID controller, I would avoid this configuration if possible, since the RAID controller will be a single point of failure, and possibly a performance bottleneck as you approach the throughput limit of the controller. Instead, I would want to have one RAID controller per DAS array (subject to the number of PCI-E slots you have available in your server). This gives you both better redundancy and better performance. Having multiple RAID controllers allows you to take advantage of the dedicated cache in each RAID controller, and helps ensure that you are not limited by the throughput capacity of the single RAID controller or the expansion slot that it is using.

Provisioning and Configuring the Storage Subsystem

Having discussed each of the basic components of the storage system, it's time to review the factors that will determine the choices you make when provisioning and configuring the storage subsystem.

The number, size, speed, and configuration of the disks that comprise your storage array will be heavily dependent on the size and nature of the workload. Every time that data required by an application or query is not found in the buffer cache, it will need to be read from the data files on disk, causing read I/O. Every time data is modified by an application, the transaction details are written to the transaction log file, and then the data itself is written to the data files on disk, causing write I/O in each case.

In addition to the general read and write I/O generated by applications that access SQL Server, additional I/O load will be created by other system and maintenance activities.

- **Transaction log backups** – create both read and write I/O pressure. The active portion of the transaction log file is read, and then the transaction log backup file must be written.

- **Index maintenance**, including index reorganizations and index rebuilds – creates read I/O pressure as the index is read off the I/O subsystem, which then causes memory pressure as the index data goes into the SQL Server Buffer Pool. There is CPU pressure as the index is reorganized or rebuilt, and then write I/O pressure as the index is written back out to the I/O subsystem.

- **Full text catalog and indexes for Full Text Search** – the work of crawling the base table(s) to create and maintain these structures and then writing the changes to the Full Text index(es) creates both read and write I/O pressure.

- **Database checkpoint operations** – the write activity to the data files occurs during database checkpoint operations. The frequency of checkpoints is influenced by the recovery interval setting and the amount of RAM installed in the system.

- **Use of High Availability / Disaster Recovery (HA/DR)** – features like Log Shipping or Database Mirroring will cause additional read activity against your transaction log, since the transaction log must be read before the activity can be sent to the Log Shipping destination(s) or to the database mirror. Using Transactional Replication will also cause more read activity against your transaction log on your Publisher database.

The number of disks that make up your storage array, their specifications in terms of size, speed and so on, and the physical configuration of these drives in the storage array, will be determined by the size of the I/O load that your system needs to support, both in terms of IOPS and I/O throughput, as well as in the nature of that load, in terms of the read I/O and write I/O activity that it generates.

A workload that is primarily OLTP in nature will generate a high number of I/O operations and a high percentage of write activity; it is not that unusual to actually have more writes than reads in a heavy OLTP system. This will cause heavy write (and read) I/O pressure on the logical drive(s) that house your data files and, particularly, heavy write pressure on the logical drive where your transaction log is located, since every write must go to the transaction log first. The drives that house these files must be sized, spec'd and configured appropriately, to handle this pressure.

Furthermore, almost all of the other factors listed previously that cause additional I/O pressure are almost all more prominent for OLTP systems. High write activity, caused by frequent data modifications, leads to more regular transaction log backups, index maintenance, more frequent database checkpoints, and so on.

Backup and data compression

Using data and backup compression can reduce the I/O cost and duration of SQL Server backups at the cost of some additional CPU pressure – see Chapter 1 for further discussion.

A DSS or DW system usually has longer-running queries than a similar size OLTP system. The data in a DSS system is usually more static, with much higher read activity than write activity. The less volatile data means less frequent data and transaction log backups – you might even be able to use read-only file groups to avoid having to regularly back up some file groups – less frequent index maintenance and so on, all of which contributes to a lower I/O load in terms of IOPS, though not necessarily I/O throughput, since the complex, long-running aggregate queries that characterize a DW/DSS workload will often read a lot of data, and the data load operations will write a lot of data. All of this means that, for a DSS/DW type of workload, I/O throughput is usually more important than IOPS performance.

Finding the read/write ratio

One way of determining the size and nature of your workload is to retrieve the read/write ratio for your database files. The higher the proportion of writes, the more OLTP-like is your workload.

The DMV query shown in Listing 2.1 can be run on an existing system to help characterize the I/O workload for the current database. This query will show the read/write percentage, by file, for the current database, both in the number of reads and writes, and in the number of bytes read and written.

```
-- I/O Statistics by file for the current database
SELECT  DB_NAME(DB_ID()) AS [Database Name] ,
        [file_id] ,
        num_of_reads ,
        num_of_writes ,
        num_of_bytes_read ,
        num_of_bytes_written ,
        CAST(100. * num_of_reads / ( num_of_reads + num_of_writes )
                        AS DECIMAL(10,1)) AS [# Reads Pct] ,
        CAST(100. * num_of_writes / ( num_of_reads + num_of_writes )
                        AS DECIMAL(10,1)) AS [# Write Pct] ,
```

```
        CAST(100. * num_of_bytes_read / ( num_of_bytes_read
                                + num_of_bytes_written )
                    AS DECIMAL(10,1)) AS [Read Bytes Pct] ,
        CAST(100. * num_of_bytes_written / ( num_of_bytes_read
                                + num_of_bytes_written )
                    AS DECIMAL(10,1)) AS [Written Bytes Pct]
FROM    sys.dm_io_virtual_file_stats(DB_ID(), NULL) ;
```

Listing 2.1: Finding the read/write ratio, by file, for a given database.

Three more DMV queries, shown in Listing 2.2, can help characterize the workload on an existing system, from a read/write perspective, for cached stored procedures. These queries can help give you a better idea of the total read and write I/O activity, the execution count, and the cached time for those stored procedures.

```
-- Top Cached SPs By Total Logical Writes (SQL 2008 and 2008 R2)
-- This represents write I/O pressure
SELECT   p.name AS [SP Name] ,
         qs.total_logical_writes AS [TotalLogicalWrites] ,
         qs.total_logical_reads AS [TotalLogicalReads] ,
         qs.execution_count , qs.cached_time
FROM     sys.procedures AS p
         INNER JOIN sys.dm_exec_procedure_stats AS qs
                        ON p.[object_id] = qs.[object_id]
WHERE    qs.database_id = DB_ID()
         AND qs.total_logical_writes > 0
ORDER BY qs.total_logical_writes DESC ;
-- Top Cached SPs By Total Physical Reads (SQL 2008 and 2008 R2)
-- This represents read I/O pressure
SELECT   p.name AS [SP Name] ,
         qs.total_physical_reads AS [TotalPhysicalReads] ,
         qs.total_logical_reads AS [TotalLogicalReads] ,
         qs.total_physical_reads/qs.execution_count AS [AvgPhysicalReads] ,
         qs.execution_count , qs.cached_time
FROM     sys.procedures AS p
         INNER JOIN sys.dm_exec_procedure_stats AS qs
                        ON p.[object_id] = qs.[object_id]
WHERE    qs.database_id = DB_ID()
         AND qs.total_physical_reads > 0
ORDER BY qs.total_physical_reads DESC, qs.total_logical_reads DESC ;
```

```
-- Top Cached SPs By Total Logical Reads (SQL 2008 and 2008 R2)
-- This represents read memory pressure
SELECT    p.name AS [SP Name] ,
          qs.total_logical_reads AS [TotalLogicalReads] ,
          qs.total_logical_writes AS [TotalLogicalWrites] ,
          qs.execution_count , qs.cached_time
FROM      sys.procedures AS p
          INNER JOIN sys.dm_exec_procedure_stats AS qs
                        ON p.[object_id] = qs.[object_id]
WHERE     qs.database_id = DB_ID()
          AND qs.total_logical_reads > 0
ORDER BY qs.total_logical_reads DESC ;
```

Listing 2.2: The read/write ratio for cached stored procedures.

As discussed, a workload with a high percentage of writes will place more stress on the drive array where the transaction log files for your user databases are located, since all data modifications are written to the transaction log. The more volatile the data, the more write I/O pressure you will see on your transaction log file. A workload with a high percentage of writes will also put more I/O pressure on your SQL Server data file(s). It is common practice, with large volatile databases, to have multiple data files spread across multiple logical drives to get both higher throughput and better IOPS performance. Unfortunately, you cannot increase I/O performance for your transaction log by adding additional files, since the log file is written to sequentially.

The relative read/write ratio will also affect how you configure the cache in your RAID controllers. For OLTP workloads, write cache is much more important than read cache, while read cache is more useful for DSS/DW workloads. In fact, it is a common best practice to devote the entire RAID controller cache to writes for OLTP workloads.

How many disks?

One common mistake that you should avoid in selecting storage components is to only consider space requirements when looking at sizing and capacity requirements. For example, if you had a size requirement of 1 TB for a drive array that was meant to hold a SQL Server data file, you could satisfy the size requirement by using three 500 GB drives in a RAID 5 configuration. Unfortunately, for the reasons discussed relating to disk latency, the performance of that array would be quite low. A better solution from a performance perspective would be to use either 8x146 GB drives in RAID 5, or 15x73 GB drives in RAID 5 to satisfy the space requirement with many more spindles. You should always try to maximize your spindle count instead of just using the minimum number of drives to meet a size requirement with the level of RAID you are going to use. So, after all of this discussion, how many disks do you actually need to achieve acceptable performance?

Here is one formula for estimating the number of disks required for a given workload and RAID level that Australian SQL Server MVP Rod Colledge has written about:

```
n = (%R + f (%W))(tps)/125
Required # Disks = (Reads/sec + (Writes/sec * RAID adjuster)) / Disk IOPS
```

It is important to consider both IOPS, to calculate the number of disks needed, and the I/O type, to ensure the I/O bus is capable of handling the peak I/O sequential throughput.

Configuration: SAN vs. DAS, RAID levels

For OLTP systems, the seek time and rotational latency limitations for a single disk, discussed at the start of this chapter, have led to the proliferation of large SAN-based storage arrays, allowing data to be segmented across numerous disks, in various RAID configurations. Many larger SANs have a huge number of drive spindles and so this architecture is able to support a very high random I/O rate. Use of a SAN for the I/O subsystem in OLTP workloads makes it relatively easy (but expensive) to support dozens to hundreds of disk spindles for a single database server.

The general guideline is that you will get roughly 100 IOPS from a single 10,000 rpm magnetic drive and about 150 IOPS from a single 15,000 rpm drive. For example, if you had a SAN with two hundred 15,000 rpm drives, that would give the entire SAN a raw IOPS capacity of 30,000 IOPS. If the HBAs in your database server were older, 4 Gbps models, your sequential throughput would still be limited to roughly 400 MB/second for each HBA channel.

If you don't have the budget or in-house expertise for a large SAN, it is still possible to get very good IOPS performance with other storage techniques, such as using multiple DAS enclosures with multiple RAID controllers along with multiple SQL Server file groups and data files. This allows you to spread the I/O workload among multiple logical drives that each represent a dedicated DAS enclosure. You can also use SSDs or Fusion-IO cards to get extremely high IOPS performance without using a SAN, assuming you have the hardware budget available to do that.

When you are using non-SAN storage (such as DAS enclosures) it is very important to explicitly segregate your disk activity by logical drive. This means doing things like having one or more dedicated logical drives for SQL Server data files, a dedicated logical drive for the log file (for each user database, if possible), a dedicated logical drive for your TempDB data and log files, and one or more dedicated logical drives for your SQL Server backup files. Of course, your choices and flexibility are ultimately limited by the number of drives that you have available, which is limited by the number of DAS enclosures you have, and the number of drives in each enclosure.

However, for DW/DSS systems, a SAN storage array may not be the best choice. Here, I/O throughput is the most important factor, and the throughput of a SAN array can be limited to the throughput capacity of a switch or individual HBA. As such, it is becoming more common for DW/DSS systems to use multiple DAS devices, each on a dedicated RAID controller, to get high levels of throughput at a relatively low cost.

If you have the available budget, I would prefer to use RAID 10 for all of your various SQL Server files, including data files, log files, `TempDB`, and backup files. If you do have budget constraints, I would consider using RAID 5 for your database backup files, and RAID 5 for your data files (if they are relatively static). Depending on your workload characteristics and how you use `TempDB`, you might be able to use RAID 5 for `TempDB` files. I would fight as hard as possible to avoid using RAID 5 for transaction log files, since RAID 5 does not perform nearly as well for writes.

Summary

Having an appropriate storage subsystem is critical for SQL Server performance. Most high-volume SQL Server workloads ultimately run into I/O bottlenecks that can be very expensive to alleviate. Selecting, sizing, and configuring your storage subsystem properly will reduce the chances that you will suffer from I/O performance problems.

In addition, using powerful multi-core processors and large quantities of RAM, as discussed in *Chapter 1*, provides relatively cheap extra protection from expensive I/O bottlenecks. Having more RAM reduces read I/O pressure, since more data can fit into the SQL Server buffer cache, and it can also reduce write I/O pressure by reducing the frequency of checkpoints. Using modern, multi-core processors can give you the excess processor capacity that can allow you to use various compression features, such as data compression and backup compression, which can also reduce I/O pressure in exchange for additional CPU utilization.

Ultimately, however, the only way to know that your chosen hardware, including the processor, disk subsystem and so on, is capable of handling the expected workload is to perform benchmark tests, as described in the next chapter.

Chapter 3: Benchmarking Tools

Having read *Chapters 1* and *2*, you hopefully have a better understanding of server hardware from a SQL Server perspective, and of how your hardware choices can be affected by the types of SQL Server workload that must be supported.

However, as well as understanding the factors that will influence hardware selection and provisioning, it is vitally important to **measure** and **validate** the performance of the various major hardware components (such as the processor(s), memory, or disk subsystem) as well as SQL Server itself, in order to verify that performance targets will be met.

One way to evaluate and compare hardware performance, and to make sizing and capacity estimates, is to use benchmark test results. There are many different kinds of benchmarks in use today, but this chapter will focus on two main types, which are:

- **application benchmarks** – use one or more real applications (such as Microsoft SQL Server) to measure the actual performance, throughput, and response time of an entire system while running the application

- **component benchmarks** – focus on one or more components in a computer system, usually using a synthetic workload that is designed to measure the absolute performance of that part of the system.

We will discuss some of the industry standard database application benchmarks (such as TPC-C, TPC-E, and TPC-H), including how they work and how they can be useful in helping you evaluate and properly size database server hardware.

We'll then move on to the component benchmarks that you can carry out yourself and that will help you to compare the relative performance of different components of the system in a focused manner, without actually using SQL Server. For example, tools such as HD Tune Pro, CrystalDiskMark, and SQLIO allow us to measure and validate SQL Server storage performance, before we even install SQL Server.

Likewise, a component benchmark tool, such as Geekbench (from Primate Labs) WWW.PRIMATELABS.CA/GEEKBENCH/ can be very useful for estimating and comparing CPU and memory performance between an existing server and a proposed new server, allowing the DBA to make much more accurate sizing and capacity estimates. In my opinion, it is always preferable to make use of component benchmarks to actually measure performance instead of just guessing about the relative performance of different components across different systems.

Application Benchmarks

The Transaction Processing Performance Council (TPC) is a non-profit organization, founded in 1988, which aims to define transaction processing and database benchmarks, and to disseminate objective, verifiable, TPC performance data to the industry.

TPC benchmarks are used widely in evaluating the performance of database systems. TPC benchmark results are listed by Performance, Price/Performance, and Watts/Performance. The TPC organization has very strict rules about how results must be submitted and audited, including very detailed disclosure rules. TPC results are published on the TPC website, at WWW.TPC.ORG/.

Both hardware and software vendors have a tendency to use good TPC benchmark results as marketing tools, which is fine by me, but which leads some people to treat with skepticism, or even completely disregard, the value of TPC benchmarks. One argument I have heard is that the database vendors (such as Microsoft, IBM, and Oracle) are so familiar with the various queries that are used in the TPC benchmarks that they modify their query optimizer logic to make their products artificially perform better on the benchmarks. I tend to discount this argument, since I believe all of the major database vendors have more integrity than that, and I believe it would be extremely difficult and counterproductive to make those types of code modifications to the query optimizer.

Another argument I hear against the TPC benchmarks is that they don't represent a realistic workload and that the types of systems that are built for TPC benchmarks are extremely expensive; that they are not representative of a typical system that would actually be purchased by a real customer, and so have little real-world value and should be ignored.

I think this attitude is a mistake; as long as you know how to interpret the results, and realize their purpose and limitations, I believe there is real value to be had in comparing the TPC benchmarks for various systems. There is a rigorous set of rules in place for how TPC benchmark testing is conducted and submitted to TPC for final auditing and approval. Results that are listed on the TPC website must include an Executive Summary, a Full Disclosure Report (FDR), and a full set of Supporting Files, all of which make very interesting reading for the true database and hardware geek.

Furthermore, taken alongside the results from component benchmarks and your own common sense and experience, you can apply and extrapolate the results from formal TPC submissions to your own, probably smaller-scale, systems. There are three current benchmarks used by TPC, the **TPC-C**, **TPC-E**, and **TPC-H** benchmarks.

TPC-C benchmark

The TPC Benchmark C (TPC-C) benchmark is an old OLTP benchmark, originally released in 1992, which simulates the OLTP workload of a wholesale supplier. The business model of the wholesaler is organized into Warehouses, Districts, and Customers. The TPC-C data model is very simple, with only nine tables and four data types, and is hierarchical in nature – districts are subsets of warehouses, while customers are subsets of districts.

There are five different transaction types in the TPC-C benchmark. The TPC-C data model does not enforce referential integrity, and the data in the database is mostly random strings of gibberish (for columns like customer names). A frequent criticism of the TPC-C benchmark is that it does not require fault-tolerant storage media, which is not especially realistic for a database benchmark. The TPC-C benchmark also has an unrealistic dependency on disk I/O, meaning that vendors would often configure systems with an extremely high number of disk spindles in a quest to get the best absolute TPC-C benchmark score. There is some validity to these criticisms, in my opinion, so I tend to ignore the TPC-C benchmark and focus on the much newer TPC-E benchmark.

TPC-E benchmark

The TPC Benchmark E (TPC-E) is an OLTP performance benchmark that was introduced in February 2007. TPC-E is not a replacement for the older TPC-C benchmark, but a completely new OLTP benchmark. It is an OLTP, database-centric workload that is meant to reduce the cost and complexity of running the benchmark compared to the older TPC-C benchmark. It simulates the OLTP workload of a brokerage firm that interacts with customers using synchronous transactions and with a financial market using asynchronous transactions.

The business model of the brokerage firm is organized by Customers, Accounts, and Securities. The data model for TPC-E is significantly more complex, but more realistic than TPC-C, with 33 tables and many different data types. The data model for the TPC-E database does enforce referential integrity, unlike the older TPC-C data model. Some of the differences in the data model for the TPC-C and TPC-E databases are shown in Figure 3.1.

Characteristic	TPC-C	TPC-E
Tables	9	33
Columns	92	188
Primary Keys	8	33
Foreign Keys	9	50
Tables w/Foreign Keys	7	27
Check Constraints	0	22
Referential Integrity	No	Yes

Figure 3.1: TPC-C and TPC-E database schema summary.

The TPC-E database is populated with pseudo-real data, including customer names from the year 2000 US Census, and company listings from the NYSE and NASDAQ. Having realistic data introduces data skew, and makes the data compressible. Unlike TPC-C, the storage media for TPC-E must be fault tolerant (which means no RAID 0 arrays). Overall, the TPC-E benchmark is designed to have reduced I/O requirements compared to the old TPC-C benchmark, which makes it both less expensive and more realistic, since the sponsoring vendors will not feel as much pressure to equip their test systems with disproportionately large disk subsystems in order to get the best test results. The TPC-E benchmark is also more CPU-intensive than the old TPC-C benchmark.

The TPC-E implementation is broken down into a **Driver** and a **System Under Test** (SUT), separated by a mandatory network. The Driver represents the various client devices that would use an N-tier client-server system, abstracted into a load generation system. The SUT has multiple Application servers (Tier A) that communicate with the database server and its associated storage subsystem (Tier B). TPC provides a transaction harness component that runs in Tier A, while the test sponsor provides the other components in the SUT.

The performance metric for TPC-E is transactions per second, **tpsE**. The actual tpsE score represents the average number of Trade Result transactions executed within one second. To be fully compliant with the TPC-E standard, all references to tpsE results must include the tpsE rate, the associated price per tpsE, and the availability date of the priced configuration.

It seems interesting that, as of early 2011, Microsoft is the only database vendor that has submitted any TPC-E results, even though the TPC-E benchmark has been available since early 2007. Whatever the reasons why other database vendors haven't posted results, there are certainly many results posted for SQL Server, which makes it a very useful benchmark when assessing SQL Server hardware.

TPC-H benchmark

The TPC Benchmark H (TPC-H) is a benchmark for Decision Support Systems (DSS). It consists of a suite of business oriented, ad hoc queries and concurrent data modifications. The queries, and the data populating the database, have been chosen to have broad industry-wide relevance. This benchmark illustrates decision support systems that examine large volumes of data, execute queries with a high degree of complexity, and give answers to critical business questions.

The performance metric reported by TPC-H is called the TPC-H Composite Query-per-Hour Performance Metric (**QphH@Size**), and reflects multiple aspects of the capability of the system to process queries. These aspects include the selected database size against which the queries are executed, the query processing power when queries are submitted by a single stream and the query throughput when queries are submitted by multiple concurrent users. The TPC-H Price/Performance metric is expressed as **$/QphH@Size**.

TPC-H results are grouped by database size, with database size groups of 100 GB, 300 GB, 1,000 GB, 3,000 GB, 10,000 GB, and 30,000 GB. You should not compare TPC-H results across database sizes, which means that the TPC-H score for a 100 GB database should not be compared with the TPC-H score for a 1,000 GB database.

Analyzing benchmark test results

Now that you have a better idea about the purpose and composition of the three current TPC benchmarks, it is time to talk about how to analyze and interpret the results. First, you need to focus on the benchmark that is closest to your type of workload. If you have an OLTP workload, that would be TPC-C or TPC-E, while if you have a DSS/DW workload you would focus on TPC-H. The TPC-E benchmark is newer and more realistic than the old TPC-C benchmark, but there are fewer submitted results for TPC-E than for TPC-C.

When analyzing the submitted results, I like to view **All Results**, sorted by performance, and look for systems that are similar to the one I am considering. Since TPC-E results go back to 2007, it is likely that you can find a system that has the same number of processors, of the same processor generation and family, as your candidate system.

TPC-E benchmark analysis sample

As an example, let's consider that you are upgrading an existing OLTP system, and want to understand what sort of performance and scalability improvement you might expect for your hardware investment.

Among the submitted TPC-E benchmark scores, you see one from August 24, 2007 for a Dell PowerEdge 6850 system with (4) dual-core, 3.4 GHz , Xeon 7140 processors and 64 GB of RAM, with 184 disk spindles. This system was running x64 SQL Server 2005 Enterprise Edition SP2 on top of x64 Windows Server 2003 Enterprise Edition SP1. The initial database size was 856 GB. This system is the closest match to the existing system that you are looking to consolidate or replace, and its tpsE score was 220.

You also see a more recent submission, March 30, 2009, for a Dell PowerEdge T610 system, with (2) quad-core 2.93 GHz Xeon X5570 processors and 96 GB of RAM, with 396 disk spindles. The T610 was running on x64 SQL Server 2008 Enterprise Edition on top of x64 Windows Server 2008 Enterprise Edition. The initial database size on the T610 system was 2,977 GB. lts tpsE score was 766.

At first glance, the newer, two-socket system offers about 3.5 times the performance of the older, four-socket system. Looking deeper, you notice the newer system is running a newer version of both SQL Server and the operating system, and it has 50% more RAM and has slightly over twice the number of disk spindles, while the initial database size is about 3.5 times as large.

There are many competing factors at play here. The newer version of SQL Server and of the operating system would give about a 10–15% advantage with OLTP workloads, on the same hardware. This 10–15% performance advantage comes primarily from improvements in the SQL Server query optimizer, better memory management in SQLOS, and low-level kernel and network stack improvements in Windows Server 2008.

The newer system has more RAM and more disk spindles, which are required to drive the system hard enough to max out the processors during the test. Having more RAM and more disk spindles in the newer system is somewhat counterbalanced by having a much larger initial database size, which places more stress on the memory and I/O subsystem.

The newer system would have much better single-threaded performance, which is very important for OLTP workloads. Given all of this information, I would feel very confident that I could replace my existing, four-socket system with the newer, two-socket system and have lots of scalability headroom to spare.

If two benchmarked systems were not exact matches to my existing and prospective systems, I would try to use the results of component benchmarks to help adjust for the differences. For example, I might use the results of the Geekbench component benchmark to help determine by how much to adjust a TPC-E score (for my sizing calculations) to allow for differences in the processors and memory types between two systems.

This is a relevant adjustment technique because the TPC-E benchmark is primarily CPU limited, assuming you have enough I/O capacity to drive the workload to capacity, which is a pretty safe assumption for any TPC submitted score, due to the expense and time required to submit an official TPC-E result.

The overall idea here is to use all of the available information from the TPC-E benchmark submissions and component benchmark results, along with your own judgment and common sense, to get the most accurate impression of the performance and scalability differences between two systems.

TPC-E benchmark analysis by CPU type

As an experiment, I imported the current official TPC-E results spreadsheet (available at HTTP://TPC.ORG/INFORMATION/RESULTS_SPREADSHEET.ASP) into a SQL Server database, so that I could easily query and analyze the results. I did a little data cleansing so that the data would always use the same terms for CPU model, SQL Server version, and so on. I also added a few columns that are not in the original official results spreadsheet, such as the MemorySize, SpindleCount, and OriginalDatabaseSize, and added that data to each row in the table, using the information from the Executive Summary for each submitted TPC-E result. Luckily, there were only 41 TPC-E results at the time this was written.

Having done all this, I was ready to write a few queries to see if anything interesting might reveal itself from the actual raw data. Since SQL Server is licensed by physical socket when you buy a processor license, I ranked the results by **TpsE per Socket**, by simply dividing the TpsE score by the number of sockets. This provides a rough guide as to which processor gives you the most "bang for the buck" on the TPC-E benchmark, assuming that the rest of the system was properly optimized.

The abridged results (repeat tests for the same processor model, with the same number of cores and threads, are not included) for the top tier of processors are shown in Figure 3.2. At the top of the list, we have a system using the Intel Xeon X5680 (Westmere-EP) processor. After that come four- and eight-sockets systems using the Intel Xeon X7560 processor (Nehalem-EX). Notice that the TpsE performance scales very well, i.e., the eight socket scores are pretty close to double the four-socket scores for that processor, which is indicative of the effectiveness of the NUMA memory architecture, used in these newer processors.

Next in line is a two-socket AMD Opteron 6176 SE (Magny Cours) system, which does 10% better than the following Intel Xeon X5570 system, which is about a year older. After that, we have a mix of Intel Nehalem- and AMD Magny Cours-based systems.

CPU Type	Sockets	Cores	Threads	TpsE	TpsE per socket
Intel Xeon X5680	2	12	24	1,110.1	555.05
Intel Xeon X7560	4	32	64	2,022.64	505.66
Intel Xeon X7560	8	64	128	3,800	475
AMD Opteron 6176 SE	2	24	24	887.38	443.69
Intel Xeon X5570	2	8	16	800	400
Intel Xeon X7560	8	64	128	3,141.76	392.72
Intel Xeon X5570	2	8	16	766.47	383.23
AMD Opteron 6174	4	48	48	1,464.12	366.03
AMD Opteron 6176 SE	4	48	48	1,400.14	350.035

Figure 3.2:   The top tier of TPC-E results, by CPU type.

The first interesting point to note, on examining the second tier of processor benchmark scores, shown in Figure 3.3 (again, abridged), is just how much of a drop we see in the TpsE per Socket score; the four-socket Intel Xeon X7460 (Dunnington), which was no slouch in its day, shows a drop of nearly 50% compared to the lowest system in the top tier, and a drop of almost 65% compared to the system using its four-socket Nehalem-EX counterpart, the Intel Xeon X7560. This shows what a huge improvement the Intel Nehalem is, compared to the older Intel Dunnington.

You can also see that newer, two-socket Intel systems (X5680 and X5570) do much better than the older, four-socket X7460 systems, both in absolute and per socket terms. Finally, notice the poor performance of the listed 16-socket Intel Xeon X7460 systems, showing the weakness of the old shared front-side bus architecture in older Intel Xeon processors, compared to the newer NUMA architecture (see *Chapter 1* for more details). As you add more and more processors to a front-side bus architecture machine, you get increased memory contention, and your scaling factor goes down.

CPU Type	Sockets	Cores	Threads	TpsE	TpsE per socket
Intel Xeon X7460	4	24	24	721.4	180.35
AMD Opteron 8384	4	16	16	635.43	158.85
Intel Xeon X5460	2	8	8	317.45	158.72
Intel Xeon X7460	8	48	48	1,165.56	145.69
Intel Xeon X5355	1	4	4	144.88	144.88
Intel Xeon X5460	2	8	8	268	134
Intel Xeon X7460	16	96	96	2,012.77	125.79
Intel Xeon X7350	4	16	16	492.34	123.08
Intel Xeon X7460	12	64	64	1,400	116.66
Intel Xeon X7350	8	32	32	804	100.5
Intel Xeon X7460	16	64	64	1,568.22	98.01

CPU Type	Sockets	Cores	Threads	TpsE	TpsE per socket
Intel Xeon 5160	2	4	4	169.59	84.79
Intel Xeon X7350	16	64	64	1,250	78.12
Intel Xeon 7140	4	8	16	220	55
Intel Xeon 7140	16	32	64	660.85	41.30
Intel Itanium 9150N	32	64	64	1,126.49	35.20

Figure 3.3: The 2nd tier of TPC-E results, by CPU type.

The main point to take away from this simple analysis is that any system with processors older than the Intel Nehalem or the AMD Magny Cours (Intel 55xx, Intel 75xx or AMD 61xx) will be pretty severely handicapped compared to a system with a modern processor. This is especially evident with older Intel four-socket systems that use Xeon 74xx or older processors, which are easily eclipsed by two-socket systems with Intel Xeon X5570 or X5690 processors. The Xeon 74xx series had six cores per physical processor (but no hyper-threading) so a typical four-socket machine would have 24 total physical cores available. The newer Xeon 55xx series has four cores per physical processor (plus hyper-threading), so you can have up to 16 total logical cores available in a two-socket machine. The Xeon 56xx series has up to six cores per physical processor (plus hyper-threading), so you can have up to 24 total logical cores available in a two-socket machine.

Component Benchmarks

Component benchmarks are micro-benchmarks that purposely *do not* simulate an actual application workload, but instead generate a synthetic workload that is designed to heavily stress one component of a system. Rather than measure the performance of the entire system, including SQL Server, component benchmarks allow us to assess the performance characteristics of a specific component, or group of related components, such as the processor(s), memory, disk subsystem, and so on.

Performing a component benchmark can be very useful when, for example:

- assessing the suitability of the disk subsystem to cope with the predicted I/O load
- assessing the true performance benefit of an investment in more expensive components (such as processors)
- measuring and documenting the performance of a component (such as the I/O subsystem) before and after making a change
- validating the effects of configuration changes.

I think it is important to remember that component-level benchmarks should be used, primarily, to compare the *relative* performance of different components in different systems. Try not to be overly concerned with the absolute performance results for a single-component benchmark.

Over the coming sections, we will take a closer look at a few useful component benchmarks for testing various aspects of the hardware system for a SQL Server installation, including processor power, memory, and I/O capacity.

CPU and memory testing

There is an age-old, and still prevalent, tradition among many DBAs to attempt to solve SQL Server-related performance issues by throwing more hardware at the problem. Even though the cost of CPU and memory has come down in recent years, it can still represent a substantial investment, and it's vital that you understand, from an engineering perspective, exactly what performance benefit this investment can be expected to deliver.

In this section, we'll briefly review two very useful benchmark tools for CPU sizing, capacity or consolidation planning: **SPEC benchmarks** and **Geekbench**.

SPEC benchmarks

The Standard Performance Evaluation Corporation (SPEC) is a non-profit corporation, the purpose of which is to *"establish, maintain and endorse a standardized set of relevant benchmarks that can be applied to the newest generation of high-performance computers."*

SPEC develops benchmark suites to test the performance of a range of different systems, including workstations, web servers, mail servers, network file systems, and so on. SPEC also reviews and publishes the results submitted by their member organizations.

Most relevant to the DBA, are the SPEC CPU benchmarks, the current one being **SPEC CPU2006**, which is a widely-used and useful benchmark for measuring and comparing CPU performance. It has two separate benchmark suites for measuring computer intensive performance. The first is CINT2006, which measures integer performance, and the second is CFP2006, which measures floating point performance. You can buy these tools (from the SPEC website WWW.SPEC.ORG/ORDER.HTML) and run benchmarks on your own systems, or you can analyze published results on the SPEC website. SPEC CPU2006 benchmark results are published at WWW.SPEC.ORG/CGI-BIN/OSGRESULTS?CONF=CPU2006, and you can search the results by hardware vendor, server model number, or particular processor model number.

Geekbench

Geekbench is a cross-platform, synthetic benchmark tool from Primate Labs. It provides a comprehensive set of benchmarks designed to quickly and accurately measure processor and memory performance. There are 32-bit and 64-bit versions of Geekbench, but in trial mode you can only use the 32-bit version, which is available from WWW.PRIMATELABS.CA/GEEKBENCH/.

One nice thing about Geekbench is that there are no configuration options whatsoever. All you have to do is just install it and run it, and within two to three minutes you will have an overall benchmark score for your system, which is further broken down into four sections, two measuring processor performance, **Integer** (12 scores) and **Floating Point** (14 scores), and two measuring memory bandwidth performance, **Memory** (5 scores), and **Stream** (8 scores).

I tend to focus first on the overall Geekbench score, and then look at the top level scores for each section, as shown in Figure 3.4. These scores can be used to measure and compare the absolute processor and memory performance between multiple systems, or between different configurations on the same system.

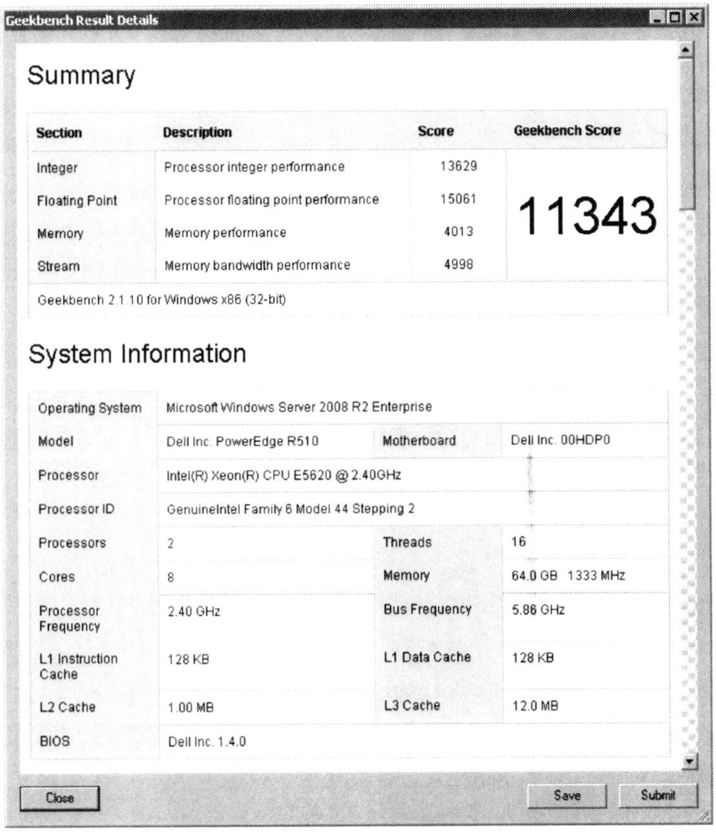

Figure 3.4: Geekbench Summary and System Information results.

I always run each test at least three times in succession, and take the average overall Geekbench score. This, in just a few minutes, gives me a pretty good idea of the overall processor and memory performance of the system.

To get the best performance on Geekbench (and in real-life database usage), it is important that you make sure that Windows is using the High performance Power Plan instead of the default Balanced Power Plan. On most new server systems, there are also Power Management settings in the main system BIOS that need to be set correctly to get the best performance from a system. Otherwise, the system will try to minimize electrical power usage (at the cost of performance) despite what your Windows power plan setting is trying to do. Generally speaking, you either want to disable power saving at the BIOS level or set it to OS control (so that you can dynamically control it from within Windows). This will be discussed in more detail in *Chapter 5*.

Verifying memory configuration

It is common that you can get significantly different levels of memory performance depending on the number and type of memory sticks you use in a server. For example, with Nehalem-EP and Westmere-EP based servers, you have three memory channels allocated to each processor, since these processors have their own integrated memory controller. The memory speed (in MHz) of each channel depends on the memory config-uration. By "memory configuration," I mean the type of memory modules, which could be single-rank, dual-rank, or quad-rank, registered dual in-line memory modules (RDIMMs), and the number of memory modules installed per channel. Single-rank and dual-rank RDIMMs offer more flexibility than quad-rank DIMMs, in that you can install more memory modules per channel at a higher performance level.

For example, with a dual-rank RDIMM, you could install two memory modules per channel, and still get the fastest 1,333 MHz memory speed. If you used quad-rank RDIMMs, and installed two memory modules per channel, you would only get 800 MHz memory speed. This may sound like a dramatic difference but, in most benchmarks I have seen, the real-life performance difference is in the 10–15% range. I would tend to err on the side of having more physical memory available (using dual-ranked RDIMMs), and worry less about the effective memory speed. I say this because even slower memory is much faster than your I/O subsystem, and having more memory will relieve stress on your I/O subsystem.

Fujitsu has an excellent white paper, *Memory Performance of Xeon 5600 (Westmere-EP)-Based Systems*, available at HTTPS://GLOBALSP.TS.FUJITSU.COM/DMSP/DOCS/WP-WESTMERE-EP-MEMORY-PERFORMANCE-WW-EN.PDF that goes into much more detail about this subject. You should check with your system vendor to see what advice they have on how to configure your memory.

Geekbench will accurately measure those differences, which will show up in the Memory and Stream memory bandwidth scores. This can help you validate that you have your memory installed and configured correctly.

Capacity and consolidation planning

I like to run Geekbench on every available non-production system, so that I can save the various system configurations and Geekbench score results in a spreadsheet. Then, I can use this information to roughly compare the overall CPU/memory "horsepower" of different systems. This is very useful if you are doing capacity or consolidation planning.

For example, let's say that you have an existing database server with (4) dual-core 3.4 GHz Xeon 7140M processors and 64 GB of RAM, and this system has an averaged Geekbench score of 5,282. You are assessing a new system that has (2) six-core 3.33 GHz Xeon X5680 processors and 72 GB of RAM, and the new system has an averaged Geekbench score of 22,484. In this situation, you could feel extremely confident, from a CPU and RAM perspective, that the new, two-socket system could handle the workload of the old four-socket system, with plenty of room to spare. You could use the extra CPU capacity of the new system to handle additional workload, or you could use it to reduce your I/O requirements by being more aggressive with SQL Server data compression and backup compression.

In the absence of a large number of different systems on which to run Geekbench, you can still browse online the published Geekbench results for various systems at HTTP://BROWSE.GEEKBENCH.CA/GEEKBENCH2/TOP; simply look up the results for the system closest in spec to the one being evaluated. You can use the search function on that page to find systems with a particular processor, and then drill into the results to get a better idea of its relevance.

Figure 3.5 shows some of the Geekbench scores that I've taken (as of late 2010) for various processors and configurations.

Processor	Speed GHz	Sockets	Cores	Threads	Geekbench score
Intel Xeon X7560	2.26	4	24	24	27,595
Intel Xeon X5680	3.33	2	12	24	22,484
AMD Opteron 6174	2.2	4	48	48	21,132
Intel Xeon X5650	2.66	2	12	24	17,740
Intel Xeon X7460	2.66	4	24	24	16,632
AMD Opteron 6174	2.2	2	24	24	16,046
Intel Xeon X5570	2.93	2	8	16	15,228
Intel Xeon X5550	2.66	2	8	16	14,418
Intel Xeon E5620	2.4	2	8	16	11,343
Intel Xeon X7350	2.93	4	16	16	9,724
Intel Xeon E5440	2.83	2	8	8	7,953
Intel Xeon 7140	3.4	4	8	16	5,282

Figure 3.5: Selected Geekbench scores for various system configurations.

As you can see, there are several modern two-socket configurations that are extremely competitive compared with several recent and current four-socket configurations. For example, the four-socket, Intel X7460 system (24 cores in total) has a Geekbench score of 16,632, compared to the two-socket, Intel Xeon X5680 system (also 24 cores) with a Geekbench score of 22,484. Likewise, the four-socket, Intel Xeon 7140 system (16 cores) has a Geekbench score of 5,282 compared to the two-socket, Intel Xeon X5570 system with a Geekbench score of 15,228 (also 16 cores).

The relative performance seen in each case for Geekbench is similar to that seen in the submitted TPC-E results for what appear to be very similar systems. This is not to say that there is any absolute correlation between the TPC-E benchmark and the Geekbench benchmark, but the fact that we see a similar ratio between two systems, on both benchmarks, tends to reinforce my confidence in the results of both benchmarks. In my experience, the correlation between Geekbench scores and TPC-E benchmark scores is reasonably good, which makes sense, given that TPC-E is a CPU-intensive OLTP benchmark.

Keep in mind, again, when buying processor licenses, that SQL Server is licensed by physical CPU sockets, so if you can find a two-socket configuration that can handle the load of an older, four-socket system, you will be able to save a very significant amount of money in SQL Server license costs.

On the other hand, a four-socket system will have more memory slots and more expansion slots than a two-socket system from the same generation processor family. This means that a typical four-socket system could accommodate a lot more RAM and either host bus adapters or RAID controllers, than a two-socket system. Another factor to consider is that a new four-socket system may have more RAS features than a comparable two-socket system. Nevertheless, I am very impressed with the performance of the latest two-socket systems, and I believe they can handle a very high percentage of SQL Server workloads.

Disk I/O testing

As discussed in *Chapter 2*, one of the most common limiting factors in the performance of a SQL Server system is an under-provisioned disk subsystem, leading many busy OLTP systems to run into I/O bottlenecks.

In this section we'll cover two very useful tools for benchmarking the I/O capacity of your disks: **HDTune Pro** and **CrystalDiskMark**. Also useful in this regard is the **SQLIO** tool from Microsoft, covered in the later section in this chapter on *SQL Server-specific Benchmarks and Stress Tools*.

HDTune Pro benchmark

HDTune Pro is a disk benchmark program from EFD Software, allowing you to easily check the transfer rate, access time, burst rate and CPU usage of an individual drive, or an array of drives. A 15-day trial version of HDTune Pro is available from WWW.HDTUNE.COM/DOWNLOAD.HTML, after which you will need to buy a license to keep using it.

Using HDTune Pro, you can run a read or write test against any logical drive that is presented to a host in Windows. It provides a useful means to evaluate and validate the performance of a drive array with different configurations, and works with both magnetic and solid-state drives. For example, you could run a benchmark test before and after you change the RAID level or the cache policy of a disk array, and observe the effect of the change.

The HDTune benchmark result shown in Figure 3.6 was taken on the 500 GB 7,200 rpm Seagate Momentus XT Hybrid SATA drive in the laptop on which I'm writing this book. It shows an average transfer rate of 82.9 MB/second, which is not too bad for a single laptop hard drive.

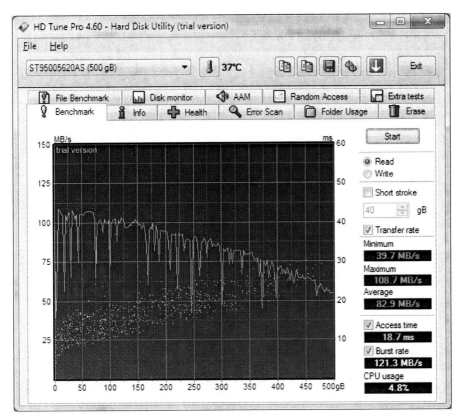

Figure 3.6: Example of HD Tune Pro read results for a single laptop drive.

CrystalDiskMark benchmark

CrystalDiskMark, available from Crystal Dew World at HTTP://CRYSTALMARK. INFO/?LANG=EN, is another widely-used I/O component benchmark. You can select the number of test runs, desired file size, and which logical drive you are testing and it allows you to measure:

- **sequential** read and write performance in megabytes/second

- **random** read and write performance for a 512 K block size, a 4 K block size, and a 4 K block size with a queue depth of 32.

There is a comment area at the bottom of the main screen where you can manually add some information about the logical drive or physical drive that you are testing. The following series of figures show some sample test results for several different logical drives in a test system. All of these tests results used five test runs and a 1,000 MB file size for the test.

Figure 3.7 shows the results from two 146 GB Seagate Cheetah 15 K SAS drives in a RAID1 configuration. Notice the 154.6 MB/s sequential read and 126.9 MB/s sequential write score. The scores for 4 K random reads and writes fall off pretty dramatically with traditional magnetic hard drives. This is an area where SSDs really do very well.

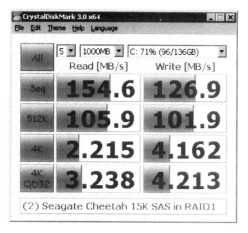

Figure 3.7:   CrystalDiskMark scores for two 15 K SAS drives in RAID1.

Figure 3.8 shows the results from four 146 GB Seagate Cheetah 15 K SAS drives in a RAID10 configuration. Notice the 414.0 MB/s sequential read and 314.8 MB/s sequential write score, which is quite a bit better than for the two-drive RAID 1 array. Adding more spindles is definitely helping performance here.

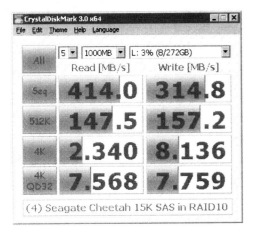

Figure 3.8: CrystalDiskMark scores for four 15 K SAS drives in RAID10.

Figure 3.9 shows the results from six 146 GB Seagate Cheetah 15 K SAS drives in a RAID10 configuration. Notice the 531.7 MB/s sequential read and 414.6 MB/s sequential write score. This shows the positive effect of having six drives compared to having four drives (using the exact same drives and RAID level). Even with six 15 K drives in RAID10, the 4 K random read and write performance is pretty low.

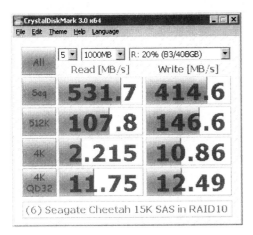

Figure 3.9: CrystalDiskMark scores for six 15 K SAS drives in RAID10.

A single, consumer-grade Multi-Level Cell (MLC) SSD drive will have much, much higher random I/O performance than this six-drive RAID10 array. This is shown if you compare random read and random write numbers between the six-drive RAID 10 array in Figure 3.9 and the single, consumer-grade MLC SSD drive in Figure 3.10.

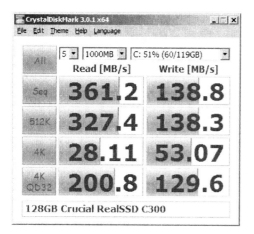

Figure 3.10:   CrystalDiskMark scores for one 128 GB Crucial SSD.

SQL Server-specific benchmarks and stress tools

After you have analyzed and compared application benchmarks and run and analyzed component benchmarks, you should consider some SQL Server benchmarks to help complete your testing and sizing efforts. You can use freely available tools, commercially available third-party tools, or you can write your own SQL Server-specific benchmark tool, if you have the time and development skills. Ultimately, the idea is to perform some SQL Server-specific testing with your environment and infrastructure, using a workload that is as similar as possible to your real workload.

You can use tools like SQL Server Trace, and some of the DMV queries presented in *Chapter 2*, to help characterize your workload in terms of read/write percentage, query execution counts and volume, and what parameters are typically passed to your queries and stored procedures. This will help you generate a more realistic SQL Server specific workload, during your testing with tools like **SQLStress**, **SQLIO** and **SQLIOSim**.

SQLStress

SQLStress, written by David Kubelka and available at www.sqlstress.com/, is a SQL Server-specific stress tool, the main purpose of which is to help find infrastructure problems within a Microsoft SQL Server installation. It can also be used for hardware sizing, system tuning or benchmarking.

The tool does a pretty good job of allowing you to create a configurable workload for SQL Server, using a small .NET 2.0 executable. This executable creates a database with one table and one stored procedure. You can choose the characteristics of workload of the benchmark, as shown in Figure 3.11, to most closely emulate the type of workload that your real applications will apply to SQL Server.

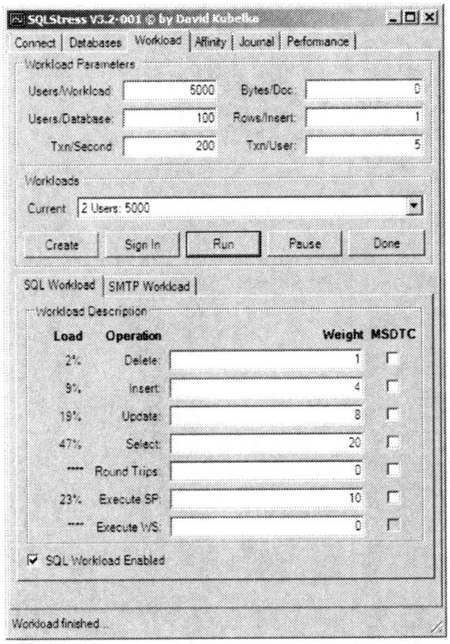

Figure 3.11:   SQLStress Workload tab.

Using the metrics you have gathered from DMV queries, SQL Profiler, and your own best judgment, you can select the breakdown of Delete, Insert, Update, and Select queries to use with SQLStress. After you have configured SQLStress to emulate your desired workload, you can run it to see what effect it has on your test system. Figure 3.12 shows Task Manager during a short SQLStress test run, showing high CPU activity and high memory utilization.

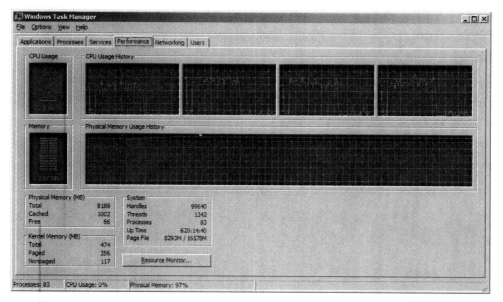

Figure 3.12: Task Manager for a system running SQLStress.

SQLIO

SQLIO is a free tool developed by Microsoft to evaluate the I/O performance capacity of a given disk configuration and it is a valuable tool for measuring the impact of file system I/O on SQL Server performance. SQLIO can be downloaded from HTTP://GO.MICROSOFT.COM/FWLINK/?LINKID=115176.

The name SQLIO is somewhat deceptive, since SQLIO does not actually use SQL Server, and it does not generate an actual SQL Server workload on your I/O subsystem. Instead, it allows you to test the limits of your I/O subsystem, in terms of IOPS and throughput (in MB/sec). Tools such as HDTune Pro and CrystalDiskMark are easier to configure and use, but they don't give you the level of control for your tests that you can get with SQLIO. I like to use all three tools to test my I/O subsystem.

You can use SQLIO before you install SQL Server on the database server, to help test whether or not the logical drives that are presented to your database server are configured correctly and performing as expected. The idea is to determine the absolute I/O capacity of a given configuration, using different parameters for SQLIO. Unfortunately, SQLIO does not have a graphical user interface, so you have to use either the command line or a batch file to run it. There are a number of different configurations and parameters to choose from, which makes the tool a little harder to use.

Set up: the param.txt file

The first thing you need to do is edit the **param.txt** file, shown in Figure 3.13, which is located at **C:\Program Files (x86)\SQLIO** (by default on an x64 operating system). On a 32-bit operating system, it would, by default, be located at **C:\Program Files\SQLIO**, but hopefully, in 2011, you are not using a 32-bit operating system for your new database server!

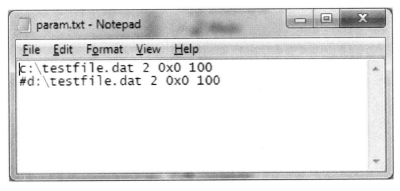

Figure 3.13: Default values in `param.txt` for SQLIO.

The first line has the location (file path) and name of the test file that SQLIO will create and use for its testing on each logical drive. You need to change this to use the logical drive(s) that you want to test. The second parameter is the number of threads per test file. Microsoft recommends that you set this value equal to the number of physical CPU cores on the host being tested. The third parameter is a mask, which you should leave set to 0x0, which is a value of zero. The final parameter is the size of the test file in megabytes. This file should be larger than the size of the cache in the RAID controller, or in the SAN. This is because we don't want the I/O requests to be served completely out of cache, which would give you unrealistically high results. However, be aware that running SQLIO on a SAN, using a large file size, could negatively affect other host systems which use the SAN for storage, since the SAN's cache will be monopolized by SQLIO.

You can actually test more than one logical drive at a time, by adding additional lines to the `param.txt` file. Notice the second line in Figure 3.13, which is commented out with a # character. You want to make sure the `param.txt` file is saved in the same directory as the `sqlio.exe` file.

Running the tests: SQLIO command-line switches

Here is an example of how you might call SQLIO, with some common command-line switches:

```
sqlio -kR -t2 -s30 -dC -o2 -frandom -b8 -BH -LS Testfile.dat.
```

The command-line switches for the example are explained in Figure 3.14.

-kR	R is for Read, W is for Write.
-t2	Two threads. The more threads, the heavier the load.
-s30	The number of seconds to run the test, 30 in this example.
-dC	The drive letter to be tested, drive C: in this example.

-o2	The number of outstanding requests. The higher the number, the more stress on the drive.
-frandom	Type of test, either random or sequential.
-b8	The block size of the request in bytes.
-BH	Buffering type. N = none, Y = all, H = hardware, S = software.
-LS	Latency timing source. S = system, P = processor.

Figure 3.14: Command-line switches for SQLIO.

The easy way to run SQLIO, with many different parameter values, is to create a batch file in the same directory as the **sqlio.exe** file. I like to create a batch file called **RunSQLIO.bat**. A small example of successive SQLIO commands is shown in Figure 3.15.

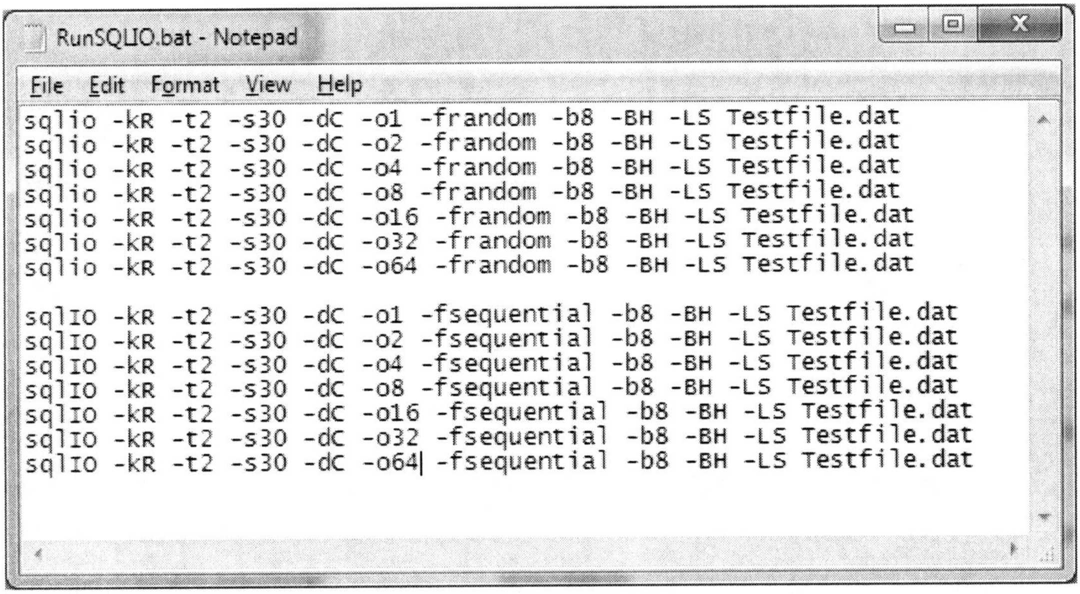

```
RunSQLIO.bat - Notepad
File  Edit  Format  View  Help
sqlio -kR -t2 -s30 -dC -o1 -frandom -b8 -BH -LS Testfile.dat
sqlio -kR -t2 -s30 -dC -o2 -frandom -b8 -BH -LS Testfile.dat
sqlio -kR -t2 -s30 -dC -o4 -frandom -b8 -BH -LS Testfile.dat
sqlio -kR -t2 -s30 -dC -o8 -frandom -b8 -BH -LS Testfile.dat
sqlio -kR -t2 -s30 -dC -o16 -frandom -b8 -BH -LS Testfile.dat
sqlio -kR -t2 -s30 -dC -o32 -frandom -b8 -BH -LS Testfile.dat
sqlio -kR -t2 -s30 -dC -o64 -frandom -b8 -BH -LS Testfile.dat

sqlIO -kR -t2 -s30 -dC -o1 -fsequential -b8 -BH -LS Testfile.dat
sqlIO -kR -t2 -s30 -dC -o2 -fsequential -b8 -BH -LS Testfile.dat
sqlIO -kR -t2 -s30 -dC -o4 -fsequential -b8 -BH -LS Testfile.dat
sqlIO -kR -t2 -s30 -dC -o8 -fsequential -b8 -BH -LS Testfile.dat
sqlIO -kR -t2 -s30 -dC -o16 -fsequential -b8 -BH -LS Testfile.dat
sqlIO -kR -t2 -s30 -dC -o32 -fsequential -b8 -BH -LS Testfile.dat
sqlIO -kR -t2 -s30 -dC -o64| -fsequential -b8 -BH -LS Testfile.dat
```

Figure 3.15: Example of contents of batch file to run SQLIO with different parameters.

When running the test you can redirect the output of SQLIO to a text file to capture the performance information for later analysis, using a command like that shown in Figure 3.16.

Figure 3.16: Example of calling batch file to run SQLIO and pipe results to a text file.

After the batch file completes, the SQLIOResults.txt file will contain summarized performance data that was collected during the test run. The results will vary pretty wildly, based on several factors including your hardware, how it is configured, the type of test (read, write, sequential, or random), and the various other parameters you passed into SQLIO for the test runs. Rather than focus on the absolute numbers, I think it is more valuable to focus on the *relative* numbers, as you make configuration changes to your storage infrastructure.

Interpreting storage test results

All of the I/O benchmark tools we have covered so far give us metrics about **IOPS**, **throughput** (MB/sec) and **latency** (ms), for different storage configurations, with different workloads. After you have run these benchmarks, you need to spend some time analyzing the results to determine whether your storage subsystem is configured correctly to get the best performance from your available hardware. Configuration covers many different factors, including the type of storage, the number of Logical Unit Number (LUN)s, the number of spindles behind each LUN, the RAID level, and the RAID controller or HBA settings.

You also need to consider the purpose of a logical drive in your system. For example, with DAS, you would want to configure separate logical drives for each specific purpose, such as storing SQL Server data files, log files, `TempDB`, and SQL Server backup files. Depending on the purpose of the LUN, you will need to be more concerned with IOPs and latency for random I/Os, or throughput (MB/s) for sequential I/Os.

A LUN that was meant for a SQL Server data file would see lots of random I/O (for both reads and writes) with OLTP workloads, and you would want higher IOPS and lower latency numbers for the best performance. A backup file drive would see mostly sequential writes during a database backup, and sequential reads during a database restore, and you would want high throughput numbers.

As you increase the number of spindles in a LUN, you should see increased throughput numbers (until you saturate the bandwidth of the RAID controller or HBA). With more spindles, you could also eventually saturate the network bandwidth of the fiber channel switch (or Ethernet switch for iSCSI), or the front end port on the storage array. Using an Active/Active Multiple Path I/O (MPIO) driver can help take care of this by using both (or all) of the HBAs within the server, as well as both switches, and more than one (or all) of the front end ports on the storage array.

Generally speaking, disk benchmarks are not CPU-intensive, but you should monitor your CPU utilization during your testing to make sure that there are no CPU bottlenecks that might affect the results. Using larger I/O sizes with SQLIO will result in higher latency numbers.

Figure 3.17 shows the results for two test runs on the `C:` drive of my laptop. My laptop has a 500 GB Seagate Momentus XT Hybrid hard drive. This drive is a 7,200 rpm conventional magnetic hard drive with a 32 MB cache, along with a fairly small 4 GB SLC NAND chip on board that acts as a read cache. As data is read from the magnetic portion of the disk, it is cached in the 4 GB NAND chip in case it is needed again. If that same data is needed again, it can be retrieved from the 4 GB NAND (if it is not found in the 32 MB cache). That is why Figure 3.17 shows an unusually high number of I/Os per second from a single drive. The throughput figures (at around 80 MB/sec) are about what you would expect from a single magnetic drive.

```
SQLIOResults.txt - Notepad
File  Edit  Format  View  Help
C:\SQLIO>sqlIO -kR -t2 -s30 -dC -o32 -fsequential -b8 -BH -LS Testfile.dat
sqlio v1.5.SG
using system counter for latency timings, 2208066 counts per second
2 threads reading for 30 secs from file C:Testfile.dat
        using 8KB sequential IOs
        enabling multiple I/Os per thread with 32 outstanding
        buffering set to use hardware disk cache (but not file cache)
using current size: 12228 MB for file: C:Testfile.dat
initialization done
CUMULATIVE DATA:
throughput metrics:
IOs/sec: 10270.06
MBs/sec:    80.23
latency metrics:
Min_Latency(ms): 0
Avg_Latency(ms): 5
Max_Latency(ms): 202
histogram:
ms: 0  1  2  3  4  5  6  7  8  9 10 11 12 13 14 15 16 17 18 19 20 21 22 23 24+
%:  1  1  1  1  5 30 46 14  1  0  0  0  0  0  0  0  0  0  0  0  0  0  0  0  0

C:\SQLIO>sqlIO -kR -t2 -s30 -dC -o64 -fsequential -b8 -BH -LS Testfile.dat
sqlio v1.5.SG
using system counter for latency timings, 2208066 counts per second
2 threads reading for 30 secs from file C:Testfile.dat
        using 8KB sequential IOs
        enabling multiple I/Os per thread with 64 outstanding
        buffering set to use hardware disk cache (but not file cache)
using current size: 12228 MB for file: C:Testfile.dat
initialization done
CUMULATIVE DATA:
throughput metrics:
IOs/sec: 11360.01
MBs/sec:    88.75
latency metrics:
Min_Latency(ms): 0
Avg_Latency(ms): 10
Max_Latency(ms): 115
histogram:
ms: 0  1  2  3  4  5  6  7  8  9 10 11 12 13 14 15 16 17 18 19 20 21 22 23 24+
%:  0  1  1  1  1  1  1  1  1  1 11 51 25  3  1  0  0  0  0  0  0  0  0  0  0
```

Figure 3.17: Example of contents of `SQLIOResults.txt` text file.

Mike Ruthruff, from Microsoft's SQLCAT wrote an excellent white paper called *Pre-deployment I/O Best Practices*, which is available from HTTP://TECHNET.MICROSOFT.COM/EN-US/LIBRARY/CC966412.ASPX and goes into great detail on how to configure and test your I/O subsystem before you deploy SQL Server in production.

SQLIOSim

SQLIOSim is another free tool, released by Microsoft in 2006, which generates the typical read and write activity patterns of SQL Server by simulating the user activity and the system activity of a SQL Server system. SQLIOSim is a useful tool to use as a final I/O testing step, before you install SQL Server, in order to validate that your I/O subsystem is working correctly with a workload that is similar to a SQL Server workload. SQLIO is more useful to measure the absolute throughput and performance limits of your I/O subsystem, especially after you make configuration changes.

The SQLIOSim utility performs this simulation independently of the SQL Server engine, so SQL Server does not have to be installed to use the utility. It is available for download from HTTP://SUPPORT.MICROSOFT.COM/KB/231619.

In the **Files and Configuration** screen shown in Figure 3.18, you specify the size, growth amount and location of the data file(s) and the log file (being very careful not to use actual, existing SQL Server database file names), since they would be overwritten by the utility.

You can also specify that SQLIOSim uses other configuration parameters that you can specify in `configuration.ini` text files to simulate different types of workload, such as high volumes of sequential writes or a very large hardware cache. This is explained in more detail in the Microsoft KB article available at HTTP://SUPPORT. MICROSOFT.COM/KB/231619.

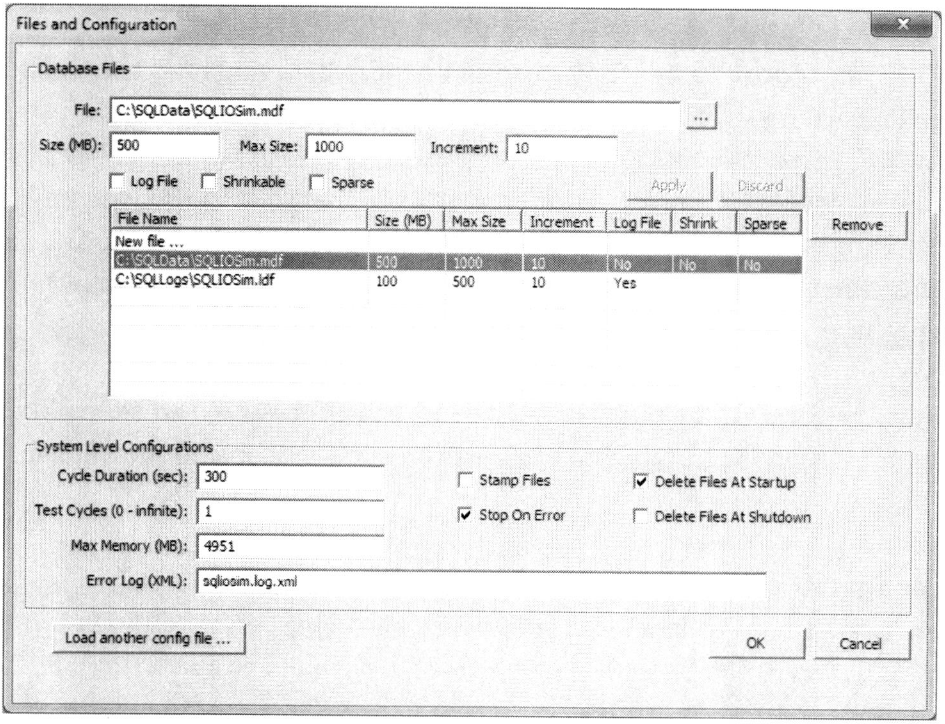

Figure 3.18: Files and Configuration screen for SQLIOSim.

Figure 3.19 displays the SQLIOSim results for each file that was tested. In this example, I had a single data file and a single log file, both on the **C:** drive of my laptop. In real life, you would probably have a number of data files and a log file that were on dedicated, separate LUNs on your test system.

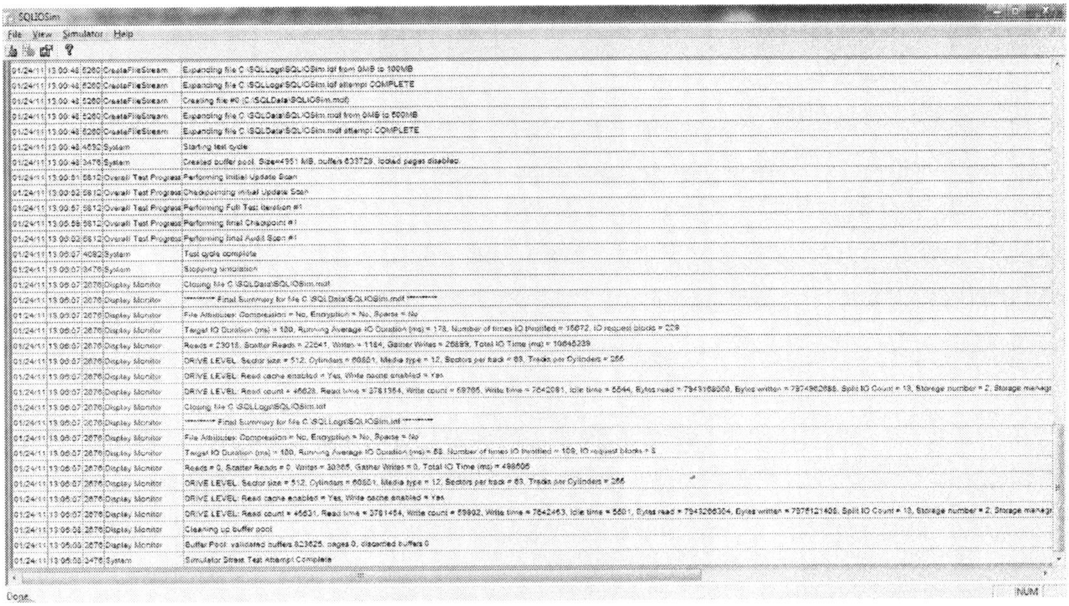

Figure 3.19: SQLIOSim results.

Summary

In this chapter, several different types of benchmarks were introduced, along with some guidelines for how to use them in your hardware evaluation and sizing efforts. Both standardized application benchmarks and component benchmarks can be very useful in comparing different types and generations of server hardware from a scalability and performance perspective. Used intelligently, benchmarks can help you properly select and size hardware to meet both hardware upgrade or hardware consolidation needs.

We have done some analysis of TPC-E scores and of Geekbench scores for different systems with different numbers of sockets and different types of processors from both AMD and Intel. I think this analysis reinforces my contention that modern two-socket Intel systems perform very well for most OLTP workloads. It also shows how well the latest Intel systems perform on OLTP workloads, compared both to older Intel systems and to AMD systems. Given the cost of SQL Server licenses, it is very hard to justify using old hardware for SQL Server usage.

This chapter has also covered some commonly-used disk I/O benchmarks, including how to run them and how to interpret the results. These include HD Tune Pro, CrystalDiskMark, and SQLIO. We have also discussed how to use two SQL Server specific benchmarks, SQLStress, and SQLIOSim to get an even better idea how SQL Server will perform on your system, in your environment, with your workload.

Chapter 4: Hardware Discovery

This short chapter will cover a number of useful tools and techniques that can identify, precisely, what kind of hardware is being used in an existing system, from the motherboard to the processor(s), to the memory and storage subsystem, and how that hardware is configured.

I am always disappointed when I ask a DBA what kind of hardware is in one of their database servers, and I get some vague answer like, "I don't know for sure. I think it is a Xeon?" As a database professional, you really do need to know the gory details of the hardware that you are using to run SQL Server. Old, under-powered hardware can make even the best designed and optimized database run poorly, making you, the DBA look bad. Having modern, powerful hardware supporting a well-designed and tuned database will make you look like a rock star. After all, nobody has ever complained about their database being too fast!

This chapter will help you remove the guesswork, and provide you with the tools you need to uncover all of the sometimes gory details of your existing hardware infrastructure. Specifically, it will cover the **CPU-Z, MSINFO32**, **Windows Task Manager**, and **Computer Properties Dialog** tools. The first one, CPU-Z, provides the most extensive and detailed information regarding your hardware specification and configuration, but the others provide good overview details too, and are installed and available on more or less every system.

Finally, this chapter will show how to identify exactly what version, edition and build of SQL Server you have installed. Many performance-related features are only available in newer versions and higher-cost editions of SQL Server. Microsoft often fixes SQL Server performance and reliability defects in subsequently released Service Packs and Cumulative Updates, so knowing the exact version, edition and build of SQL Server that you have installed is very important.

CPU-Z Tool

CPU-Z is a freeware system profiler (WWW.CPUID.COM/) that can provide interesting and important details regarding the low-level hardware of any SQL Server machine that is running on a recent version of Windows.

I always use the "no install" version, which is just an executable file inside of a zip file. You simply copy the small executable out of the zip file. By running this executable, you can analyze the system in a few seconds, answering several important questions that you may have about the machine, including those below.

- Is the hardware 64-bit capable?

- What is the size of the installed memory sticks – e.g. is it four 1 GB sticks or two 2 GB sticks)?

- How many cores? How many threads (which equates to logical CPUs visible to the operating system)?

- What processor(s) are in use (processor model number, codename, manufacturing technology, clock speed, supported instruction sets and cache types and sizes)?

This tool is also very popular with hardware enthusiasts, who like to use it to document how much they have been able to over-clock their processor, meaning how far above the factory-rated clock speed they have gotten their processor to run, by manipulating BIOS settings. This tends to increase the heat dissipation of the processor and reduce its stability and operating life, so it is not recommended for database server use. Of course, the BIOS of actual servers from major hardware vendors such as Dell, HP, and IBM do not have the required over-clocking BIOS settings anyway.

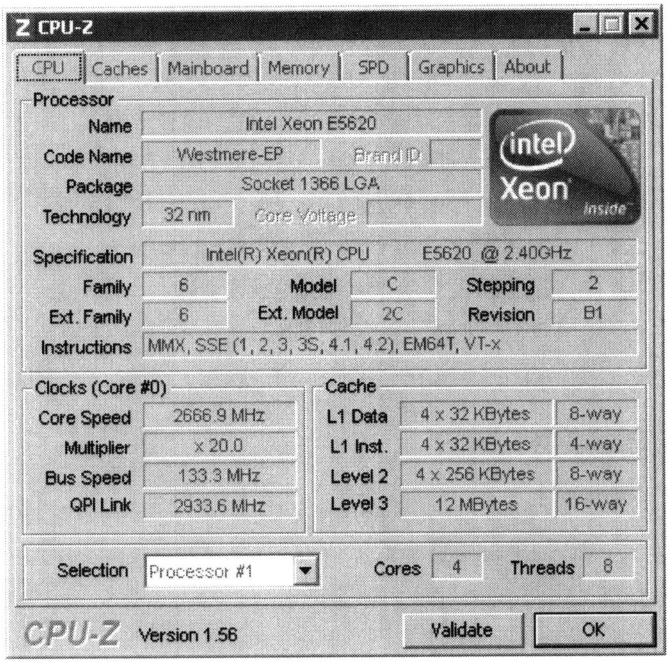

Figure 4.1:   Example of CPU tab in CPU-Z.

Figure 4.1 shows the **CPU** tab of the tool, for a quad-core Intel Xeon E5620 (Westmere-EP) processor, and gives you a good feel for the very high level of detail you can get about the CPU(s) in a machine. This screen also confirms whether the processor is 64-bit capable, (which it is, in this case, since EM64T is listed in the **Instructions** list), and whether the processor supports hardware virtualization (which it does, since VT-x is also in the list). When you see the number of Threads listed at double the number of Cores, that tells you that the processor has hyper-threading enabled. The Cores and Threads listing is per physical processor. If you want to know the number of physical processors, you need to look at the Selection drop-down, to list each physical processor.

With AMD processors, you will see **x86-64** in the **Instructions** list to indicate that the processor is 64-bit capable, and you would see **AMD-V** (which means AMD Virtualization) to indicate hardware virtualization support.

The **Caches** tab, shown in Figure 4.2, provides more information about the various CPU caches, including the L1 Data Cache, L1 Instruction Cache, L2 Cache, and L3 Cache (if the processor has one). Remember, SQL Server is very dependent on L2 and L3 cache size for performance. Depending on the exact processor, these various caches are either exclusive to individual cores or shared among all physical (and logical) cores of the entire physical processor. For example, in the Intel Xeon E5620 shown in Figures 4.1 and 4.2, the L1 Data, L1 Instruction, and Level 2 caches are in each physical core (indicated by the "4 x 32 Kbytes" or "x 4" nomenclature). The 12 MB Level 3 cache is shared across all four physical cores.

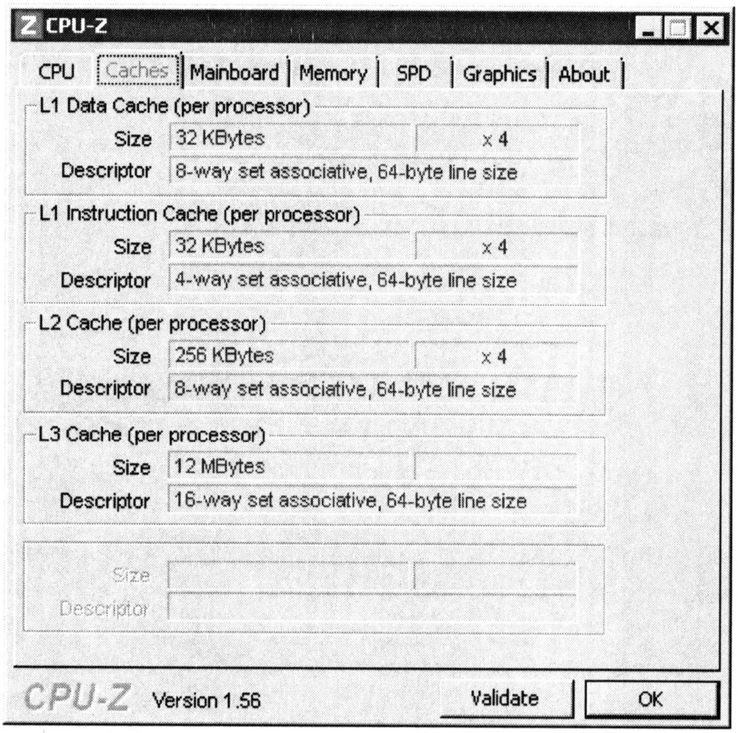

Figure 4.2: Example of Caches tab in CPU-Z.

The **Mainboard** tab, shown in Figure 4.3, reveals information about the manufacturer, model number, chipset and main BIOS version of the server motherboard. It is generally a good idea to keep your main BIOS firmware up to date to prevent stability problems with your server hardware. It will also save time if you ever need to call your hardware vendor for support, since they will probably want you to upgrade to a current version of the main BIOS firmware (and any other firmware) as part of their troubleshooting efforts.

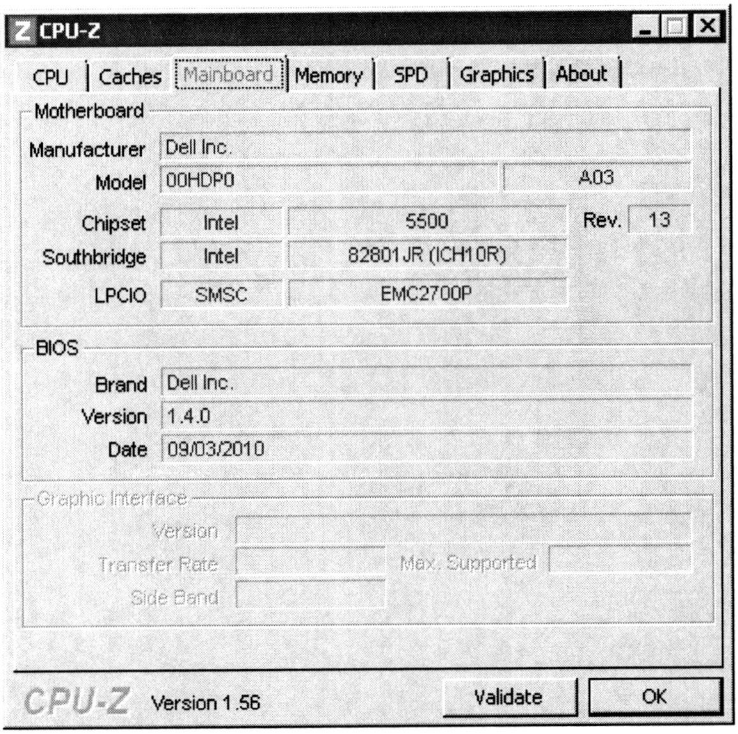

Figure 4.3: Example of Mainboard tab in CPU-Z.

The **Memory** tab, shown in Figure 4.4, reveals the type and total amount of RAM installed in the system. You can compare the values you find here with the specifications for your server model to see if you can add any additional RAM.

You can also determine what type of RAM (DDR2, DDR3, and so on) you have installed in your system. This tab also shows information about your memory timings and the number of memory channels being used.

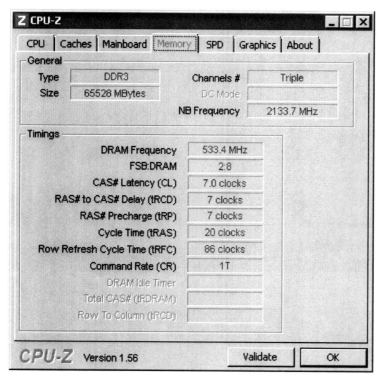

Figure 4.4: Example of Memory tab in CPU-Z.

The **SPD** (Serial Presence Detect) tab, shown in Figure 4.5, tells you how many memory slots are available in the system, and the size, type, speed, and manufacturer of the memory stick that is installed in each slot. This is extremely useful information when you are considering whether you can add more RAM to an existing system. You need to determine whether you have any empty slots and/or whether your chipset and motherboard will let you use larger capacity memory modules to add additional RAM to your system.

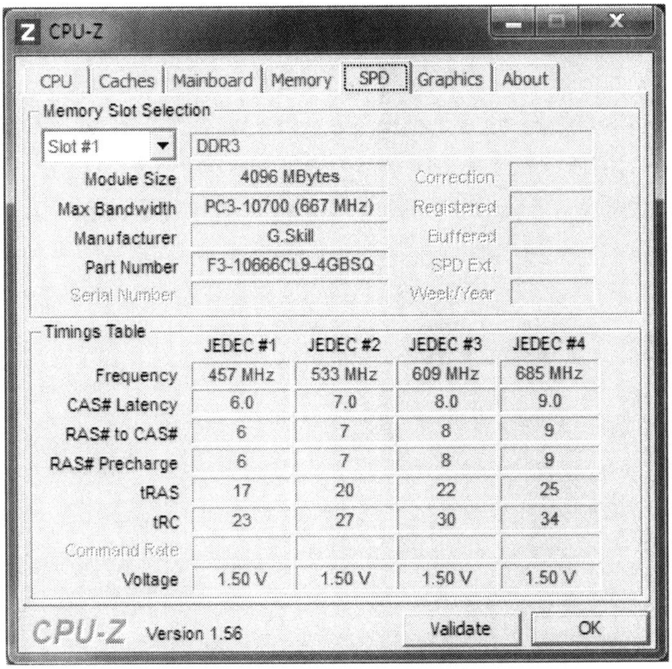

Figure 4.5: Example of SPD tab in CPU-Z.

Unfortunately, on some server systems, this tab will be blank, due to limitations of CPU-Z when it tries to read the hardware information on certain newer systems. If that is the case, you may have to use a system administration tool such as the Dell Open Manage System Administrator (OMSA) to get detailed information about each installed memory module. Another possible solution is to see if you have the very latest version of CPU-Z, which is updated about every 3–4 months. The latest version will work with newer hardware that may not be supported on older versions of the tool.

As you can see, using CPU-Z removes all doubt about the details of the processor(s) and memory installed in an existing system. The tool really comes into its own when comparing information for two different processors, or for the same processor with different configurations.

Figures 4.6 and 4.7 show the CPU tab for a 2.83 GHz Intel Xeon E5440 Harpertown, with four cores and four threads (no hyper-threading), and a newer, 2.66 GHz Intel Xeon X5550 Gainestown, with four cores and eight threads (hyper-threading enabled), respectively. You'll see some similarities – for example both are 64-bit capable and support hardware virtualization – but also some important differences in the supported instructions (SSE 4.2 adds seven new instructions, mainly for text manipulation), along with differences in the size and types of cache, in each case.

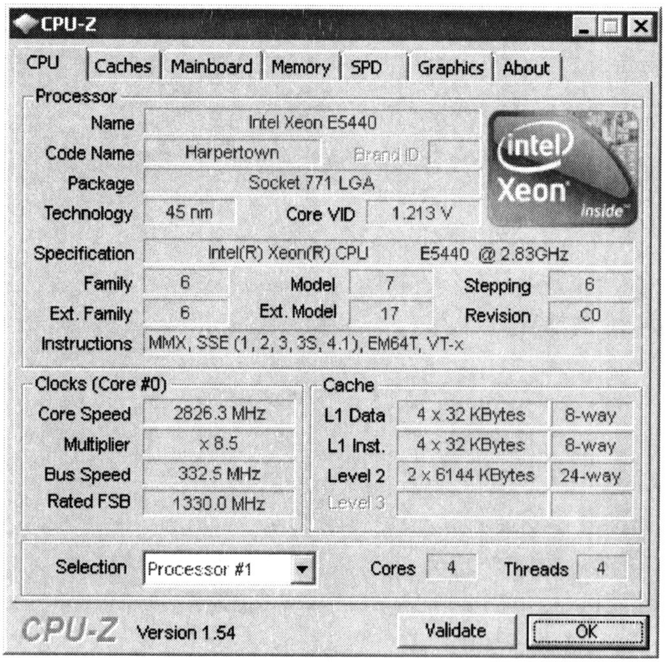

Figure 4.6: Intel Xeon E5440 CPU details.

For example, notice in Figure 4.6 that the rated speed of the Harpertown processor is 2.83 GHz (see the **Specification** entry) and that the current **Core Speed** is 2,826 MHz, indicating that it is running at its full rated speed, which is good.

In contrast, in Figure 4.7, we can see that while the Gainestown is rated at 2.67 GHz, it is only running at 1,596 MHz. This is bad for performance and indicates that some form of power management technology, such as Enhanced Intel Speed Step (EIST), is in effect.

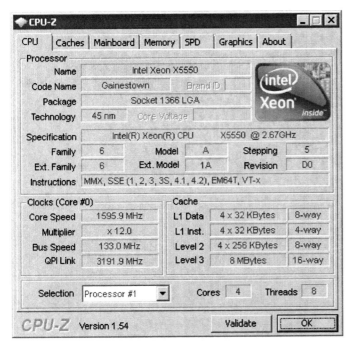

Figure 4.7:   Intel Xeon X5550 CPU details.

Electrical power-saving technologies like EIST are great for laptop computers, since they can help extend battery life significantly, and they can be a good idea for desktop workstations since they can reduce power usage quite dramatically. However, as has been stressed in previous chapters, they are not a good idea for a mission-critical database server.

The switching mechanism that is used to vary the processor speed in response to the workload does not react quickly enough to spikes in the database server's workload to avoid hurting query response times, especially with OLTP workloads. It is a good idea, if you are concerned about performance, to disable any power-saving features in the BIOS of your database server (or set it to **OS Control**), and to make sure that Windows is using the High Performance Power Plan.

If you have an Intel Xeon 55xx, 56xx, 65xx, or 75xx processor, you may notice that the current **Core Speed** is actually higher than the rated clock speed for the processor. This means that the processor is using Intel Turbo Boost technology, which actually works quite well despite the somewhat silly name. Turbo Boost technology allows individual processor cores to be over-clocked if the overall processor is lightly loaded, which allows that processor core to handle a typical OLTP type query faster, assuming that the query is not waiting on non-processor resources. The upcoming Intel Sandy Bridge processor will have an improved version of Turbo Boost that will more aggressively over-clock more cores, based on the ambient temperature of the system. AMD's upcoming Bulldozer processor will also have the ability to temporarily over-clock all of the processor cores by 500 MHz based on the processor load.

MSINFO32

A useful tool that is present on all versions of Windows since Windows 2000 is `MSINFO32.exe`, which provides a comprehensive overview of your hardware, system components, and software environment. By simply typing `msinfo32` into a **Run** dialog, you will open a System Information dialog that offers information about your server such as:

- operating system and build number

- NetBios name of the system

- manufacturer and model number of the server

- information about the processors

- physical and virtual memory details

- size and location of the page file.

If, for some reason, you were not allowed to run CPU-Z on a system, then MSINFO32 offers some of the same information, albeit with a lot less detail. The most relevant information from a hardware perspective is in the **System Summary** section, shown in Figure 4.8.

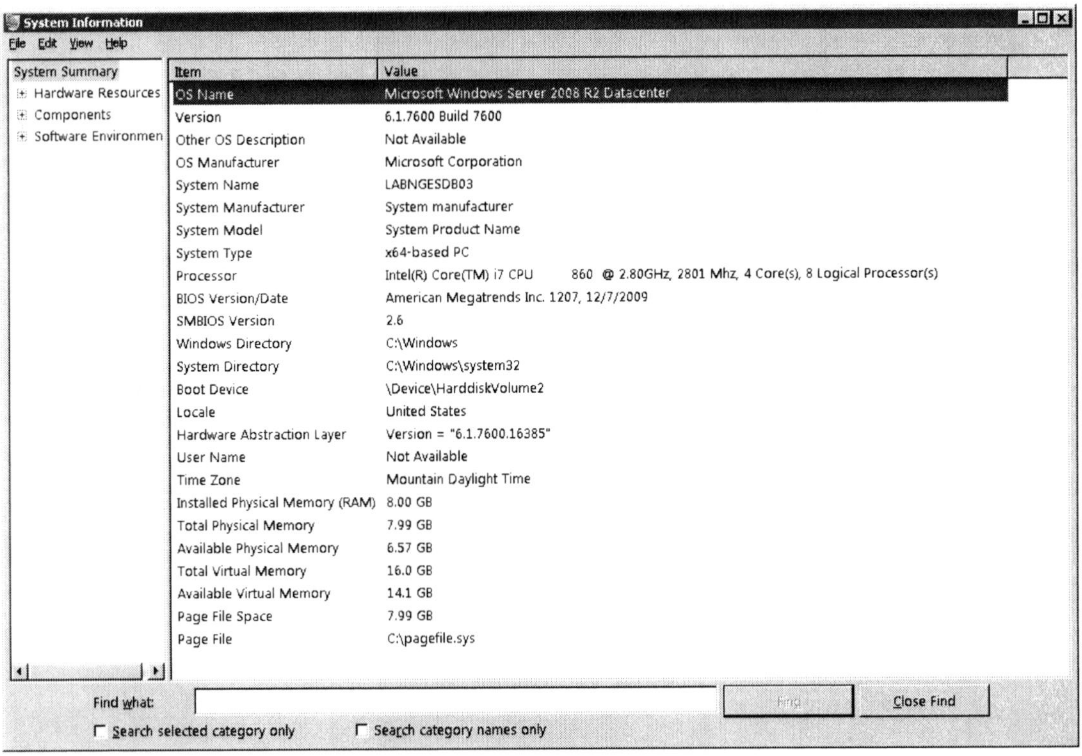

Figure 4.8:   Example of MSINFO32 System Summary results.

There are a number of command-line switches that you can use with MSINFO32, a few of which are summarized in Table 4.1.

`msinfo32 /computer ServerName`	Allows you to run MSINFO on a remote machine.
`msinfo32 /nfo C:\TEMP\TEST.NFO`	Creates an nfo file of the results at the specified location.
`msinfo32 /nfo syssum.nfo /categories +systemsummary`	Creates an nfo file with System Summary info.
`msinfo32/report FileName`	Saves the exported file as a .txt file.

Table 4.1: Command-line switches for MSINFO32.

Windows Task Manager

Windows Task Manager is a useful tool for gathering and confirming hardware information; it is present on all Windows-based systems. The **Performance** tab of Windows Task Manager, as shown in Figure 4.9, reveals how many logical CPUs are visible to the operating system, and how much physical memory is visible to the operating system. It also gives you a very rough idea of the current workload on the server.

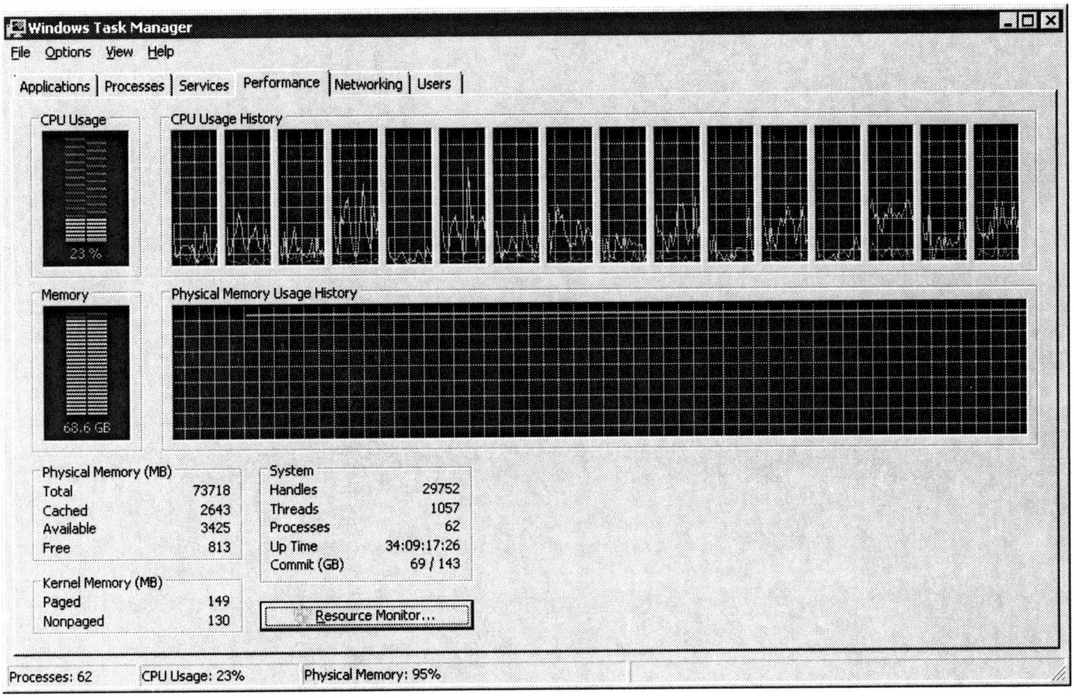

Figure 4.9: Performance tab in Windows Task Manager.

Computer Properties dialog

The Computer Properties dialog, accessed by simply right-clicking on **Computer**, and selecting **Properties**, reveals the Windows Version and Edition, the type and number of physical processors, the amount of installed memory, and whether the operating system is 32-bit or 64-bit.

Different versions and editions of Windows have different limits for the amount of RAM and number of processors (both physical and logical) that they support, so it is very important to know the exact version and edition of Windows that you have installed, along with whether it is 32-bit or 64-bit. For example, the x86 version of Windows Server 2003 R2 Standard Edition has a limit of 4 GB for physical memory, so even if you install more than 4 GB memory on such a machine, the operating system will only recognize 4 GB of memory. The limits of the various versions and editions of Windows Server are covered in much more detail in *Chapter 5*.

The system shown in the Computer Properties dialog in Figure 4.10 is running Windows Server 2008 R2 Enterprise Edition. It has two Intel Xeon X5550 2.66 GHz processors and 72 GB of RAM. In the case of Windows Server 2008 R2, note that this dialog will only ever show 64-bit, since there is no 32-bit version of Windows Server 2008 R2, or newer operating systems.

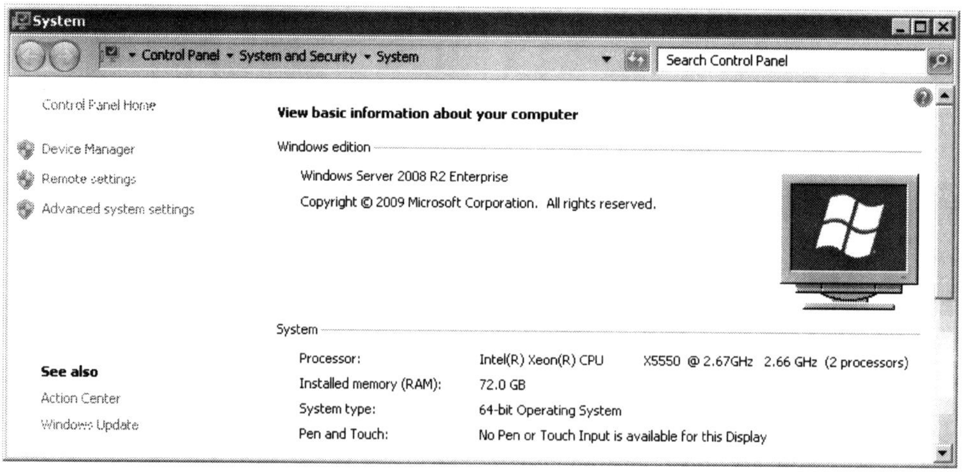

Figure 4.10: Computer Properties for a Windows Server 2008 R2 Enterprise system.

SQL Server version information

On any existing SQL Server system, it is very important to know the exact version, edition, and build of SQL Server being used, where:

- **Version** refers to whether you are using, for example, SQL Server 2005, SQL Server 2008, SQL Server 2008 R2, or SQL Server Denali

- **Edition** refers to whether you have Express, Workgroup, Standard, Developer, Enterprise, or Datacenter Edition

- **Build** identifies the exact build number, which you can use to identify the Service Pack (SP) and Cumulative Update (CU) that you have installed for a SQL Server instance.

This information determines what features are available to you and how current your SQL Server versions and builds are. For example, if you are using SQL Server 2005 or SQL Server 2008 Standard Edition, then you cannot use data compression, since it isn't supported at all in the former case, and is an Enterprise Edition feature in the latter. One good website that maintains a complete list of SQL Server builds (going back to SQL Server 7.0) is HTTP://SQLSERVERBUILDS.BLOGSPOT.COM/.

If you are running an old build of your version of SQL Server, it may mean that you are running on an unsupported Service Pack, which means that you can only get limited support from Microsoft CSS if you ever run into problems (see *Chapter 5* for a fuller discussion of this).

The simple query shown in Listing 4.1 reveals all of the necessary SQL Server information, along with some OS version information (including whether it is 32- or 64-bit).

```
-- SQL and OS Version information for current instance
SELECT  @@VERSION AS [SQL Server and OS Version Info] ;

SQL Server and OS Version Info
------------------------------
Microsoft SQL Server 2008 R2 (RTM) - 10.50.1753.0 (Intel X64)
    Dec 10 2010 10:27:29
    Copyright (c) Microsoft Corporation
    Enterprise Edition on Windows NT 6.1 <X64> (Build 7600: Service Pack 2)

(1 row(s) affected)
```

Listing 4.1:   SQL Server version information displayed in SSMS.

The query results shows x64 SQL Server 2008 R2 (RTM) Build 10.50.1753, (which is Cumulative Update 5) Enterprise Edition running on x64 Windows NT 6.1 (which is either Windows 7 or Windows Server 2008 R2).

Summary

Knowing exactly what hardware you currently have is extremely important for analysis and planning purposes. You can use free tools like CPU-Z to identify many important details about your current server hardware, including whether it is being affected by any form of power management. Other tools, such as msinfo32, and the Computer Properties dialog can give you additional details about your current servers.

Knowing exactly what version and edition of Windows Server and SQL Server you have, or plan to have, on a database server is also very important for your design and planning efforts. Different versions and editions of Windows Server and SQL Server have differing features and limitations that you should be aware of. These differences are covered in much more detail in subsequent chapters.

Chapter 5: Operating System Selection and Configuration

Having selected and configured the appropriate hardware for a SQL Server installation, the next job is to install and configure the chosen operating system. For a production server running SQL Server 2005 or later (we don't cover earlier versions in this book), this means choosing between the various editions of Windows Server 2003 and 2008, and their respective R2 counterparts.

This choice may be narrowed depending on the minimum OS requirements of your specific SQL Server version; for example, when SQL Server Denali hits production, you'll need to be running it on Windows Server 2008 and later. Nevertheless, where choice exists, it's important to understand the features and characteristics of the Operating Systems at your disposal.

Of course, generally speaking, newer versions of Windows Server are better than older ones; they are more secure, perform better, and bring many usability and manageability improvements. In an ideal world, everyone would be running the x64 version of SQL Server 2008 R2 on Windows Server 2008 R2, and it's true that SQL Server 2008 R2 has some low-level optimizations that mean it is *designed* to work better on Windows Server 2008 R2.

However, for those who don't always have the luxury of the "latest and greatest," this chapter will explain the tangible differences between the various Windows Server versions, to help you make the best choice for your SQL Server installation. It will also describe how to install and configure each Windows Server version to get the best results with SQL Server 2005 and above. Along the way, I hope the advice about specific improvements and advantages of the more recent versions of Windows Server will give you some ammunition you need to convince your boss that you need to be running on the current, latest version which, at time of writing (Q1 2011), is Windows Server 2008 R2.

Specifically, this chapter will cover:

- advantages of 64-bit versions of Windows Server and SQL Server over 32-bit versions

- advantages of newer versions of Windows Server over older versions

- advantages of high-end editions of Windows Server over lower-end editions

- how Windows Server is serviced by Microsoft

- important configuration settings for Windows Server.

32-bit or 64-bit?

Most recent releases of Windows Server are available in three different versions: x86 (32-bit), x64 (64-bit), and IA64 (64-bit Itanium). The sole exception is Windows Server 2008 R2, which only has x64 and IA64 versions, and will be the last version of Windows Server that will support IA64.

I have been advocating for some time that people use 64-bit versions of SQL Server 2005 and above, since the biggest barriers to its adoption, namely lack of hardware support, have largely been removed. All server-grade processors released in the last six to seven years have native 64-bit support. The other major obstacle, lack of 64-bit drivers for hardware components such as NICs, HBAs, and RAID controllers, is not really an issue any more, as the advent of 64-bit Windows Server 2008 R2 in 2009 has meant that 64-bit drivers are much more readily available for nearly all devices.

One sticking point, and the bane of many a DBA's life when it comes to upgrades, is third-party databases. Some common reasons for still using an x86 version of Windows Server include: third-party, ISV databases that require x86; third-party, ISV databases that have not been "certified" on x64; and third-party applications using older data access technology, such as 32-bit ODBC drivers or 32-bit OLE-DB providers that do not work with an x64 database server.

I am one of the lucky ones; at NewsGator, we have no third-party databases, and we are a 100% Microsoft shop, so all of the applications that use my databases use the ADO.NET Provider. As a result, NewsGator's production SQL Server environment has been 100% 64-bit since April 2006.

Advantages of 64-bit versions of Windows for SQL Server

The main advantage of running x64 over x86 is that you can more fully and easily take advantage of all of your installed memory, beyond 4 GB.

By default, in 32-bit versions of Microsoft Windows operating systems, each 32-bit process has access to 4 GB of virtual address space (a 32-bit pointer cannot hold a memory address larger than 4 GB). 2 GB of this address space are reserved for the operating system (kernel-mode VAS) and 2 GB are available to the application (user-mode VAS), in this case SQL Server. All threads initiated by the application share this user-mode VAS.

In the x86 world, you have to enable Address Windowing Extensions (AWE) for SQL Server, in order to allow allocation of memory beyond this 4 GB limit. To enable AWE, you must perform the actions below.

1. Boot the system with the `/PAE` switch added to the `boot.ini` file, to enable support for use of more than 4 GB of memory.

2. On your SQL Server instance, set `awe enabled` to 1, using `sp_configure` to make available to SQL Server AWE-mapped memory.

3. Using the Windows Group Policy tool (`gpedit.msc`), assign the **Lock Pages in Memory** option to the SQL Server Service account.

4. Restart the SQL Server Service, after enabling **Lock Pages in Memory**.

The **Lock Pages In Memory** option (more details later in this chapter, and also *Chapter 7*) essentially gives the SQL Server process permission to keep pages in memory, and prevent the OS from trimming the working set of SQL Server. Depending on the Build of SQL Server that you are on, you may need to have Enterprise Edition in order to use **Lock Pages in Memory**. Having performed these operations, SQL Server would get allocated 2 GB memory that it could use for any purpose, plus the additional AWE memory, which could be used for the *buffer pool only*.

You could also decide to add the /3GB switch in `boot.ini` to let applications use 3 GB of RAM instead of 2 GB of RAM (so limiting to 1 GB of kernel-mode VAS). However, you would **not** want to do this if you had more than 16 GB of RAM installed, since when you have more than 16 GB of RAM the operating system requires 2 GB of virtual address space for system purposes, and can therefore support only a 2 GB user-mode virtual address space.

Overall, it's needlessly complicated to make the right choices necessary to be able to use any of your memory beyond 4 GB in any x86 versions of Windows; and even after you've done all of this, only the SQL Server Buffer Pool can use the AWE memory. Another issue with using AWE memory on 32-bit systems is the extra CPU overhead that is required to manage the AWE memory. I have heard of systems reaching between 20–40% CPU utilization to manage large amounts of AWE memory.

With the x64 or IA64 version of Windows Server, SQL Server 2005 and above can use all installed RAM (up to the operating system limit) for pretty much any purpose, with none of the 32-bit limitations. The availability of significantly larger amounts of virtual memory means that SQL Server can use larger paged and non-paged pools, which allows much larger blocks of code and data to be kept in memory without swapping, and also leads to a dramatically expanded internal system cache (1 TB versus 1 GB). The internal system cache is memory that Microsoft Windows allocates to file caching (which is not usually that important to SQL Server). System cache resources are partitioned during startup and do not change.

All of this means that 64-bit SQL Server handles memory-intensive workloads much more efficiently than 32-bit versions. Use of 64-bit also benefits SQL Server engine components requiring memory for items other than the SQL Server Buffer Pool. Some of the non-Buffer Pool memory consumers in SQL Server include:

- **Procedure Cache** – used for cached stored procedures and dynamic SQL batches

- **Workspace Memory** – used for processing hash joins or GROUP BY queries, and for large-scale sorts; also for Index builds and rebuilds

- **Connection Memory** – used for each connection to SQL Server

- **Lock Memory** – used to track lock information for database objects

- **Thread Memory** – memory allocation to worker threads

- **CLR Garbage Collector Heap Memory** – used for the CLR garbage collector when you use .NET assemblies in your database(s).

The performance and scalability of highly-concurrent, large-scale OLTP workloads, typified by high numbers of user connections, cached procedures, and concurrent queries and modifications, will be enhanced greatly by the additional memory available to each of these consumers. DW/BI workloads will often also benefit, for example, from the increased thread memory available to process complex parallel query plans.

Overall, native 64-bit versions of Windows and SQL Server offer significantly better performance and scalability than 32-bit, and are especially beneficial for memory-intensive workloads. Any Intel or AMD server CPU sold since 2004–2005 should be x64 capable; if you are unsure, it's easy to check with a tool like CPU-Z, as described in *Chapter 4*.

Disadvantages of 64-bit versions of Windows for SQL Server

There are some differences between 32-bit and 64-bit processes, in general, which apply to SQL Server. The working set of 64-bit SQL Server is larger than 32-bit both in code and data; mainly due to doubling the size for pointers, 64-bit instructions, and so on.

This means that 64-bit SQL Server will be more sensitive to the size of the onboard L2 and L3 processor caches, which may be used less efficiently when compared to 32-bit, resulting in a higher Cost per Instruction (CPI). This could have a small negative effect on processor performance, depending on your hardware.

The end result is that some applications (especially OLTP) that are not memory constrained on 32-bit Windows may incur a very slight performance penalty when running on 64-bit, using the same hardware. However, the x64 platform will provide *much better* scalability in the long term so it is important not to be shortsighted when evaluating minor performance differences between the two platforms. The huge scalability advantage of being able to use much larger amounts of memory for any purpose far outweighs the small performance hit (from a processor and memory perspective) you may see with some workloads, on older processors.

Windows Server: Versions and Editions

Over the past eleven years, five different versions of Windows Server have been released: Windows 2000 Server, Windows Server 2003, Windows Server 2003 R2, Windows Server 2008, and Windows Server 2008 R2. Each of these Windows Versions has been available in a number of different Editions, such as Standard, Enterprise, Datacenter, and so on, and most have been available in x86, x64, and IA64 versions.

The focus here will be on the 2003 and 2008 versions. I am not going to waste too much time on Windows 2000 Server and I'll start with a short-but-stern lecture: *you should not be using Windows 2000 Server in the year 2011!*

Windows 2000 Server

Windows 2000 Server was released in March 31, 2000, near the end of the first dot-com boom. In order to make development and adoption as easy as possible for corporations and third-party developers, Microsoft ensured that nearly all features and components of the operating system were installed and enabled by default. This led to a raft of serious security issues that caused Microsoft and its customers a lot of problems; fortunately this lax attitude to security is very much "old Microsoft" but, nevertheless, the company has only recently started recovering from the resulting dent to their security reputation.

Aside from security concerns, Windows Server 2000 also suffers from a now outdated architecture that is not conducive to scalability. For example, although Windows Server 2000 was HT-compliant, it was not HT-aware, i.e. it was unable to distinguish a logical processor from a physical processor. This meant that it was possible to install Windows 2000 Server on a four-socket machine with hyper-threaded processors, and have the operating system only use two of the actual physical processors in the server, since Windows 2000 Server allowed a maximum of four processors – logical or physical – per machine and each logical processor was counted against that limit.

Windows 2000 Server was only widely available in an x86 version, but there was a special Limited Edition for Itanium and x64 processors, which was only available from hardware OEMs. There were three editions of Windows 2000 Server, as shown in Figure 5.1 along with their processor- and memory-related license limits.

Version	Processor limit	Memory limit in x86
Windows 2000 Server	4	4 GB
Windows 2000 Advanced Server	8	8 GB
Windows 2000 Datacenter Server	32	32 GB

Figure 5.1: Windows 2000 license limits.

While you can install SQL Server 2005 on Windows 2000 Server SP4, you *really* should not do that, especially since Windows 2000 Server fell out of Extended Support from Microsoft on July 13, 2010.

Windows Server 2003

Windows Server 2003 was released on May 28, 2003 and, to a large extent, was a result of the hard security lessons Microsoft had learned over three years of supporting Windows 2000 Server. One of the guiding principles for the release was **Secure by Default**, which meant that most features and components of the operating system were *not* installed by default and, even when they were installed, they were disabled until a system administrator explicitly enabled them. This dramatically reduced the "attack surface" and thus the threat of security breach.

There are still, in 2011, many systems running SQL Server 2005 on top of Windows Server 2003. This is a testament to the performance and stability improvements in Windows Server 2003, but it is also a potential problem, since Windows Server 2003 fell out of Mainstream Support from Microsoft on July 13, 2010. We will discuss the implications of this later in the chapter.

Windows Server 2003 was available in x86, x64, and IA64 versions and a number of different editions, which included Web Edition, Standard Edition, Enterprise Edition, and Datacenter Edition. One thing to keep in mind is that, from a licensing perspective, you are not allowed to install or use SQL Server on Windows Server 2003 Web Edition, which would not be a good idea anyway, because of the low memory and processor limits present in Windows Server 2003 Web Edition.

Performance and scalability enhancements

Windows Server 2003 took advantage of advances in computer hardware to offer support for 64-bit processors, Intel processor hyper-threading, and Non-Uniform Memory Access (NUMA). It also features optimizations to components of the Windows kernel that make up the core OS, such as the memory and I/O managers, and the system process scheduler, as well as architectural changes to improve core Windows services, such as Internet Information Service (IIS) 6.0.

All of this substantially improved performance and scalability compared to Windows Server 2000 and made Windows Server 2003 a much better host operating system for SQL Server.

HT and NUMA optimizations

Windows Server 2003 addressed two limitations of Windows 2000 that complicated the use of hyper-threading. Firstly, Windows Server 2003 became HT-aware, meaning that it could distinguish a logical from a physical processor, and count only *physical* processors for licensing purposes (just like SQL Server does). Secondly, Windows Server 2003 became much more efficient at scheduling threads among processors. Windows 2000 simply assigned threads to logical processors sequentially. Windows Server 2003 will dispatch threads to inactive physical processors whenever possible, to minimize resource contention and improve performance.

As discussed in *Chapter 1*, AMD processors, and more recently Intel processors, support a NUMA, in which each processor in a multiple CPU system uses a dedicated local "node" for CPU and memory allocation, and an external bus is used from cross-node data traffic. To benefit from this architecture, both the OS and applications (such as SQL Server) must be designed to minimize cross-node data traffic. SQL Server 2008 R2 has some NUMA-related optimizations that will be covered in *Chapter 6*.

Windows Server 2003 introduced optimizations for NUMA machines in the thread scheduler and memory manager. It improved the way the OS assigns threads and memory pools to nodes, increasing the degree to which threads, and the memory they consume, are physically located in the same node. Having an application run locally within a NUMA node reduces data transfer on the system interconnect and resource contention with other applications, which improves performance of applications on NUMA-based systems, if they are properly designed.

Kernel enhancements

Windows Server 2003 also included a variety of performance improvements in the Windows kernel. Performance improvements in the OS kernel meant better service and application performance, since all services and applications run under the guidance of the kernel. In Windows Server 2003, Microsoft improved the way the kernel scheduled thread execution and synchronized requests for resources, which helped to reduce contention-related performance problems on large, multi-processor servers (such as database servers).

Microsoft also optimized the Windows Server 2003 memory manager to better handle systems with large memory, and improved the heap manager, which is used by applications to allocate and free memory. Windows Server 2003 included hot-add memory, allowing servers with dynamic memory support to use RAM as soon as an administrator adds it. On previous operating systems, you would have to shut down the server, add memory, and then restart the server for the memory to be recognized and used.

Editions and specifications

Windows Server 2003 Web Edition was intended as an affordable way to get a Windows operating system onto web servers that might otherwise have run Linux. It has a very low limit of 2 GB for RAM, along with a processor limit of two sockets. It is also 32-bit only, and specifically not licensed for use with SQL Server. This is not really a surprise, since it was meant for use as a web server, but I have had many people ask me over the years whether they could use SQL Server on Windows Server 2003 Web Edition, and the answer is "No."

Windows Server 2003 Standard Edition does allow you to use SQL Server, and it increases the license limits for both RAM and processor sockets with both the 32-bit and 64-bit versions, as shown in Figures 5.2 and 5.3. The one big gap is that Standard Edition does not have Windows fail-over cluster support, which precludes its use as part of your high availability strategy.

Windows Server 2003 Enterprise Edition also allows you to use SQL Server, and it increases the license limits even further for both RAM and processor sockets with both the 32-bit and 64-bit versions. Enterprise Edition is required for Windows fail-over cluster support, which allows you to use fail-over clustering for high availability.

Finally, **Windows Server 2003 Datacenter Edition** raises the license limits even further for both maximum RAM and processor sockets, but with no change to the maximum number of fail-over nodes, as shown in Figures 5.2 and 5.3. Simply stated, if you needed more than 64 GB of RAM or more than eight processor sockets, you needed to use the Datacenter Edition.

As noted, Windows Server 2003 was widely available in both 32-bit and 64-bit versions, and Figure 5.2 summarizes the license limits of the various editions of the 32-bit OS.

Specification	Web	Standard	Enterprise	Datacenter
Maximum RAM (x86)	2 GB	4 GB	32 GB	128 GB
Processor sockets	2	4	8	32
Fail-over cluster nodes	0	0	8	8
Hot-add memory	No	No	Yes	Yes

Figure 5.2:   Windows Server 2003 32-bit license limits.

Likewise, Figure 5.3 shows the equivalent table for 64-bit OS versions.

Specification	Standard	Enterprise	Datacenter	Itanium
Maximum RAM (x64)	32 GB	64 GB	512 GB	512 GB
Processor sockets	4	8	32	64
Fail-over cluster nodes	0	8	8	8
Hot-add memory	No	Yes	Yes	Yes

Figure 5.3:   Windows Server 2003 64-bit license limits.

Windows Server 2003 R2

Windows Server 2003 R2 was released on March 5, 2006. It primarily added improved manageability features to Windows Server 2003, with a series of optional components that could be installed from a second CD disc. A few examples that are relevant for SQL Server include Microsoft Management Console (MMC), and Storage Manager for SANs (which is an MMC snap-in).

Even though it was released nearly three years after Windows Server 2003, it shares the same Mainstream and Extended Support deadlines as Windows Server 2003. This means that Windows Server 2003 R2 also went out of Mainstream Support on July 13, 2010.

Windows Server 2008

Windows Server 2008 was released on May 6, 2008, 18 months after the release of Windows Vista. It shares much of the Windows Vista code base but, fortunately, performs significantly better than Windows Vista. In fact, in the mid-2008 to late-2009 timeframe, it was fairly common for Windows developers to use Windows Server 2008 Standard Edition on their workstations instead of Windows Vista, to get better stability and performance.

Windows Server 2008 was available in x86, x64, and IA64 versions and a number of different editions, which included Web Edition, Standard Edition, Enterprise Edition, and Datacenter Edition. One important change, compared to Windows Server 2003, was that Windows Server 2008 Web Edition allowed the use of up to 32 GB of RAM (in the x64 version), and was licensed for use by SQL Server. This allowed smaller standalone SQL Server installations to use x64 Windows Server 2008 Web Edition instead of a more expensive edition of Windows Server 2008.

Performance and scalability enhancements

One of the key enhancements to Windows Server 2008 was support for Server Message Block 2.0 (SMB 2.0), in order to tackle issues with data transfer latency. It also features various hardware-related improvements, including improved NUMA support and support for hot-adding processors (in the Datacenter Edition). The most significant service enhancement was the addition of support for virtualized environments, via Hyper-V.

Support for SMB 2.0

With previous versions of Windows Server, many DBAs encountered very slow data copy times, when performing SQL Server backups to a remote file share, or copying large SQL Server backup files from one location to another.

Windows Server 2008 introduced SMB 2.0, also known as the Common Internet File System (CIFS), which offers a number of improvements over its SMB 1.0 predecessor, including support for:

- **sending multiple SMB commands in a single network packet** – this significantly reduces the network overhead required for communication, which is especially important for high latency WAN links
- **buffer sizes larger than 64 K** – offering improved performance compared to SMB 1.0 for large file-transfers over fast networks.

Overall, SMB 2.0 enables significant throughput improvements and a significant reduction in file copy times for large transfers.

For backwards compatibility with older systems, Windows Server 2008 supports both SMB 1.0 and SMB 2.0 and automatically uses the version most appropriate for communication. SMB 2.0 is used only between Windows Server 2008 systems and Windows Vista, Windows 7, and Windows Server 2008 R2 systems. SMB communication with all other operating systems uses the older SMB 1.0 protocol.

CPU- and memory-related enhancements

Windows Server 2008 offers NUMA optimizations in the I/O manager and extends the memory manager's NUMA optimizations, compared to Windows Server 2003. Windows Server 2008 does a much better job of allocating memory to a thread's "ideal node," which reduces latency and improves performance by reducing "foreign" memory access.

Windows Server 2008 also supports hot addition and hot replacement of processors, although this should be done with caution (see *Chapter 7* for further discussion). Hot processor addition allows an administrator to upgrade a server's processing capabilities without down-time. SQL Server is CPU-addition capable, so when a new CPU arrives, Windows notifies device drivers of the impending arrival, starts the CPU, and then notifies device drivers and applications (such as SQL Server) that the new CPU is available. This capability is only available in Windows Server 2008 Datacenter Edition, on hardware that also supports it. If you've assigned specific CPU affinity mask settings, SQL Server would honor these settings and ignore the new processor until you changed the affinity mask setting.

Hot-adding a new processor will be a rare event; it requires pretty high-end hardware and, in any event, most servers will be fully populated with processors when they are initially purchased.

Kernel enhancements

The Windows kernel is, as noted previously, responsible for scheduling thread execution across multiple processors, and synchronizing requests for various resources. It does this via a variety of techniques, including the use of various types of spinlock to synchronize and coordinate the actions of the many threads.

Windows Server 2008 reduced context switches via improved **I/O Completion Port handling**. A context switch occurs when the kernel switches the processor from one thread to another, for example, when a thread with a higher priority than the running thread becomes ready. Completion ports are a Windows synchronization API, which is used to minimize switching between the multiple execution-threads that comprise I/O operations. In doing so, it removed the need for use of the dispatcher lock, a system-wide scheduler spinlock, used by all low-level synchronization operations.

This minimization of context switches, together with the resulting reduction in CPU synchronization overhead, can dramatically improve the scalability of heavily loaded server applications, such as SQL Server, on multi-processor systems.

Hyper-V

One of the core service improvements in Windows Server 2008 is Windows Hyper-V, which is a hypervisor-based, hardware-accelerated server virtualization environment that supports 64-bit guests, Virtual Machine (VM) snapshots, VM relocation, and reservation of physical peripherals and CPU cores for exclusive use by specific guest OS instances.

Unfortunately, the vi release of Hyper-V in Windows Server 2008 had a number of issues. These included:

- an inability to do a zero down-time migration of a VM from one host to another

- a limit of 16 logical processors (for the Hyper-V host)

- a lack of support for dynamically provisioning virtual machines, e.g. dynamic memory provisioning.

If you're going to use virtualization and Hyper-V, this is another very good reason to make sure you're running on Windows Server 2008 R2, and the new v2 release of Hyper-V that comes with it.

Virtualization is becoming more popular for database use, since it allows you to increase your physical server utilization by running multiple virtual machines on a single physical machine. It is particularly useful for development and testing purposes, and can be used in production scenarios, as long as you make sure that you have adequate hardware resources (RAM, CPU, and I/O) to support your total workload on the machine.

If you are going to use Windows Hyper-V, you should make sure that your processor(s) support hardware virtualization, and that hardware virtualization is enabled in the main system BIOS.

Editions and specifications

Windows Server 2008 was available in both 32-bit and 64-bit versions, and Figure 5.4 summarizes the license limits of the various editions of the 32-bit OS. Notice that the 32-bit versions have maximum memory limits that are quite low, for all editions.

Specification	Web	Standard	Enterprise	Datacenter
Maximum RAM (x86)	4 GB	4 GB	64 GB	64 GB
Processor sockets	4	4	8	64
Fail-over cluster nodes	0	0	16	16
Hot-add memory	No	No	Yes	Yes
Hot-add processors	No	No	No	Yes
Hot-replace memory	No	No	No	Yes
Hot-replace processors	No	No	No	Yes
Virtual image use rights	Guest	Host + 1 VM	Host + 4 VM	Unlimited

Figure 5.4: Windows Server 2008 32-bit license limits.

Figure 5.5 shows the equivalent table for 64-bit OS versions.

Specification	Web	Standard	Enterprise	Datacenter	Itanium
Maximum RAM (x64)	32 GB	32 GB	2 TB	2 TB	2 TB
Processor sockets	4	4	8	64	64
Fail-over cluster nodes	0	0	16	16	8
Hot-add memory	No	No	Yes	Yes	Yes
Hot-add processors	No	No	No	Yes	Yes
Hot-replace memory	No	No	No	Yes	Yes
Hot-replace processors	No	No	No	Yes	Yes
Virtual image use rights	Guest	Host + 1 VM	Host + 4 VM	Unlimited	Unlimited

Figure 5.5:   Windows Server 2008 64-bit license limits.

Windows Server 2008 R2

Windows Server 2008 R2, released on October 22, 2009, is the first Windows Server operating system that is only available in a 64-bit architecture (in x64 and IA64 versions). It shares the Windows 7 code base, but is 64-bit only.

It supports WoW64 (Windows 32-bit On Windows 64-bit), a subset of the Windows OS that deals with structural and functional differences between 32-bit Windows and 64-bit Windows so that many 32-bit applications run on a 64-bit operating system, such as Windows Server 2008 R2. It is basically an x86 emulator that allows 32-bit Windows applications to run seamlessly on 64-bit Windows. Wow64 is also supported on IA64 (Itanium) but is does not perform as well as it does on x64 versions of the operating system.

Editions and specifications

Windows Server 2008 R2 is available in a number of different editions, which include: Foundation Edition, Windows Web Server 2008 R2, Standard Edition, Enterprise Edition, and Datacenter Edition.

Windows Server 2008 R2 Foundation Edition is aimed at small business users, with a limit of 15 user accounts and 15 user connections. This means that it is not very useful for use with SQL Server.

Windows Web Server 2008 R2 allows you to use up to 32 GB of RAM, and up to four processor sockets. It also allows you to install and use SQL Server, so it is suitable for smaller, standalone SQL Server installations.

Windows Server 2008 R2 Standard Edition lets you use Windows Hyper-V, but with a limit of only one running virtual machine. The maximum RAM limit is 32 GB, which is still rather low. You can use up to four physical processor sockets, but I think it would be pretty wasteful to have a four-socket database server with only 32 GB of RAM. There is no Windows fail-over clustering support in Standard Edition.

Windows Server 2008 R2 Enterprise Edition is the most suitable edition for a large number of database servers. It raises the RAM limit to 2 TB, and raises the physical processor limit to eight. It also allows you to have four virtual machines running in Windows Hyper-V (unless you pay for additional virtual operating system licenses). Most importantly, it adds Windows fail-over clustering support for up to 16 nodes. This will allow you to use the traditional SQL Server fail-over clustering for high availability, and it will also allow use of the new SQL Server AlwaysOn features in SQL Server Denali. I consider Windows Server 2008 R2 Enterprise Edition to be the minimum "serious" edition for SQL Server usage.

Windows Server 2008 R2 Datacenter Edition is required if you need more than eight processor sockets in your database server. You will also need it if you want to run more than four virtual machines at once in Windows Hyper-V, without paying for additional licenses. Datacenter Edition also gives you more RAS features, such as hot add and replace of processors and hot replace of memory. If these features are important to you, you will need to use Datacenter Edition.

Performance and scalability enhancements

Perhaps the most important change to Windows Server 2008 R2 was to add support for up to 256 logical processors (the limit in Windows Server 2008 was 64 logical processors). However, there were also significant improvements to Hyper-V, which addressed many of the issues in the initial release of Hyper-V that was included with Windows Server 2008.

CPU- and memory-related enhancements

Both Windows Server and SQL Server use the logical processor terminology based on the following nomenclature:

- **processor/package/socket** – this refers to one physical processor and may consist of one or more cores

- **core** – this refers to one processing unit and may consist of one or more logical processors

- **logical processor (or thread)** – this refers to one logical computing engine in the OS and application view.

As noted, Windows Server 2008 R2 increased the total number of logical processors that could be supported from 64 to 256. In order to take advantage of this, the SQL Server Engine team did a lot of work on improving the scalability of some of the base components of the engine, including Latches, Buffer Pool, Log Manager, XEvents, and so on. The Scheduler also went through changes to support more than 64 logical processors.

In addition, they did work on the base primitives (used for inserts and updates). These low-level scalability and performance enhancements are also just as relevant on smaller machines with fewer processors (for example, INSERT performance is important, regardless of how many processors you have) and you'll benefit from these improvements, even if you have no need for anything approaching 256 logical processors, just by upgrading to SQL Server 2008 R2, running on Windows Server 2008 R2.

Hyper-V enhancements

Windows Server 2008 R2 Hyper-V supports a new feature named **Second Level Address Translation** (SLAT). SLAT leverages AMD-V Rapid Virtualization Indexing (RVI) and Intel VT Extended Page Tables (EPT) technology to reduce the overhead incurred during the virtual-to-physical address mapping performed for virtual machines. Through RVI or EPT respectively, AMD-V and Intel VT processors use SLAT to maintain address mappings and perform, in hardware, the two levels of address space translations required for each virtual machine. This reduces the complexity of the Windows hypervisor and also the number of context switches needed to manage virtual machine page faults.

With SLAT, the Windows hypervisor does not need to shadow the guest operating system page mappings. The reduction in processor and memory overhead associated with SLAT improves scalability with respect to the number of virtual machines that can be concurrently supported on a single Hyper-V server. Windows Server 2008 R2 Hyper-V can now use up to 64 logical CPUs on host computers, which is twice Windows Server 2008 Hyper-V's initial number of supported logical CPUs. This allows you to take better advantage of newer multi-core systems and it allows greater virtual machine consolidation ratios per physical host. There is still a limit of four virtual CPUs per virtual machine. This means that your entire Hyper-V infrastructure on a single host machine can use up to 64 logical CPUs on that host machine, but that each individual guest virtual machine can only have between one and four virtual CPUs.

In plain English, all of this means that you will be able to run more virtual machines on a single Hyper-V server, with better performance. This will give you more flexibility if you need to add more virtual machines as part of a consolidation effort.

Windows Server 2008 R2 Service Pack 1 also added a new feature called **Dynamic Memory**, which offers greater flexibility in terms of how memory settings are configured within Hyper-V. It allows Hyper-V hosts to dynamically adjust the amount of memory available to virtual machines in response to changing workloads, and generally means that you can get better use out of your available physical memory, and so increase the Virtual Machine (VM) density on the host server. This is also a good thing for the DBA, since it will allow more effective use of available physical memory, and so the ability to support more virtual machines on a single Hyper-V server.

SMB 2.1

Server Message Block (SMB) 2.1, introduced with Windows 7 and Windows Server 2008 R2, introduces a new opportunistic locking mechanism, which reduces locking, and optimizations to reduce network chattiness, which improves overall network performance.

Editions and specifications

The license limits for the primary Editions of Windows Server 2008 R2 are shown in Figure 5.6.

Specification	Web	Standard	Enterprise	Datacenter	Itanium
Maximum RAM	32GB	32GB	2TB	2TB	2TB
Processor sockets	4	4	8	64	64
Fail-over cluster nodes	0	0	16	16	8
Hot-add memory	No	No	Yes	Yes	Yes
Hot-add processors	No	No	No	Yes	Yes
Hot-replace memory	No	No	No	Yes	Yes
Hot-replace processors	No	No	No	Yes	Yes
Virtual image use rights	Guest	Host + 1 VM	Host + 4 VM	Unlimited	Unlimited

Figure 5.6: Windows Server 2008 R2 license limits.

Microsoft Support Policies for Windows Server

For Business and Developer products, which include Windows Server and SQL Server, Microsoft provides ten years of support; five years of Mainstream Support and five years of Extended Support, at the supported Service Pack level. The term "supported Service Pack" means that you cannot be running a retired Service Pack if you want the normal level of Mainstream or Extended support from Microsoft. Note that the RTM branch of a SQL Server release can be considered a non-supported Service Pack. For example, the SQL Server 2008 RTM is considered an unsupported Service Pack.

This policy is very important when you are using and maintaining SQL Server, because it affects what type of support you will receive when you contact Microsoft's Customer Service and Support (CSS) team.

Mainstream Support

Mainstream Support is offered during the first phase of the product lifecycle. At the supported Service Pack level, Mainstream Support includes:

- incident support (no-charge incident support, paid incident support, and support charged on an hourly basis)
- security update support
- the ability to request non-security hot-fixes through CSS or the Product Team.

Ideally, as a database professional, you want all of your SQL Server installations to be running under Mainstream Support. You should be ringing the alarm bell, and pushing your organization to upgrade to a newer, supported version of Windows Server, before the version you are running on falls out of Mainstream Support.

Extended Support

The Extended Support phase follows Mainstream Support and, at the supported Service Pack level, includes:

- paid support – i.e. you will have to pay for any support calls to Microsoft CSS
- security update support at no additional cost
- non-security related hot-fix support, but only upon purchase of a separate Extended Hotfix Support Agreement (per-fix fees also apply).

Once a version of Windows Server enters the Extended Support phase, no more Service Packs will be available for that operating system. There will be security-related updates available through Windows and Microsoft Update, but nothing else, unless you pay for an Extended Hotfix Support Agreement.

Another factor to consider, as a DBA, is that if your operating system is in Extended Support, it is quite likely that your hardware is rather old (and probably also out of warranty), which means that it will be less reliable, and extremely slow compared to modern hardware. It is also probable that you are running SQL Server 2005, which will fall out of Mainstream Support on April 12, 2011.

The relevant release and support end dates for Windows Server are shown in Figure 5.7, and release dates, and their accompanying mainstream and extended support dates for SQL Server, are shown in Figure 5.8.

Operating System	Release date	Mainstream Support ends	Extended Support ends
Windows 2000 Server	3/31/2000	6/30/2005	7/13/2010
Windows Server 2003	5/28/2003	7/13/2010	7/14/2015
Windows Server 2003 R2	3/5/2006	7/13/2010	7/14/2015
Windows Server 2008	5/6/2008	7/9/2013	7/10/2018
Windows Server 2008 R2	10/22/2009	7/9/2013	7/10/2018

Figure 5.7: Operating System release and support timelines.

SQL Server Version	Release date	Mainstream Support ends	Extended Support ends
SQL Server 2005	1/14/2006	4/12/2011	4/12/2016
SQL Server 2008	11/7/2008	1/14/2014	1/8/2019
SQL Server 2008 R2	7/20/2010	1/14/2014	1/8/2019

Figure 5.8: SQL Server release and support timelines.

One thing that may surprise you, because I know it surprised me, is that the support dates are identical for Windows Server 2003 and Windows Server 2003 R2, just as they are for Windows Server 2008 and Windows Server 2008 R2, which means that, from a support point of view, there is no benefit to being on the R2 version of those operating systems. A similar situation exists for SQL Server 2008 and SQL Server 2008 R2. However, as we have discussed, there are tangible performance and scalability advantages from using Windows Server 2008 R2 instead of Windows Server 2008.

Out-of-support case study

Imagine that it is May 1, 2011. You have a Dell PowerEdge 6850 server that your company purchased on January 15, 2007. This server has four 3.4 GHz dual-core Xeon 7140M processors and 32 GB of RAM. You installed the latest version of the Windows operating system and of SQL Server when you purchased the hardware, so it is running x64 Windows Server 2003 R2 Enterprise Edition, with x64 SQL Server 2005 Enterprise Edition, Service Pack 4.

Even though you have been very conscientious about maintaining this server, by installing firmware, BIOS, and driver updates, and you have kept both the operating system and SQL Server 2005 completely up to date with Service Packs, Cumulative Updates, and Windows hot-fixes, this poor server has really reached the end of its useful life.

Unless you paid dearly to extend it, the warranty on the hardware expired on January 15, 2010. That means that you will be paying to replace any parts that fail, and waiting longer for them to be delivered. There will be no more firmware, BIOS or driver updates for this server. This server is also extremely under-powered by modern standards. It has less overall CPU capacity than many modern laptop computers.

The Windows Server 2003 R2 operating system fell out of Mainstream Support on July 13, 2010, while SQL Server 2005 SP4 fell out of Mainstream Support on April 12, 2011. This means there will be no more Service Packs for either Windows Server 2003 R2 or for SQL Server 2005. There will be no more Cumulative Updates for SQL Server 2005. All you will get, for either the OS or for SQL Server 2005, will be security-related hot-fixes. If anything goes wrong with the hardware, the operating system or with SQL Server, you will be essentially on your own, unless you have paid for extended hot-fix support. Is this really where you want to be?

Of course, I can hear the objections and excuses now. Many people struggle to find the budget, or development and testing resources, to upgrade their existing applications to a newer version of Windows Server and SQL Server; they have problems with the fact that their third-party vendor has not certified their application on SQL Server 2008; they don't have the hardware budget to buy a new server to replace their old, out-of-warranty server, and so on.

Yes, upgrading is sometimes difficult, and expensive, but I will say, firstly, that there is little excuse for an ISV not to have certified their applications on SQL Server 2008 by now. Of course, there are always exceptions and extenuating circumstances, for example, if you work in an industry, such as the medical industry, that requires government certification for new versions of SQL Server.

Secondly, it really is normally not that difficult to update an existing user database (as opposed to the SQL Server instance itself) from SQL Server 2005 to SQL Server 2008 or SQL Server 2008 R2. In fact, if you're clever, you can use something like database mirroring to fail-over from the old server to the new server, and perform the database version upgrade with a sub-minute outage.

In my mind, it does not make much sense to upgrade to a newer version of Windows Server or SQL Server, but keep using the same old existing hardware. Instead, you should make the case for buying new hardware, with a fresh copy of Windows Server 2008 R2, and SQL Server 2008 R2 (which work much better together).

Of course, this adds to the cost, but it makes the upgrade process much easier to plan and manage. If you purchased Software Assurance from Microsoft, your software license costs for upgrading to these new versions would be zero. Buying a new server means you can get the server racked, the OS installed and patched, and configured, and SQL Server installed, patched, and configured in a low risk and low stress manner. You can also offset, or in some cases more than cover, the upgrade cost by exploiting the new hardware and software features to, for example:

- move from a four-socket machine down to a two-socket machine, reducing SQL Server license costs considerably while obtaining better performance and scalability than your old four-socket machine
- take advantage of opportunities for server consolidation or virtualization.

Overall, a new database server, running the latest versions of SQL Server and Windows Server, will serve you so much better than a 3–4 year old server, from every perspective. I would argue that you should be pushing your organization to upgrade sooner rather than later.

Installing Windows Server and Service Packs

When Microsoft releases a new version of Windows Server, the initial build is called the **Release to Manufacturing (RTM)** build of the operating system. It is what you get on the installation media when you buy a copy of the operating system. At some point, usually between 12–18 months after the release of the RTM, Microsoft will release Service Pack 1 (SP1) for that version of the operating system. A Service Pack will include all of the previously released hot-fixes, and will sometimes include some new features for the operating system. For example, Windows Server 2008 R2 SP1 added the new Dynamic Memory feature, as discussed earlier.

During the period after RTM, but before SP1, Microsoft will release hot-fixes for the operating system, through Windows Update. If you also install the optional Microsoft Update components (a superset of Windows Update), you will also receive updates, hot-fixes, and so on, for other Microsoft products, such as SQL Server. Microsoft typically pushes out these updates once a month, on the second Tuesday of the month (called Patch Tuesday). These hot-fixes will continue to be released throughout the life of that version of Windows Server, until it falls out of Extended Support.

If you are installing Windows Server on a new server, you will initially install the RTM version that comes on the installation media. Then, you should install the latest Service Pack that is available for that version of Windows Server. Windows Service Packs are cumulative, so there is no need to install SP1 before SP2; just install the latest one. I always download the setup program for the required Service Pack onto another server, copy it to a USB thumb drive, and then from there to the new, unpatched server. This means that I can install the Service Pack *before* I connect that new server to the Internet. Finally, I use Microsoft Update to get all of the released hot-fixes for that version and Service Pack of Windows Server.

Now that Windows Server 2008 R2 Service Pack 1 is available, you can save quite a bit of installation and patching time by using a slipstreamed version of the OS installation media that includes SP1 in the initial installation. This will allow you to install Windows Server 2008 R2 with Service Pack 1 in a single step, which is much faster than installing the RTM version, then installing SP1 as a separate step.

Configuring Windows Server

Having selected and installed your Windows operating system, there are several settings that can be tweaked in order to optimize the overall performance of your SQL Server installation. This section will discuss the following Windows settings:

- **Windows Power Plans** – designed to let you manage how your server uses power, this setting can have a dramatic effect on processor performance, and is controlled through Windows as well as the firmware BIOS settings

- **Windows Instant File Initialization** – designed to decrease the time required to create and restore SQL Server data files by skipping the default zeroing out behavior

- **Lock Pages in Memory** – designed to allow SQL Server to control whether the operating system can arbitrarily page out SQL Server memory.

Windows Power Plans and CPU performance

The Windows Power Plans feature is designed to enable you, if possible, to adopt a greener strategy with regard to the power consumption of your servers. Its settings are **Balanced** (the default), **Power saver**, and **High performance**. As worthwhile a goal as it may be to run in Balanced, or even Power saver mode in order to minimize consumption, it's also important to understand exactly what impact this might have on your processor performance, and so the overall performance of your database server.

Note, also, that your server's power consumption characteristics aren't solely controlled through this Windows setting; most new server models from major system manufacturers, such as Dell and HP, have a section in the main system BIOS (firmware) that moderates the amount of control allowed by the Windows OS in regard to power usage. Usually, you have three choices for this BIOS setting (the names may be different in your particular BIOS, depending on the manufacturer, but the function is the same).

1. **None** – your processors will run at full rated speed at all times, regardless of the processor load or temperature, and regardless of the Windows Power Plan setting.

2. **OS Control** – Windows will dictate and control the power management for the server, using one of the Windows Power Plans.

3. **Hardware** – the processor itself controls its power usage based on its load and temperature; I think that is the least desirable setting, since it takes control out of the DBA's hands and out of Windows hands.

I have seen many DBAs change the Windows Power Plan from the default **Balanced** setting to the **High performance** setting, and then wonder why their processors are still running at lower than their rated clock speed. The answer, of course, is that the BIOS setting was set to hardware control.

Therefore, it's important to investigate the effect of both the BIOS setting and the Windows Power Plan setting, on the power usage and the CPU performance of the server. You can use the CPU-Z tool (see *Chapter 4*) to measure the current processor speed compared to the rated processor speed, to confirm whether you are seeing the effects of processor power management.

In order to explore this issue deeply, my goal was to offer more concrete guidance on which settings you should choose depending on your performance and power usage objectives. In order to do this, I used the Geekbench tool (see *Chapter 3*) to measure CPU performance, while simultaneously using a simple Kill-A-Watt meter to measure the overall power consumption (in watts) of the server.

In February 2010, I performed some initial Geekbench-only tests on the effects on processor performance of the Windows Power Plans setting in Windows Server 2008 R2. In this round of testing, based on a 2.8 GHz Intel Core i7 860 processor in an ASUS desktop board, I measured a 22% increase in the Geekbench score when switching from the default, Balanced power plan to the High performance power plan, which seemed pretty significant.

In September 2010, I performed the more detailed testing that I report here, using proper server hardware, and measuring the Geekbench performance alongside the actual power usage of the entire system, for various combinations of BIOS settings and Windows Power Plans.

I also measured, as part of these tests, the impact on CPU performance and power usage of the following:

- having one physical CPU and two physical CPUs in an otherwise identical two-socket server

- enabling the processor Turbo Boost option

- enabling hyper-threading.

The hardware

NewsGator had just received a couple of nearly identical Dell PowerEdge R410 1U rack mount servers that were destined be used as middle-tier servers, so I took the opportunity to run these benchmark tests as part of the burn-in process.

Both of these servers have 16 GB of DDR3 RAM, one 15 K 146 GB 3.5" SAS drive and dual power supplies. The only difference is that one server has two Intel Xeon E5620 processors, while the other server only has one Intel Xeon E5620 processor. The 32 nm Intel Xeon E5620 Westmere-EP processor has a rated speed of 2.4 GHz, with the ability to go to 2.66 GHz with Turbo Boost. It is a quad-core processor that also supports hyper-threading, so the operating system can see eight logical processors for each actual physical processor, when hyper-threading is enabled.

Figure 5.9 presents the details for one of these Intel Xeon E5620 processors, using the CPU-Z utility (described in *Chapter 4*). It shows the effects of Turbo Boost raising the clock speed from 2.40 GHz to 2.66 GHz.

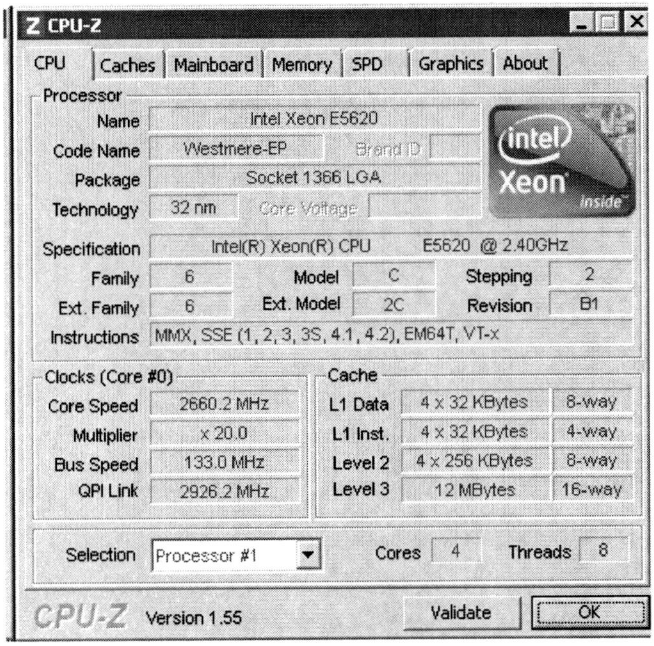

Figure 5.9: Intel Xeon X5620 with hyper-threading and Turbo Boost enabled.

Tweaking the Windows, BIOS, and hardware settings

In the main BIOS setup screen of the Dell R410, navigate to the **Power Management** section, where you can change the setting to **OS Control**, which lets Windows manage the various power settings more completely.

In the **Processor Settings** section, you can enable or disable Turbo Mode (the default is enabled), as well as hyper-threading, via the Logical Processor setting (this default is also enabled).

C1E and C States settings

As energy efficiency becomes more of a mainstream concern, each new generation of processors from both Intel and AMD have become more energy efficient and include more power management features. These C states, which can be enabled and disabled in the same Processor Settings section, refer to different sleep modes, and are only relevant when a processor goes into a sleep mode after a period of inactivity.

To set the Windows Power Plan setting in Windows Server 2008 and Windows Server 2008 R2, you can reach the **Power Options** screen, shown in Figure 5.10, by typing **powercfg.cpl** in a **Run** prompt. There you will see three default power plans; **Balanced**, **High performance** and **Power saver**. By default, it is set to **Balanced**, which is what Microsoft recommends for general use. Unfortunately, as my tests will prove, the default **Balanced** power plan is not necessarily the best choice for database server performance.

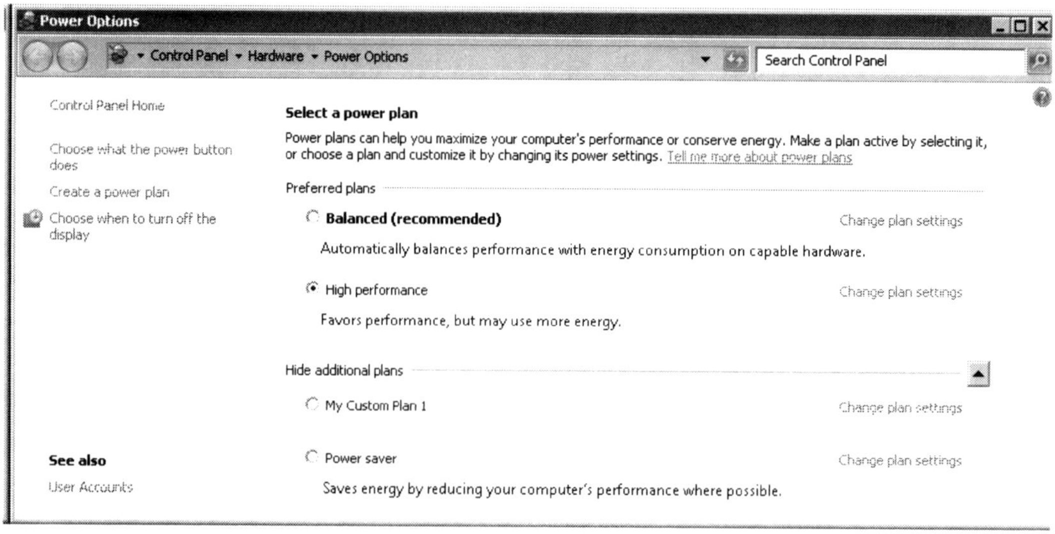

Figure 5.10: Windows Power Options dialog with High performance plan selected.

By running the CPU-Z utility, you can find out how the core speed and multiplier of Core #0 of any of your physical processors varies, on a nearly real-time basis, as you change

Windows Power plans and run benchmarks. This enables the DBA to track what is going on with the processor(s) based on the power plan setting and the current processor load.

The multiplier value shows the relationship between the bus speed of your system and the clock speed of your processor. Power management features will vary this multiplier value to change the clock speed of the processor.

Effect of Windows Power Plan setting on power usage and CPU performance

These test results report the effect on overall power usage of the various Windows Power Plan settings, for both the 1- and 2-CPU systems. The power usage figures quoted are the peak figures observed while running the Geekbench tests.

Of course, there are a lot of other components using electrical power in the server besides the processors, so you will have a baseline electrical usage that exists despite anything that you do with processor power management. It is actually quite interesting to watch what happens to the real-time power usage of a modern server as you turn it on and watch it go through the Power On Self-Test (POST) process and boot into Windows.

The single-processor Dell PowerEdge R410 peaked at 144 watts during boot and then settled down to an average usage of about 95 watts, after Windows finished loading and became idle. The two-processor Dell PowerEdge R410 peaked at 174 watts during boot and then settled down to an average "idle" power usage of about 110 watts. In each case, the startup and idle power usage figures were unaffected by the hyper-threading or Turbo Boost settings.

For the power usage figures acquired during the Geekbench tests, shown in Figure 5.11, Turbo Boost and hyper-threading are enabled, and the BIOS setting is **OS Control**. The tests for each Power Plan setting were repeated three times, and the power usage figures displayed are averages taken over those four runs.

Power Plan	Power usage (watts)	
	1-CPU system	**2-CPU system**
Power saver	147	200
Balanced	169	217
High performance	180	244

Figure 5.11:   Power usage variation with Windows Power Plan.

There is a power usage **increase** of approximately 6% (for 1 CPU) and 11% (for 2 CPU) when moving from the default Balanced plan to the High performance plan.

There is a power usage **decrease** of approximately 13% (for 1 CPU) and 8% (for 2 CPU) when moving from the default Balanced plan to the Power saver plan.

So, in both cases, there is an approximately 18% increase in power use when moving from the Power saver plan to the High performance plan, while the processor(s) are running at nearly 100% utilization. There was no power saving when the processor is idle.

Figure 5.12 shows the equivalent results for the effect of the Power Plan setting on the Geekbench CPU performance score.

Power Plan	Geekbench score	
	1-CPU system	**2-CPU system**
Power saver	4746.5	7577.3
Balanced	6080.5	9109.3
High performance	6971.3	11157.3

Figure 5.12:   Geekbench score variation with Windows Power Plan.

There is an **increase** of approximately 14.6% (for 1 CPU) and 22.4% (for 2 CPU) in Geekbench performance when moving from the default Balanced plan to the High performance plan.

There is a **decrease** of approximately 21.9% (for 1 CPU) and 16.8% (for 2 CPU) in Geekbench performance when moving from the default Balanced plan to the Power saver plan. So, in each case, there is an increase in performance of approximately 32% when moving from the Power saver plan to the High performance plan.

So, to summarize, I would say the following:

- you can achieve a 15–22% increase in CPU performance, for a cost of a 6–11% increase in power usage, by switching from the default Balanced power plan, to High performance

- by running in Power saver mode, you can achieve a power usage saving of around 18% but at the substantial cost to performance of running **almost a third slower** than you could be.

Effect of Turbo Boost and hyper-threading

The results in Figure 5.13 show the effect of enabling Turbo Boost for each of the Power Plan settings. For each Power Plan, four tests were run with Turbo Boost disabled and four with it enabled, and the average Geekbench scores are quoted in each case. In all these tests, hyper-threading was disabled.

Power Plan	Geekbench score			
	1-CPU system		2-CPU system	
	Turbo OFF	Turbo ON	Turbo OFF	Turbo ON
Power saver	3877.5	3877.8	5930	5964.5
Balanced	4839.5	4810.3	6625.8	6686.5
High performance	5318.5	5606.8	8066	8831.8

Figure 5.13:   Effect of Turbo Boost on average Geekbench score, for each Power Plan.

As you can see, Turbo Boost has a negligible effect when running in Power saver or Balanced mode. However, when using the High performance power plan, enabling Turbo Boost increases the Geekbench score by 5.4% (1 CPU) and 9.5% (2 CPUs).

In a similar manner, Figure 5.14 shows the effects of enabling hyper-threading on both systems, for each Power Plan setting, with Turbo Boost disabled in all cases.

Power Plan	Geekbench Score			
	1-CPU system		2-CPU system	
	HT OFF	HT ON	HT OFF	HT ON
Power saver	3877.5	4729	5930	7670.5
Balanced	4839.5	6028.5	6625.8	9058.3
High performance	5318.5	6529.8	8066	10558.3

Figure 5.14:   Effect of HT on average Geekbench score, for each Power Plan.

For the High performance power plan, enabling HT boosts the Geekbench score by 22.8% (1 CPU) and 30.9% (2 CPUs).

Finally, in Figure 5.15, we see the effect of enabling both HT and Turbo Boost, for each Power Plan.

Power Plan	Geekbench Score			
	1-CPU system		2-CPU system	
	HT and TB OFF	HT and TB ON	HT and TB OFF	HT and TB ON
Power saver	3877.5	4746.5	5930	7577.3
Balanced	4839.5	6080.5	6625.8	9109.3
High performance	5318.5	6971.3	8066	11157.3

Figure 5.15: Effect of HT and Turbo Boost on average Geekbench score, for each Power Plan.

For the High performance power plan, enabling both HT and Turbo Boost together boosts the Geekbench score by 31.1% (1 CPU) and 38.3% (2 CPU).

Results summary

My conclusions, based on these Geekbench benchmark tests are as follows, assuming that pure processor performance is a primary concern:

- use the High performance Windows Power Plan instead of the default Balanced Power Plan

- make sure the server BIOS power management setting is **OS Control**, which allows Windows to control power management instead of letting the hardware control it

- always enable hyper-threading (for some database workloads,such as DW or DSS, you might want to disable hyper-threading; you should test in your environment

- always enable Turbo Boost (assuming you use the High performance power plan).

It really pains me to make these recommendations, since I think reducing electrical usage in datacenters is a very worthy goal, for both economic and environmental reasons. However, for database servers, the overall electrical power savings you get from using a more green power plan are pretty negligible, especially compared to the performance loss you incur. This would be more significant for an OLTP workload, which is usually more CPU dependent (assuming you have enough I/O capacity to support your workload).

Overall, using power saving settings makes a lot more sense for middle-tier servers than it does for a database server. Upgrading to new hardware, and consolidating multiple older servers into fewer new servers is a better strategy for reducing the overall power usage of your database servers. This can save you a significant amount of money in monthly operating costs.

Windows Instant File Initialization

One Windows setting that I think is extremely important for SQL Server usage is the **Perform volume maintenance tasks** right, which enables Windows Instant File Initialization. On a Windows Server 2003 or newer operating system, using SQL Server 2005 or newer, you can take advantage of this feature to dramatically reduce the amount of time required to create or grow a SQL Server data file. This only works on SQL Server data files, not on SQL Server log files.

Normally when you create a SQL Server data file, the operating system goes through and zeros out the entire file after the file is allocated.

This can take quite a bit of time for a large data file, and this process comes into play in several situations, including:

- creating a new database

- adding a new data file to an existing database

- growing an existing data file to a larger size

- restoring a database from a full database backup

- restoring a database from a full database backup to initialize a database mirror

- restoring a database from a full database backup to initialize a secondary replica using SQL Server Denali AlwaysOn technology.

Windows Instant File Initialization allows the operating system to skip the zeroing out process (for authorized Windows users), which makes the file allocation process nearly instantaneous even for very large files (hence the name). This can have a huge effect on how long it takes to restore a database, which could be very important in a disaster recovery situation.

You have to grant this right to the Windows account that the SQL Server Service is using. This would normally be a Windows domain account. You can do this by using the Local Group Policy Editor on the machine where SQL Server will be running. You can just type GPEDIT.MSC in a **Run** window, which will bring up the Local Group Policy Editor shown in Figure 5.16.

In the left-hand panel, navigate **Computer Configuration | Windows Settings | Security Settings | Local Policies | User Rights Assignment**. Next, in the right-hand section of the dialog window, right-click on **Perform volume maintenance** tasks, select **Properties**, and click on the **Add User or Group** button. Then you need to add the name of the SQL Server Service account, and click **OK**. You must restart the SQL Server service in order for this change to go into effect.

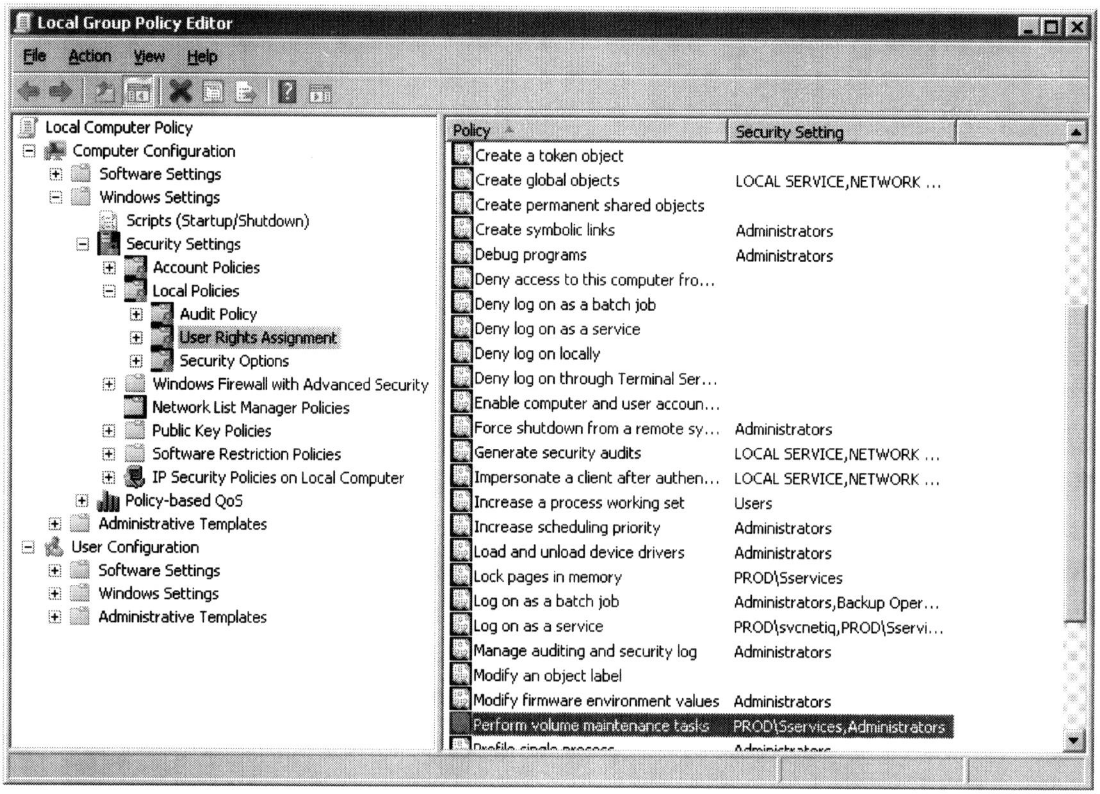

Figure 5.16: Using the Local Group Policy Editor to grant the **Perform volume maintenance tasks** right to the SQL Server Service account.

Personally, I always use this feature with any SQL Server instance under my control. I think you should strongly consider doing the same thing. One thing to keep in mind is that if you are using Transparent Data Encryption (TDE) with SQL Server 2008 or greater, you cannot use Windows Instant File Initialization.

One last caveat with using Windows Instant File Initialization is that there is a potential security risk involved. The risk is that any previously deleted content that existed on the disk(s) where you decided to create, grow, or restore a SQL Server data file might be accessed by an unauthorized principal (a "bad guy"). You can, and should, be using

Windows security to control who has access to your directories and files on your database server, so I think the risk is pretty minimal.

Lock pages in memory

Another Windows setting you might want to enable is **Lock pages in memory**. There is some controversy within the SQL Server community and within Microsoft about whether, and when, you should enable this setting on 64-bit systems. Before you decide if you want to do this, let me give you some background.

When SQL Server 2005 was first released, in early 2006, and was installed on systems running x64 Windows Server 2003, or x64 Windows Server 2003 R2, it quickly became very common to enable **Lock pages in memory**, to try to prevent the operating system from periodically paging out a large amount of memory from SQL Server's working set, which would have a very noticeable bad effect on SQL Server performance.

This would happen when the operating system ran low on available memory, typically due to buggy device drivers, or an issue with the Remote Desktop Protocol service in Windows Server 2003, and so would page out a large portion of the working set of the SQL Server process in order to free up memory for the operating system. This made the operating system happier, but had a terrible effect on the performance of SQL Server, since it would have to heavily access the storage subsystem to read back in the data that had recently been the buffer pool.

SQL Server 2005 and above are designed to perform dynamic memory management, based on the memory requirements of the current load on the system. On a Windows Server 2003 or later operating system, SQL Server can use the memory notifications from the `QueryMemoryResourceNotification` Windows API. This is meant to keep the operating system from paging out the working set of the SQL Server process, and it helps keep more database pages available in memory to reduce the level of physical I/O.

The problem was that SQL Server 2005 did not always react quickly enough to a low memory notification from the operating system, so the operating system would take matters into its own hands, and force SQL Server to release a large portion of its working set. Using **Lock pages in memory** prevented this from happening.

Initially, this setting would only be honored by SQL Server 2005 Enterprise Edition. Microsoft's official stance was that, if you encountered this issue, you should open a support incident with Microsoft CSS to try to find the root cause of the problem. Their opinion was that it was better to find the cause of the problem instead of using **Lock pages in memory** as a Band-Aid.

Many production DBAs agreed in principle but disagreed in harsh reality. Once you have been affected by this issue a couple of times, and had to explain to your management team or your customers why an application suddenly started timing out for no apparent reason, you were usually quite ready to enable **Lock pages in memory**. Later, after a lot of pressure from the SQL Server MVP community, Microsoft finally made **Lock pages in memory** available in Standard Edition (in later builds of SQL Server 2005, 2008, and 2008 R2), by using a startup trace flag of 845.

Microsoft has published conflicting information about this issue over the years. The current official stance is that you should not have to use **Lock pages in memory** with Windows Server 2008 and newer, because of improvements in memory management and improved device drivers. Off the record, I have heard several Microsoft employees concede that it may still be necessary to use this setting in some situations.

Again, you have to grant the **Lock pages in Memory** right to the Windows account that the SQL Server Service is using, which would normally be a Windows domain account. So, as described previously, type `GPEDIT.MSC` in a **Run** window, which will bring up the Local Group Policy Editor, and navigate to the **User Rights Assignment** directory. In the right-hand section of the dialog window, right-click on **Lock pages in memory**, select **Properties**, and click on the **Add User or Group** button. Add the name of SQL Server Service account, and click **OK**. Again, you have to restart the SQL Server Service for this setting take effect.

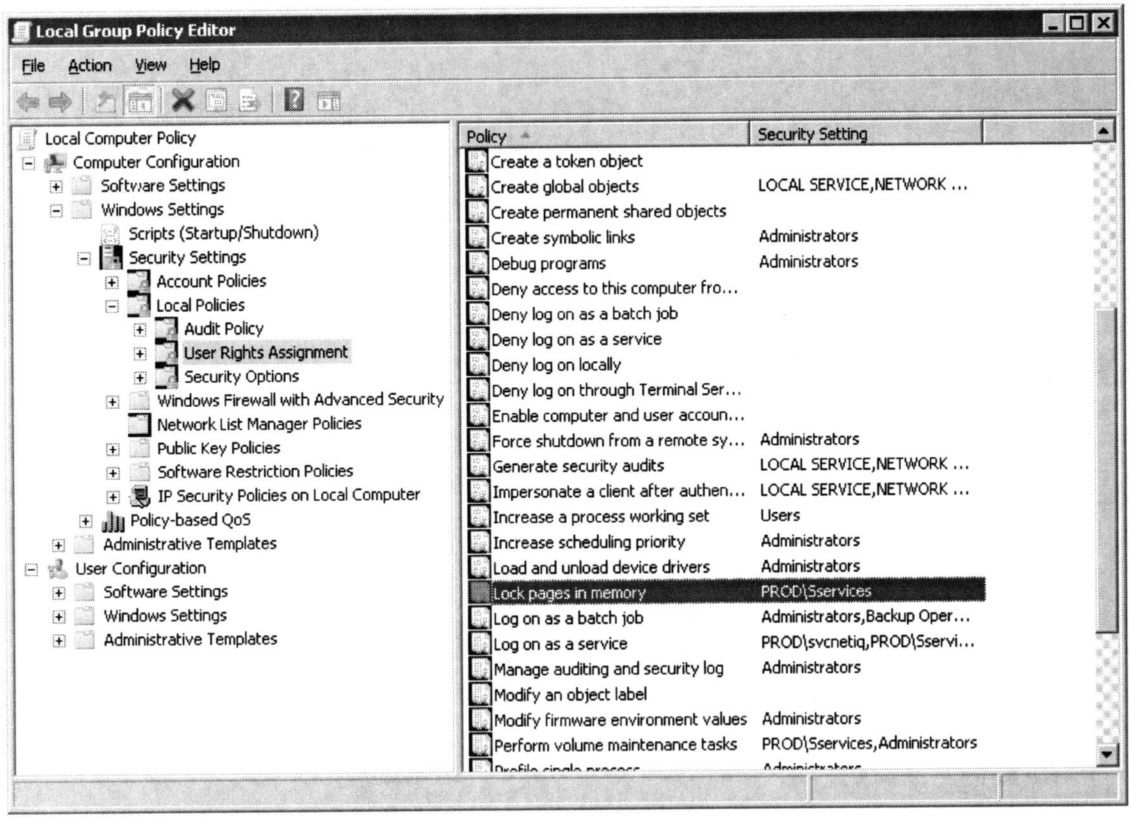

Figure 5.17: Using the Local Group Policy Editor to grant the **Lock pages in memory** right to the SQL Server Service account.

You can confirm that the LPIM user right is in being by the instance of SQL Server, checking that the following message is written in the SQL Server Error Log at startup: **Using locked pages for buffer pool.**

If you do enable **Lock pages in memory**, it is very important that you also set an explicit `MaxServerMemory` setting for your SQL Server instance, which is discussed in more detail in *Chapter 7*.

Summary

We have covered a lot of ground in this chapter. We have talked about every version of Windows Server since Windows 2000 Server, covering many of the more important improvements in each new version of Windows Server. This has hopefully given you more incentive to want to upgrade to the latest version, along with evidence to help convince your boss.

We have also talked about the differences between 32-bit and 64-bit versions of Windows Server, and why you really want to be using a 64-bit version of Windows Server. Remember, Windows Server 2008 R2 is 64-bit only, and the next version of Windows Server will be x64 only (since Itanium support will be dropped).

Next, we covered how Microsoft Support Policies work, with Mainstream Support and Extended Support. Windows 2000 Server is no longer even on Extended Support, while both Windows Server 2003 and Windows Server 2003 R2 have gone from Mainstream Support to Extended Support as of July 13, 2010. We also talked about how Windows Service Packs work, and when they are released. Windows Server 2008 R2 SP1 was released on February 16, 2011.

We spent some time covering the effects of Windows Power Plans on CPU and memory performance, and on actual total electrical power consumption for the entire server, measured at the electrical outlet. My experiments show that you can take a significant performance decrease in exchange for a relatively small electrical power saving when you don't use the High performance power plan.

Finally, we discussed the use of Windows Instant File initialization feature and the **Lock pages in memory** right for SQL Server usage, including the different considerations for their use. In *Chapter 6*, we will be exploring the different versions and editions of SQL Server since SQL Server 2005, giving more guidance on how to select the most appropriate version and edition for your workload and budget.

Chapter 6: SQL Server Version and Edition Selection

With the hardware and operating systems purchased, installed and configured, it's time to consider which version and edition of SQL Server makes the most sense, bearing in mind your organization's business needs and budget, as well as the productivity and sanity of you, the DBA.

As a database professional, in 2011, I always *want* to be running my SQL Server instances on SQL Server 2008 R2 Enterprise Edition or better, on top of Windows Server 2008 R2 Enterprise Edition. This is not just a personal predilection for all things shiny and new; it's a firm belief that they offer tangible benefits that far outweigh the additional license fees and upgrade expenses.

Some of the new features and technology enhancements offer better performance and scalability; some help reduce down-time; others simply provide more flexibility and better options to the solution architect; many will make your day-to-day life as a DBA easier, so you can spend less time in reactive, firefighting mode, and more time being productive.

The hard part, of course, is convincing your boss of all this. I've been a DBA for ten years and I've never once had a boss just walk up and *ask* me if I'd like to upgrade to a newer version of SQL Server, on some shiny, new hardware. I have always had to do research, gather evidence, and make a solid business case for why it made good technical and business sense to upgrade. I have not always won the battle on the first attempt but I share the traits of many DBAs, of tenacity and persistence.

I hope this chapter will make this battle a little easier for you. It will cover the major differences between the various versions and editions of SQL Server, with a particular focus on the database engine and SQL Server Enterprise Edition features. I firmly believe that you should be running x64 SQL Server 2008 R2 Enterprise Edition on top of

Windows Server 2008 R2, on top of new, powerful hardware. The idea here is to give you as much evidence as possible to make your case to get there.

32-bit or 64-bit SQL Server

I strongly believe that, for new installations, you should *only* be using 64-bit SQL Server. The only reason you should even consider using a 32-bit version of SQL Server is if you have a legacy application or data source that only works with a 32-bit version of SQL Server.

The whole "32-bit versus 64-bit" question will be moot fairly soon for new installs, since I strongly suspect that SQL Server Denali will be the last version of SQL Server that will even have 32-bit support. Windows Server 2008 R2 is 64-bit only and other server products from Microsoft, such as Exchange 2010 and SharePoint 2010, are also 64-bit only. The 32-bit era is close to being over, and I will not miss it one bit.

SQL Server Versions and Editions

As discussed earlier, I have a strong preference for using the latest and greatest version whenever possible. At the time of writing, that means SQL Server 2008 R2. That means that whether you are currently running an older version of SQL Server or you are looking at a new installation, you are better off on SQL Server 2008 R2. Hopefully, the information in this section will convince you of the reasons why, and give you the necessary ammunition to convince your boss of the same.

After the version decision has been made, the next big question is whether you need to invest in SQL Server Enterprise Edition, or can get by with a lower-cost edition. As an experienced production DBA, I firmly believe that you (and your organization) will be much better off if you are using Enterprise Edition for production use. It has so many features and benefits that we will cover in this chapter and that more than make up for its extra initial license cost.

With SQL Server 2008 R2, Microsoft has further complicated matters by introducing a new **Datacenter Edition**, which is even more expensive, but has higher licensing limits than Enterprise Edition. I will explain the differences between those two editions later in this chapter.

SQL Server 2005

SQL Server 2005, which was code-named Yukon during development, was released to manufacturing in October 2005, and was officially released on January 14, 2006, over five years ago at time of writing. It was a huge improvement over SQL Server 2000, as well it should have been, since it took so long to be developed and released by Microsoft.

Out in the field, there are still very many SQL Server 2005 instances, running perfectly well. This begs the question, "Why not leave well enough alone?" Well, not only are you missing out on a raft of new features and improvements in SQL Server 2008 and 2008 R2 that are genuinely valuable for both you and your organization, but you're also probably running on highly sub-optimal hardware, and you are about to run into some interesting support issues.

If you are still using SQL Server 2005, whether by choice or otherwise, it is very likely that these SQL Server 2005 instances are running on Windows Server 2003 or Windows Server 2003 R2. It is also likely that these SQL Server 2005 instances are running on hardware that is at least three years old. Why is all of this a problem?

Firstly, SQL Server 2005 went out of Mainstream Support from Microsoft on April 12, 2011. Secondly, Windows Server 2003 (and 2003 R2) went out of Mainstream Support on July 13, 2010. This means no more Service Packs or Cumulative Updates will be released for either, after these dates. Thirdly, your three-year-old server hardware is woefully underpowered by today's standards, and it is probably out of warranty. Hopefully, all of this provides powerful motivation to push for an upgrade to SQL Server 2008 R2, as soon as possible.

Microsoft support policies

The full details of Microsoft's support policies for Windows Server and SQL Server can be found in Chapter 5.

SQL Server 2008 Editions

SQL Server 2008, code-named Katmai during development, was released to manufacturing on August 6, 2008 and officially released on November 7, 2008. At NewsGator, we had been in the Katmai Technology Adoption Program (TAP) since the middle of 2007, and I literally could not wait to move from SQL Server 2005 to SQL Server 2008, since there were so many important new features that we needed at the time. The two most compelling for us were **Integrated Full Text Search** and **Data Compression**. We actually upgraded our entire production infrastructure from SQL Server 2005 to SQL Server 2008 in September of 2008, so we were very early adopters!

Since several of the features we needed, including data compression, were Enterprise Edition-only, our choice of edition was never in doubt, but SQL Server 2008 has a number of different editions from which you can choose, all based on the same core engine.

- **Express Editions**, including *Express with Tools* and *Express with Advanced Services*
  - for very small-scale usage where cost is the overriding factor.
- **Web Edition**
  - for commercial web application hosting.

- **Workgroup Edition**

  - for small applications that do not require robust database hardware support.

- **Standard Edition**

  - for general purpose use, where you don't need Enterprise features.

- **Developer Edition**

  - for development and testing only, at low cost.

- **Enterprise Edition**

  - for the best performance, scalability, and availability.

- **Evaluation Edition**

  - for 180-day trial and proof of concept usage.

SQL Server 2008 Express Editions

There are three free editions of SQL Server 2008, as follows:

- **Express Edition**

  - includes the database engine only (no SSMS), and so is targeted towards small deployments.

- **Express Edition with Tools**

  - adds SQL Server Management Studio Express (a limited version of SSMS), making it easier to develop and support SQL Server databases.

- **Express Edition with Advanced Services**

  - includes SSMS Express, Full Text Search, and Reporting Services.

All editions of SQL Server 2008 Express have a limit of one physical processor and 1 GB of RAM that the instance will recognize. There is also a maximum user database size limit of 4 GB.

There is no limit on the allowable number of databases hosted on a single Express instance but, in reality, the RAM limitations will severely limit this number. If any of your multiple databases were subject to anything more than a trivial load, you would run into memory pressure problems relatively soon. The processor limitation is less of an issue, since a modern, multi-core, single CPU will offer plenty of processor capacity for the typical SQL Server Express application.

I have often seen SQL Server Express Edition used for small Independent Software Vendor (ISV) applications where there was a need for some relational data storage, without a desire to include the cost of a SQL Server license in the cost of the ISV product. I have also seen it used as a data store for very small web applications, where SQL Server Express Edition is installed on the same machine as the web server.

SQL Server 2008 Express Edition is not a bad way to get started using SQL Server (as opposed to using something like Microsoft Access or MySQL), since you can always upgrade your instance to a more capable edition if your applications outgrow the limits of SQL Server 2008 Express Edition.

If your user databases run up against the 4 GB size limit, you can easily move them to another SQL Server 2008 instance that is running a higher edition, such as Standard Edition. Alternatively, you can upgrade to SQL Server 2008 R2 Express Edition, which has a 10 GB database size limit.

SQL Server 2008 Workgroup Edition

SQL Server 2008 Workgroup Edition is designed for remote offices or small departments that need local copies of company data. It has a license limit of two processor sockets, a maximum of 4 GB of RAM, and no database size limit.

SQL Server 2008 Workgroup Edition retails at $3,899 per processor socket, so it is not significantly less expensive than Standard Edition, but is pretty severely restricted by the 4 GB RAM limit. A Server License for SQL Server 2008 Workgroup Edition is $730, plus $146 for each Client Access License (CAL). That means that if you have fewer than about 20 users connecting to your instance, a Server License would be less expensive than a single processor license.

I would argue that it is generally a waste of money to run SQL Server 2008 Workgroup Edition on a two-socket machine. You would be paying for two processor licenses, and you would still have the 4 GB RAM limit. Certainly, in most cases, you would be hobbled by memory pressure long before you ran into CPU pressure. One way around this would be to install multiple instances of Workgroup Edition, each of which would be able to access 4 GB of RAM. In this way, you could more fully utilize a two-socket server.

SQL Server 2008 Web Edition

SQL Server 2008 Web Edition is intended for web application hosting use. It has a license limit of four processor sockets, and can use up to the operating system limit for RAM (which is currently 2 TB for Windows Server 2008 R2). It's not intended or licensed for use as an internal line-of-business (LOB) database, meaning that you are not supposed to buy or use SQL Server 2008 Web Edition for applications that run primarily inside your internal network. If you are in the business of hosting web applications that need SQL Server 2008 database support, on a shared instance of SQL Server 2008, it is a great choice.

SQL Server 2008 Standard Edition

SQL Server 2008 Standard Edition is intended for general database use in departments and businesses, small and large. It has a license limit of four processor sockets, and can use up to the operating system limit of RAM. If you cannot afford, or you don't need, the extra features in SQL Server 2008 Enterprise Edition, you will more than likely be using

SQL Server 2008 Standard Edition, which retails at $5,999 per processor socket. Standard Edition is far more scalable than Workgroup Edition because of the higher RAM and processor socket limits. At the same time, it is far less scalable and flexible than Enterprise Edition, since is lacking in so many useful Enterprise Edition features. A Server License for SQL Server 2008 Standard Edition is $885, plus $162 for each CAL. That means that, if you have fewer than about 30 users connecting to your instance, a Server License would be less expensive than a single processor license.

SQL Server 2008 Enterprise Edition

SQL Server 2008 Enterprise Edition is the most capable edition of SQL Server 2008. It is targeted at Enterprise workloads that need redundancy, high performance, and scalability. It has no limit on the number of processor sockets (but it is limited to 64 logical processors), and it can use up to the operating system limit for RAM. It has a number of very useful and valuable features that are not included in any other edition of SQL Server 2008.

In short, Enterprise Edition is the version you really want, budget permitting; it retails at $24,999 per processor socket, so it is considerably more expensive than the Standard Edition. Despite this, I firmly believe that Enterprise Edition is worth the extra license cost in most situations.

A Server License for SQL Server 2008 Enterprise Edition is $8,487, plus $162 for each CAL. That means that if you have fewer than about 100 users connecting to your instance, a Server License would be less expensive than a single processor license.

SQL Server 2008 Evaluation Edition

SQL Server 2008 Evaluation Edition is a free, fully-functional version of SQL Server 2008 Enterprise Edition, that will work for 180 days. You are allowed to use Evaluation Edition for Production use, but you need to pay attention to the calendar, since all of the various SQL Server related services will stop working after 180 days.

It is possible to upgrade in-place to a licensed version of SQL Server 2008 without having to uninstall the Evaluation Edition. You can download the Evaluation Edition from WWW.MICROSOFT.COM/SQLSERVER/2008/EN/US/TRIAL-SOFTWARE.ASPX.

SQL Server 2008 Developer Edition

SQL Server 2008 Developer Edition has the exact same features and functionality as SQL Server 2008 Enterprise Edition. It is only licensed for development, test and demonstration use, so you cannot use it in production. Microsoft practically gives it away (it costs less than $50 on Amazon) because they want you to have a tool that lets you develop and test applications and databases with all of the features that are available in Enterprise Edition.

In my opinion, every DBA should be using Developer Edition on their test instances, and every developer should be working against Developer Edition, as it is far more capable than SQL Server 2008 Express Edition that is installed by default with Visual Studio 2008 or Visual Studio 2010.

The version of SQL Server 2008 Express Edition that is installed with Visual Studio 2008 and Visual Studio 2010 does not have SQL Server Management Studio Express, so it is harder to work with for normal database development tasks. Since it is installed by default, many developers do not even know that it is installed, and it is rarely patched with SQL Server Service Packs or Cumulative Updates. SQL Server 2008 Developer Edition gives you the full, regular version of SQL Server Management Studio, and it behaves just like SQL Server 2008 Enterprise Edition in terms of features and tools support. It is a much better choice for development use.

A question I've seen asked many times concerns the existence of a configuration option in SQL Server 2008 Developer Edition that will disallow use of any Enterprise-only features. This is useful in cases where Standard Edition will be used in Production, and you want to be sure that no Enterprise-only features are accidentally used during development. Unfortunately, no such option exists, but below are a few ways around the problem.

- **Buy a copy of SQL Server 2008 Standard Edition** for every DBA and developer – of course, this is a pretty expensive proposition.

- **Buy a copy of Visual Studio Professional with MSDN** (which costs about $1,200 initially and $800 to renew) for every DBA and developer. This gives you a development license for Windows Server and SQL Server so it is a very good value.

- **Make sure that your primary test environment uses SQL Server 2008 Standard Edition** rather than SQL Server Developer Edition. That way, if any Enterprise-only features make their way into your applications or databases, they will fail in this environment.

As an additional safeguard, you can also periodically run a query against the `sys.dm_db_persisted_sku_features` DMV, looking for use of any Enterprise-only features that fundamentally affect how data is stored, and so will prevent you from restoring or attaching a database in a lower edition of SQL Server 2008, as shown in Listing 6.1.

```
-- Look for Enterprise only features in the current database
SELECT   feature_name
FROM     sys.dm_db_persisted_sku_features
ORDER BY feature_name ;
```

Listing 6.1: Detecting Enterprise-only features in the current database.

The four possible returned values in the `feature_name` column of the query are:

- **Compression** – data compression

- **Partitioning** – table or index partitioning

- **TransparentDataEncryption** – Transparent Data Encryption

- **ChangeCapture** – change data capture.

If the query returns any rows, it means that you are using one of these Enterprise-only features in your database, and you will not be able to attach or restore the database to a SQL Server 2008 instance that is running on a lower edition (such as Standard Edition). To be more precise, the database will go through the full restore process, and then fail at the end, during recovery, since the SQL Server instance has no way of knowing that any of these features is being used until the database recovery is complete.

For example, if you try to restore a database that is using data compression to an instance that is running SQL Server 2008 Standard Edition, you will get an error message similar to the following:

```
Database 'TestDatabase' cannot be started in this edition of SQL Server because
part or all of object 'TestCompressedTable' is enabled with data compression or
vardecimal storage format. Data compression and vardecimal storage format are only
supported on SQL Server Enterprise Edition.
```

It would be much more useful if the `sys.dm_db_persisted_sku_features` DMV returned multiple rows of output, by `object_id`, so that we could quickly find out which tables were using features such as data compression and partitioning. In the meantime, the query in Listing 6.2 will help you find the tables that are using data compression.

```
-- Get Table names, row counts of tables with a compressed
-- clustered index (SQL 2008 and above only)
SELECT  OBJECT_NAME(object_id) AS [Table Name] ,
        SUM(Rows) AS [Row Count] ,
```

```
          data_compression_desc AS [Compression]
FROM      sys.partitions
WHERE     index_id < 2 -- Only look at clustered index
          AND data_compression_desc <> N'NONE'
          AND OBJECT_NAME(object_id) NOT LIKE N'sys%'
          AND OBJECT_NAME(object_id) NOT LIKE N'queue_%'
          AND OBJECT_NAME(object_id) NOT LIKE N'filestream_tombstone%'
GROUP BY object_id ,
          data_compression_desc
ORDER BY SUM(Rows) DESC ;
```

Listing 6.2: Detecting tables that use data compression.

SQL Server 2008 Enterprise Edition Features

In this section, we'll run through the more valuable and important features that are included in SQL Server 2008 Enterprise Edition. I'll start with the high-level list.

Performance and scalability features

- **Data Compression** – compresses indexes to reduce I/O and memory pressure at the cost of some CPU pressure.

- **Enhanced Read Ahead** – Enterprise Edition uses more prefetching than other editions, allowing more pages to be read ahead. This speeds up base table lookups from non-clustered indexes.

- **Advanced Scanning for Reads** – allows multiple tasks to share full table scans.

- **Automatic Use of Indexed Views** – the query optimizer automatically considers the indexed view. In all other editions, the NOEXPAND table hint must be used.

- **Partitioning** – divides large tables and indexes into file groups for easier manageability and better performance.

- **Distributed Partitioned Views** – creates a view that can access multiple databases, located on multiple database servers. This is one way to scale out.

- **Scalable Shared Databases** – scale out a reporting database across multiple servers, using read-only volumes on a SAN.

- **Asynchronous Database Mirroring** – high performance, asynchronous database mirroring, which performs much better if your mirror database is hundreds of miles away.

High Availability features

- **Online Index Operations** – most index operations, such as create and rebuild, can be done without locking the entire table.

- **Fast Recovery** – databases become available at the end of the roll-forward phase of recovery, rather than at the end of the whole database recovery process.

- **Parallel Index Operations** – allows SQL Server to use multiple processor cores for creating or rebuilding an index.

- **Database Snapshots** – quickly recover accidentally deleted data from a point in time.

- **Hot-add CPU and RAM** – add additional processors and RAM without a restart of the system (if your OS and hardware support this).

- **Online Restore** – restore secondary file groups while the database is online and active.

Manageability features

- **Resource Governor** – control CPU and memory usage by different groups of logins.

- **SQL Server Audit** – audit most server and database-level events to the Windows Event Log or to a file.

- **Change Data Capture** – track DML changes to a table without requiring schema changes or using DML triggers.

- **Backup Compression** – SQL Server native backup compression reduces the I/O, time, and disk space required for a database backup.

- **Mirrored Backups** – write up to four copies of a backup file during the backup operation.

- **Oracle Replication Publishing** – use Oracle9i or later as a replication publisher to SQL Server.

- **Peer-to-Peer Replication** – maintains read/write copies of data across multiple server instances, also referred to as nodes.

- **More Instances** – up to 50 named instances, rather than the limit of 16 in other editions.

- **More fail-over clustering nodes** – with x64, up to 16 nodes in a fail-over cluster, while with IA64 the limit is 8 nodes per cluster. Standard Edition only supports two nodes in a cluster.

- **Transparent Database Encryption** – encrypts databases without need to make any application changes.

Over the coming subsections, I'll drill down into each feature in a little more detail, and explain its tangible benefits. Space precludes me from offering a complete tutorial on each feature, but you should get a good sense of the value and limitations of each one, and whether they make sense for you and your organization.

A few of these features were also available in SQL Server 2005 Enterprise Edition (I'll indicate which ones, as we proceed), but I wanted to assemble a fairly comprehensive list of SQL Server 2008 Enterprise Edition features, to make the full advantages of Enterprise Edition easier to understand (and to sell to your boss).

Performance and scalability features

Given that the focus of this book is on installing hardware, operating system, and SQL Server for maximum performance, these features will be covered in relative detail.

Data compression

Data compression is one of my favorite new features of SQL Server 2008, allowing either **Row compression** or the more effective, but more CPU-intensive, **Page compression**. Microsoft's Sanjay Mishra has written an excellent white paper called *Data Compression: Strategy, Capacity Planning and Best Practices*, which is available at HTTP://MSDN. MICROSOFT.COM/EN-US/LIBRARY/DD894051(SQL.100).ASPX.

Data compression enables compression of individual indexes on the tables and views in your databases, reducing both the I/O and memory required to access an index, and the space required in your SQL Server data files to store the index. I/O is reduced, as more data fits on a single page. Less memory is required because the index stays compressed in memory unless it is updated, or it is read for filtering, sorting, or joining as part of a query. Even in these cases, only the values that are changed or are actually needed for read filtering, sorting, or joining are decompressed in memory.

The balancing cost is increased CPU utilization. You pay a one-time CPU (and memory and I/O) cost for the initial rebuild of your index and compression of the data. Then, you pay a CPU cost to decompress and recompress the data if any data that is used by the index changes. As discussed in *Chapter 1*, modern processors often provide excess CPU capacity and so the price of somewhat higher CPU usage is a small one to pay for what is often a sizeable reduction in disk I/O and memory pressure, and better overall performance for your workload.

Nevertheless, care must be exercised when choosing where to deploy data compression. If the data in the index is very volatile, the additional CPU cost might outweigh the I/O and memory savings, in term of your overall workload performance. You should evaluate each index individually, to determine whether you should use Page, Row, or no compression. By design, Microsoft does not make it possible to simply enable data compression at the database level, forcing you to consider whether or not to use data compression on an index-by-index basis.

The perfect candidate for data compression is an index on a large table that is read-only, or relatively static in nature, where the index also has a large estimated compression ratio. Your compression ratio will be affected by the data types used by your index, and the actual data in the index. For example, if you have columns in the index with numeric or fixed-length character data types where most values don't require all the allocated bytes for that data type, such as integers where most values are less than 1,000, you will get a good compression ratio. Conversely, a bad candidate for data compression would be a small, highly volatile OLTP table that has a small estimated compression ratio.

The estimated compression ratio for an index can be obtained using the `sp_estimate_data_compression_savings` system stored procedure. Unfortunately, this stored procedure does not work in SQL Server 2008 Standard Edition, which means that you can't use it in your development environment to verify how effective data compression would be for a given index. One way round this is to restore a copy of your database to a test instance that is running Developer Edition, Evaluation Edition, or Enterprise Edition and then run the query in Listing 6.3 to assess the compressibility of your data.

```
-- Get data compression savings estimate for all indexes on a table
EXEC sp_estimate_data_compression_savings N'dbo', N'TestTable',
                                    NULL, NULL, 'ROW' ;
```

Listing 6.3: Getting estimated data compression settings.

You can also use the Data Compression Wizard in SQL Server Management Studio (SSMS) to get a data compression estimate for an index. Simply right-click on an index in Object Explorer, select **Storage**, and then select **Manage Compression** to start the wizard.

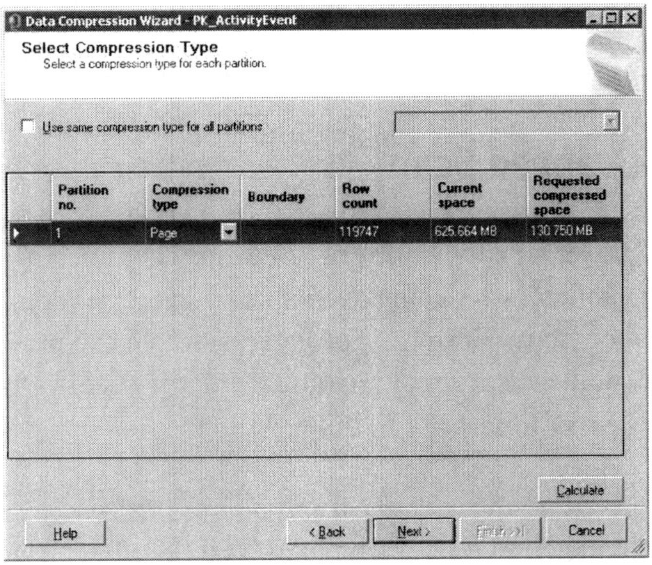

Figure 6.1: Data Compression Wizard.

In Figure 6.1, we have an index that is currently using 625 MB of space, with no compression, and the data compression wizard estimates that converting to Page compression will reduce the space usage to about 131 MB, which is nearly a five-to-one compression ratio.

The data compression wizard will let you generate the required T-SQL script to actually compress the index. I recommend that you do this, rather than letting the wizard do it directly from within the SSMS graphical user interface. I always want to look at the generated T-SQL code from SSMS rather than just letting it run generated code with no review.

You should be aware that compressing (or uncompressing) an index requires that you completely rebuild the index with the desired compression setting, which can be **Page**, **Row**, or **None**. This can take some time, and is a very resource-intensive process for large indexes; as noted, it requires CPU, memory, and I/O resources as the index is rebuilt and compressed or decompressed. A side benefit is that rebuilding the entire index during the compression process virtually eliminates any logical fragmentation in the index.

Enhanced Read Ahead and Advanced Scan

These two features were first added to SQL Server 2005 Enterprise Edition. They are both designed to increase performance and scalability by reducing overall I/O usage. It is very common for large, busy SQL Server instances to run into I/O bottlenecks, which can be difficult and expensive to alleviate, so any built-in feature or technology that seeks to alleviate I/O pressure helps to justify the cost of Enterprise Edition.

Enhanced Read Ahead uses prefetching to reduce overall logical and physical I/O usage. Prefetching is used to speed base table lookups from non-clustered indexes, by allowing the storage engine to start to asynchronously retrieve data rows from the underlying base table before it has completed a scan of the non-clustered index. The basic read ahead feature is available in other editions, but in Enterprise Edition prefetching is used regardless of whether the table has a clustered index, and it does more prefetching than the other editions of SQL Server, allowing more pages to be read ahead, and potentially reducing overall query response time (hence the name, *Enhanced* Read Ahead).

The **Advanced Scan** feature in SQL Server Enterprise Edition allows multiple queries to share full table scans (which are potentially quite expensive). If a table scan is in progress from one query, and a second query requires a table scan of the same table, the database engine will join together the two scans, sending rows from the table scan to each query until both are satisfied. Any number of table scans can be combined in this manner, and the database engine will loop through the data pages for the table, as needed, until all of the combined scans are complete. This can save a great deal of logical I/O (where the data is found in the buffer pool) as well as disk subsystem I/O (where the data is not found in the buffer pool).

This feature gives you some built-in insurance against a poorly-written stored procedure or query that ends up doing a table scan on a large table because it is missing an important index. This situation will still be expensive, and you will want to detect and correct it as soon as possible, but the fact that the database engine will combine the table scans from multiple queries will give you a little more breathing room, which is always a good thing!

SQL Server 2008 R2 Books Online has more detail about both enhanced read ahead and advanced scan at HTTP://MSDN.MICROSOFT.COM/EN-US/LIBRARY/MS191475.ASPX.

Automatic use of indexed views

An indexed view, which is essentially a clustered index on a view, can be created in any edition of SQL Server 2008. However, if you are using SQL Server 2000 Enterprise Edition or later, the query optimizer automatically considers the indexed view, provided the indexed view contains all of the columns necessary to "cover" the query, with no effort on your part. It does so via a function called **indexed view matching**. To get the optimizer to use an indexed view instead of the base tables, the NOEXPAND table hint must be used in the query in all other editions of SQL Server.

Indexed views are generally better suited to data warehouse or reporting type workloads, rather than OLTP workloads, due to the added cost of maintaining the indexes on both the indexed view and on the base table(s) included in the view.

Microsoft's Eric Hanson and Susan Price have written a very useful white paper, *Improving Performance with SQL Server 2008 Indexed Views*. It is available at HTTP://MSDN.MICROSOFT.COM/EN-US/LIBRARY/DD171921(SQL.100).ASPX.

Partitioning

Partitioning was first added in SQL Server 2005 Enterprise Edition and is used to horizontally divide the data in tables and indexes into units that can be distributed across more than one filegroup in a database. Partitioning is used to improve the scalability and manageability of large tables, and tables that have varying access patterns (i.e., older data might be read-only, while newer data might be read/write). When tables and indexes become very large, partitioning can help by separating the data into smaller, more manageable sections.

Many common operations can be performed on individual partitions, instead of dealing with an entire large table or index at once. A secondary benefit can be found in increased query performance. If your tables or indexes are partitioned properly, using the correct partitioning key, you may benefit from partition elimination, where the query optimizer, in evaluating the execution plan, is able to ignore most of the partitions in a very large table or index.

Partitioning can be used to move subsets of data quickly and efficiently with the **ALTER TABLE...SWITCH** command. This allows you, for example, to:

- load a staging table with data and then add it as a new partition to an existing partitioned table

- switch a partition from one partitioned table to another partitioned table

- remove a partition from an existing partition to create a new table.

Kimberly Tripp wrote a white paper, *Partitioned Tables and Indexes in SQL Server 2005*, which is still an excellent reference and is available at HTTP://MSDN.MICROSOFT.COM/ EN-US/LIBRARY/MS345146(SQL.90).ASPX.

Distributed Partitioned Views

Distributed Partitioned Views (DPV) is a feature that has been around since SQL Server 2000. It allows you to create a view in a database that can access multiple databases, located on multiple database servers. The idea is to **scale out** the data tier by spreading the query workload across multiple servers, instead of just **scaling up** by using a larger, more expensive server.

Unfortunately, to be effective, this approach requires very careful table and query design. It is important that the data is partitioned in such a way that the most frequent or important queries are not forced to visit multiple servers during a single query execution, to retrieve their data. What you want is each query to find all of the information it needs on a single node (a concept sometimes referred to as node elimination).

You also want to make sure that you have enabled the `lazy schema validation` option, using the `sp_serveroption` system stored procedure, for all of the linked servers that you will be using in your DPVs, to make sure SQL Server does not get slowed down by checking the schema of remote tables. SQL Server 2008 R2 Books Online has a good tutorial on how to create and use a DPV, which is available at HTTP://MSDN. MICROSOFT.COM/EN-US/LIBRARY/MS188299.ASPX.

Personally, I like to use Data Dependent Routing (DDR) in this scenario, rather than DPV. DDR is not a SQL Server product feature, but rather an engineering method whereby you design your databases and applications so that they know where to find their data, and where this data can be sharded across multiple commodity database servers. Microsoft TechNet has a good white paper called *Scaling Out SQL Server with Data Dependent Routing* that explains the concept quite well. It is available at HTTP://TECHNET.MICROSOFT. COM/EN-US/LIBRARY/CC966448.ASPX.

Scalable shared databases

This feature, first added to SQL Server 2005, is designed to scale out a reporting database across multiple servers, using read-only volumes on a SAN. It has a lot of restrictions and special requirements, and I have never used this feature, nor have I ever seen or heard of anyone else using it. I actually queried the SQL Server MVP community (via email list and Twitter), regarding use of this feature and nobody had any success stories to tell.

However, if you want to find out more, Microsoft's Denny Lee has a good blog post about *Scalable Shared Databases*, which is available at HTTP://DENNYGLEE.COM/2007/10/22/ SCALABLE-SHARED-DATABASES/.

Asynchronous database mirroring

First added in SQL Server 2005 Enterprise Edition, Asynchronous Database Mirroring (*a.k.a.* High-Performance Mode mirroring) is designed to help reduce the performance impact of database mirroring on your applications.

With conventional, synchronous database mirroring, an application must wait for transactions to be hardened on the mirror database. When data is changed by your application, it is first written to the transaction log for the Principal database, then that log activity is sent over your network to the Mirror database, where that activity is replayed. This is sometimes called a two-phase commit, and it means that an application has to wait for the data to be written to the transaction log on both sides of the database mirror. If that mirror database is located on a remote database server that is more than a couple of hundred miles away from your Principal database, the network latency will add to this delay, and your applications will be noticeably slowed down as a result.

Asynchronous mirroring does not use the same two-phase commit process, so your application does not have to wait for the transaction to harden on the Mirror database. This gives better performance, but means that the Mirror database could potentially fall behind the Principal database. For example, a low-bandwidth network connection might not be able to send data across quickly enough for the Mirror database to remain fully synchronized with the Principal; in terms of the data it contains, the Mirror could lag anywhere from seconds to hours behind the Principal database.

In such cases, you are exposed to the risk of some data loss in the event of a failure of the Principal database. There are ways to monitor your mirroring performance using DMV queries or the Database Mirroring Monitor in SSMS. For example, you can run the system stored procedure `sp_dbmmonitorresults` against a mirrored database to look at your historical database mirroring statistics for that database, as shown in Listing 6.4.

```
-- Get database monitoring history data using system SP
EXEC msdb.dbo.sp_dbmmonitorresults N'YourDatabaseName', 2, 1;
```

Listing 6.4: Checking database mirroring statistics.

You can also use the Database Mirroring Monitor from within SSMS to keep an eye on your current and historical database mirroring performance, as shown in Figure 6.2.

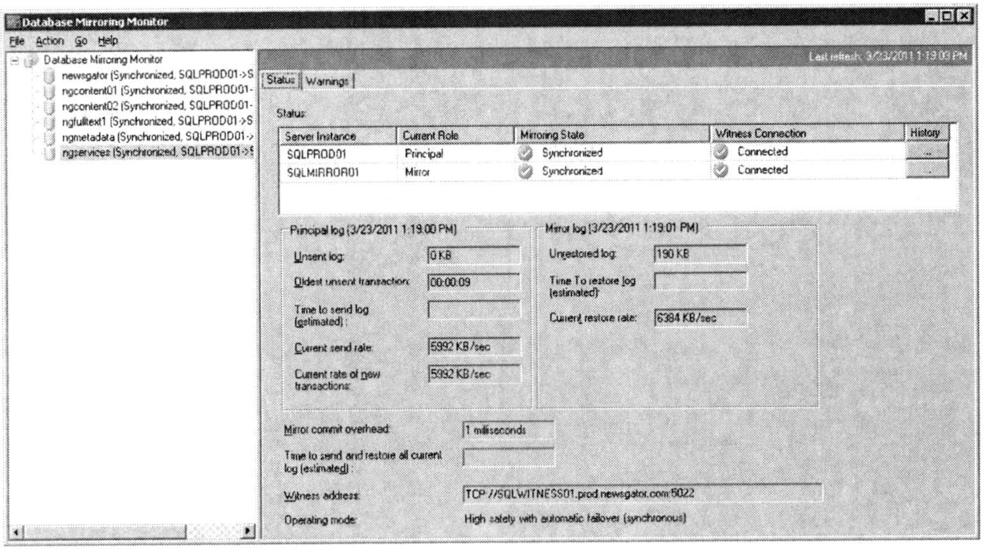

Figure 6.2: Database Mirroring Monitor.

A second case where asynchronous mirroring can be useful is when your mirrored database is running on inferior hardware (from a CPU and I/O perspective) compared to the hardware that hosts your Principal database. With synchronous database mirroring, your faster, Principal server will be slowed down, waiting for the slower Mirror server. I call this situation "dragging around a boat anchor," since I had to deal with it for several years at NewsGator. Asynchronous database mirroring gives you more flexibility to deal with this sort of situation.

At NewsGator, I was forced to use asynchronous database mirroring because my mirrored databases ran on a SQL Server instance that used an older SAN with much lower IOPS and throughput performance compared to what I had available on the SQL Server instance running my Principal databases. This meant that I had to be very vigilant about monitoring the mirroring performance of my databases. It was very common for the unrestored log on the mirrored databases to be multiple gigabytes in size, as the older SAN on the Mirror side struggled to keep up with the newer SAN on the Principal side.

One way I dealt with this was to be very careful about when and how I did index maintenance. Creating, rebuilding, or reorganizing a relational index will generate a lot of transaction log activity that must then be transferred to the Mirror, so you want to make sure you don't do all of your regular index maintenance in a very short period. In such cases, you need to spread the index maintenance activity out over time, with some gaps in between index maintenance operations in order to give your mirrored databases time to catch up.

SQL Server 2008 added a new feature to database mirroring called **log stream compression**, which compresses the log stream data before it is sent over the network to the mirror. This reduces bandwidth requirements, but does not help with network latency. You should be aware that Asynchronous Database Mirroring does not support automatic fail-over, so it is better suited to Disaster Recovery, rather than High Availability, when used alone.

Microsoft's Sanjay Mishra has written a very good technical note that goes into great detail about the performance characteristics of asynchronous mirroring, called *Asynchronous Database Mirroring with Log Compression in SQL Server 2008*, which is available at HTTP://BIT.LY/HOZAIO.

High Availability features

SQL Server 2008 Enterprise also added a range of features designed to help DBAs reach their Service Level Agreement (SLA) targets for database and application availability.

Online index operations

Online index operations are an extremely useful feature that can save you a lot of down-time and make your life as a DBA much less stressful. The `ONLINE = ON` flag can be used with most index DDL operations to allow a clustered or non-clustered index to be created, altered, or rebuilt while the table is still available for normal operation. The `ONLINE` option allows concurrent DML query access to the base table or clustered index data during index DDL operations. It does take longer to create an index with the `ONLINE` option, but since the table is available during the process, that does not matter in most situations.

For example, while a clustered index is being rebuilt, DML queries can continue to read and write to the underlying base table. When you rebuild a clustered index without using the `ONLINE` option, the rebuild operation will hold exclusive locks on the underlying data and associated indexes. This prevents reads and writes to the base table until the index rebuild operation is complete, which could be quite a long time, depending on the size of the index and your hardware capacity. As such, without online index operations, you would usually have to take a maintenance outage to create or rebuild an index on a very large table, which would obviously affect your overall High Availability numbers.

One limitation of this feature, in SQL Server 2008 R2 and earlier, is that you cannot use the `ONLINE` option on a clustered index if your table has any large object (LOB) data types, such as: `image`, `ntext`, `text`, `varchar(max)`, `nvarchar(max)`, `varbinary(max)`, and `xml`. It is very likely that this limitation will be corrected in a future version of SQL Server. Listing 6.5 demonstrates how to use T-SQL to create a non-clustered index using the `ONLINE` option.

```
-- Create a nonclustered index with ONLINE = ON
CREATE NONCLUSTERED INDEX IX_TestTable_TestName
ON dbo.TestTable (TestName ASC)
WITH (STATISTICS_NORECOMPUTE  = OFF, SORT_IN_TEMPDB = OFF,
IGNORE_DUP_KEY = OFF, DROP_EXISTING = OFF, ONLINE = ON,
ALLOW_ROW_LOCKS  = ON, ALLOW_PAGE_LOCKS  = ON, MAXDOP = 4) ON [PRIMARY] ;
```

Listing 6.5:   Creating an index with ONLINE and MAXDOP options.

Microsoft SQL Server 2008 R2 Books Online has a topic called *Guidelines for Performing Online Index Operations* that gives good advice on this topic. It is available at HTTP://MSDN. MICROSOFT.COM/EN-US/LIBRARY/MS190981.ASPX.

Parallel index operations

The Enterprise editions of SQL Server 2005 and later allow parallel index operations. In short, you can enable parallel processing of index operations (CREATE, ALTER, DROP) in a similar way to how query execution can be parallelized, via the MAXDOP option. This feature can help SQL Server Enterprise Edition create or rebuild a large index much more quickly on a modern, multi-core, multi-processor server, assuming that your I/O subsystem does not become a bottleneck.

Caution is needed, however, if MAXDOP for the SQL Server instance is set to its default value of 0, meaning that SQL Server can parallelize queries and index operations as it sees fit. This could lead to an index DDL operation monopolizing your processors for an extended period of time, negatively affecting your normal workload performance.

Limiting the number of cores to about 25% of your total logical cores will make the index DDL operation take longer, but will safeguard against this eventuality. So, for example, if there are 16 logical cores, it is wise to use a value of MAXDOP = 4 for all index DDL operations, as shown in Listing 6.5, thus limiting index DDL operations to a maximum of 4 of the available cores.

Microsoft SQL Server 2008 R2 Books Online has a topic called *Configuring Parallel Index Operations*, which goes into more detail, and is available at HTTP://MSDN.MICROSOFT.COM/EN-US/LIBRARY/MS189329.ASPX.

Fast recovery

In the Enterprise Edition of SQL Server 2005 and later, a database will become available immediately after completion of the undo phase of a crash recovery process, or a database mirroring fail-over. The redo phase of the recovery will be completed while the database is online and accessible. You can read more about recovery performance and crash recovery at HTTP://MSDN.MICROSOFT.COM/EN-GB/LIBRARY/MS189262(V=SQL.105).ASPX.

What this means in plain English is that user databases will be back online and available for use more quickly after the main SQL Server Service starts (for standalone or clustered instances), thus reducing down-time and making it easier to meet your High Availability SLA.

Likewise, it is a useful feature for both clustering fail-overs and database mirroring fail-overs. Unless you have a very effective middle-tier caching solution in place, your applications are unavailable during clustering or mirroring fail-overs; fast recovery will mean that the database will fail-over more quickly and be back online faster. Fast recovery is a silent, unheralded feature that is extremely valuable in production usage.

Paul Randal has a great blog post, *Lock logging and fast recovery*, that explains what actually happens internally with fast recovery, and is available at HTTP://WWW.SQLSKILLS.COM/BLOGS/PAUL/POST/LOCK-LOGGING-AND-FAST-RECOVERY.ASPX.

Database snapshots

The database snapshot feature was first added in SQL Server 2005 Enterprise Edition. A database snapshot is a point-in-time view of a database that you create by using a variation of the **CREATE DATABASE** command. A database snapshot is simply a file or collection of files associated with a specific source database. As data changes in the source database, the original data from the source database is copied to the snapshot file(s).

The database snapshot is not a complete copy of the source database, and it is not a replacement for a regular database backup. It is simply a set of pointers to how the data looked when the snapshot was taken. The database snapshot files will grow over time as the source database data changes. If the source database is deleted or damaged, the snapshots are worthless.

The main uses for database snapshots are for reporting, and to have some protection from accidental data changes. For example, if someone accidentally deleted some data from a database, you can simply run a query against the snapshot to retrieve the data as it looked at the time the database snapshot was taken. You can then write an **UPDATE** or **INSERT** command to pull the data from the database snapshot into the live source database. This may be a pretty easy operation if the data was deleted from a single table with no foreign keys, but it will be more challenging in cases where many tables are affected by the accidental data change.

All of this assumes that the guilty party tells you about the accidental data change in a timely manner, while you still have the database snapshot available. Maintaining a large number of database snapshots on a volatile, OLTP database can have a negative impact on performance (and disk space), since the first time that data changes for a page, the original data has to be written to each database snapshot. As the percentage of changed data in the source database approaches 100%, the database snapshot size will be nearly as large as the original source database.

In a volatile OLTP database, you would want to implement a rolling database snapshot window, where you automatically create and drop snapshots on a set schedule. The idea is that you always retain enough snapshots to let you go back in time a set number of hours, but avoid storing an unmanageable number of large database snapshots.

If you have a modern SAN and appropriate software, you can get similar functionality from a SAN snapshot. Another possibility would be to use third-party database backup software that allows you to do object level restores (where you can pull data directly from the database backup file, without having to do a full database restore). Personally, I would regularly test the functionality of any other solution you decide to implement in addition to native SQL Server backups. I would also strongly resist any suggestion you may get from your SAN administrator or your boss that you can stop doing SQL Server backups in favor of something like SAN snapshots or database snapshots. Those are fine solutions that can be used *in addition* to running SQL Server backups as needed to meet your RPO.

Microsoft's Sanjay Mishra has written an interesting white paper called *Database Snapshot Performance Considerations under I/O-Intensive Workloads*, which is available at HTTP://SQLCAT.COM/WHITEPAPERS/ARCHIVE/2008/02/11/DATABASE-SNAPSHOT-PERFORMANCE-CONSIDERATIONS-UNDER-1-O-INTENSIVE-WORKLOADS.ASPX.

Hot-add CPU and RAM

Providing your OS and hardware support these features, you can add additional processors and RAM without restarting the system. Currently only the Datacenter Edition of Windows Server 2008 or above supports hot-add of CPUs.

Personally, I don't think this is a particularly valuable feature. The need to add additional processors or RAM to a system should be relatively rare, since you usually fill up all of the processor sockets when you first buy the server. It is a little more common to add more RAM to fill empty memory slots in a server.

In either case, I would prefer to do this type of work by failing-over to a database mirror, or another node in the cluster, and then powering down the server. Too many things can go wrong when hot-adding components to a running database server, such as cables being unplugged, the OS or SQL Server becoming unstable, and so on. Paul S. Randal has a short blog post that discusses this feature, which is available at HTTP://BIT.LY/HPS9E8.

Online restore

An online restore is supported in SQL Server 2005 Enterprise Edition and later, and refers to the ability to perform a file, page, or piecemeal restore of data while the database is online. The online restore feature only works for databases that contain multiple files or filegroups (and, under the SIMPLE recovery model, only for read-only filegroups).

Under any recovery model, you can restore a file that is offline while the database is online. Under the FULL recovery model, you can also restore single database pages while the database is online, as long as transaction log backups exist from the time of the last full database backup up to the current time. More generally, you can perform piecemeal online restores that involve restoration of the primary filegroup followed, optionally, by one or more of the secondary filegroups. The database will be online, and can be used for your regular workload as soon as the primary filegroup and the transaction log are online, even if one or more of its secondary filegroups are offline. Depending on what data is in the offline filegroup, any applications that depend on that database may have reduced functionality, but that is usually better than being completely down.

The ability to restore only the filegroups or pages that are damaged, and to do it online, can further reduce your down-time. For example, if you lost a secondary filegroup due to corruption or hardware failure, the database could remain online while you were restoring that filegroup. Anyone who has seen one of Kimberley Tripp's conference presentations over recent years may be familiar with her famous demonstration of this feature. She would use a USB hub, plugged into her laptop, populated with several small USB thumb drives. She would create a database with multiple filegroups, with the filegroups spread across the available thumb drives. Finally, she would simulate a catastrophic disk array failure by simply removing one of the thumb drives that housed one of the secondary filegroups, and prove that the database remained online.

You can get more information about online restores and partial database availability from the white paper, *Partial Database Availability* which is available at HTTP://BIT.LY/DLRSOW.

Manageability features

Finally, we'll review the many manageability features that are only available in the Enterprise edition of SQL Server.

Resource Governor

Resource Governor, a new Enterprise Edition-only feature added in SQL Server 2008, allows the DBA to manage SQL Server workload and system resource consumption. Resource Governor enables you to control how much CPU and memory resources are assigned to a particular workload. The idea is to segregate different types of applications or users (by their login credentials) into resource pools. You can then set limits for CPU and memory usage for each resource pool, to prevent a rogue application or user from monopolizing your server resources with an expensive, runaway query. For example, via Resource Governor, the DBA can specify that no more than 20% of CPU or memory resources can be allocated to running reports.

One major weakness in Resource Governor is that it does not allow you to have any control over I/O usage. It is possible that this may be fixed in a future version of SQL Server, which would be very useful.

There is a good white paper on MSDN, called *Using the Resource Governor*, which is available at HTTP://MSDN.MICROSOFT.COM/EN-US/LIBRARY/EE151608(V=SQL.100).ASPX.

SQL Server Audit

SQL Server Audit uses Extended Events, a new feature added to SQL Server 2008, to help create an audit at either the instance level or individual database level. This feature lets you audit most server- and database-level events to the Windows Application Event Log, the Windows Security Log, or to a file. This is a much better choice for auditing than "rolling your own" auditing solution using DML triggers that write to auditing tables.

Microsoft SQL Server 2008 R2 Books Online has a good topic that explains this feature; it is called *Understanding SQL Server Audit*, and it is is available at HTTP://MSDN.MICROSOFT. COM/EN-US/LIBRARY/CC280386.ASPX.

Change Data Capture

Change Data Capture (CDC), a new feature added in SQL Server 2008, lets you track DML changes to a table without requiring schema changes or the use of DML triggers. Using DML triggers for auditing DML changes usually requires schema or code changes to the database.

CDC is different from Change Tracking in that it actually lets you track the data that was changed, whereas the Change Tracking feature (available in non-Enterprise editions) only gives you the PK value for the row that was changed.

CDC is designed to capture insert, update, and delete activity applied to SQL Server tables. It can be very useful if you want to do an incremental load to a data warehouse, since it lets you determine exactly what data has changed in a given period of time, and thereby load only that data.

Microsoft SQL Server 2008 R2 Books Online has a topic called *Basics of Change Data Capture* that does a good job of explaining CDC. It is available at HTTP://MSDN.MICROSOFT. COM/EN-US/LIBRARY/CC645937.ASPX.

Backup compression

SQL Server 2008 brought with it, for the first time, native compression of full, differential, and transaction log backups. The data that will be written to the backup file(s) is compressed *before* it is written out to the backup file. This makes the backup file(s):

- **much smaller** – in my experience, most databases usually see a compression ratio of around 3 or 4 to 1, but this is dependent on your data

- **2 to 3 times faster** – since disk I/O is reduced, and disk throughput is the main bottleneck when doing a database backup; restoring from a compressed backup is also faster by a similar amount.

Of course, this benefit is not completely free, since your CPUs have to do some extra work, generally 10–20% extra, depending on your hardware, in compressing and uncompressing the backup files. This is yet another argument for having modern, multi-core processors, which can usually shrug off this extra load.

One common misconception is that you will not see any benefit from backup compression if you are also using SQL Server data compression. Depending on your data, and the number of indexes that have already been compressed with data compression, you will see a *reduced* compression ratio from backup compression, but you will still see some benefit from backup compression. On the databases I manage that are subject to data compression, I find that the backup compression ratio falls from 3 or 4 to 1, down to 2 to 1.

SQL Server native backup compression does lack the advanced features available in many third-party products such as SQL Backup Pro or SQL HyperBac. For example, with native backup compression, you have no control over the compression level, and you are unable to do object level or virtual restores.

Microsoft SQL Server 2008 R2 Books Online discusses backup compression at HTTP://MSDN.MICROSOFT.COM/EN-US/LIBRARY/BB964719(V=SQL.100).ASPX.

Mirrored backups

First introduced in SQL Server 2005 Enterprise Edition, a mirrored backup is simply a database backup where up to four copies of the database backup file are simultaneously written to different locations. This introduces an extra measure of safety and redundancy, in case one of your database backup files is deleted or is otherwise unusable.

Mirrored backups are not to be confused with striped backups; mirrored backups are purely about redundancy, and are conceptually similar to using RAID 1, since you have at least two complete copies of the file in two different locations. Striped backups are all about backup performance and are conceptually similar using RAID 0; a single backup file is split into multiple files and then written simultaneously to different locations, usually using different physical I/O paths.

Samples of the different T-SQL backup commands for striped and mirrored backups (with backup compression) are shown in Listing 6.6.

```
-- Mirrored full backup with compression (Enterprise Edition)
BACKUP DATABASE [TestDB]
TO DISK = N'C:\SQLBackups\TestDBFull.bak'
MIRROR TO DISK = N'D:\SQLBackups\TestDBFull.bak' WITH FORMAT, INIT,
NAME = N'TestDB-Full Database Backup',
SKIP, NOREWIND, NOUNLOAD,COMPRESSION, STATS = 1 ;
-- Striped full backup with compression (All Editions)
BACKUP DATABASE [TestDB]
TO  DISK = N'C:\SQLBackups\TestDBFullA.bak',
DISK = N'D:\SQLBackups\TestDBFullB.bak' WITH NOFORMAT, INIT,
NAME = N'TestDB-Full Database Backup',
SKIP, NOREWIND, NOUNLOAD, COMPRESSION,  STATS = 1 ;
```

Listing 6.6: Mirrored and striped full, compressed backup commands.

I discussed this feature in a blog post called *Mirrored Database Backups vs. Striped Database Backups*, which is available at HTTP://SQLSERVERPERFORMANCE.WORDPRESS. COM/2011/03/13/MIRRORED-DATABASE-BACKUPS-VS-STRIPED-DATABASE-BACKUPS/.

Transparent Data Encryption

Transparent Data Encryption (TDE), a new feature added in SQL Server 2008, performs real-time I/O encryption and decryption of the data and log files of a SQL Server database. It also encrypts the files in `TempDB` if any user databases on the instance are using TDE. Backup files made from databases that are using TDE are also encrypted.

The purpose of TDE is to protect your data at rest by encrypting the physical files of the database, rather than the data itself. This is a much better solution than encrypting the data in individual columns or tables, since it requires no application changes and does not affect the effectiveness of indexes used by queries.

If you are using TDE, you will not be able to use Windows Instant File initialization when you create, grow, or restore SQL Server data files. TDE also makes backup compression much less effective; so much so that Microsoft recommends that you do not use the two features together. If you are in a situation where data security trumps performance and you need to use TDE, you will just have to go without the performance benefit of Windows Instant File initialization.

John Magnabosco has an excellent article on TDE called *Transparent Data Encryption*, which is available at HTTP://WWW.SIMPLE-TALK.COM/SQL/DATABASE-ADMINISTRATION/ TRANSPARENT-DATA-ENCRYPTION/.

More fail-over clustering nodes

If you need more than two nodes in a SQL Server fail-over cluster, you will need to have SQL Server 2008 Enterprise Edition, which supports up to 16 nodes when you are using x64 SQL Server, and 8 nodes when you are using IA64 SQL Server. If you are using fail-over clustering, this is a compelling feature, since a two-node cluster is pretty limiting in terms of flexibility and redundancy.

More instances

SQL Server 2008 Standard Edition supports up to 16 named instances of SQL Server installed on a single server. If you need more, you'll need to move to Enterprise Edition, which supports up to 50. If you are using a traditional Windows fail-over cluster with shared storage, you are limited to 25 instances before you run out of available drive letters.

Personally, I have never needed more than 16 instances of SQL Server on a single server, even in a development and testing environment. I also do not like using multiple instances of SQL Server in a production environment, since the multiple instances are competing for resources on that server, which can affect overall performance.

Oracle Replication Publishing

SQL Server Enterprise Edition has supported this feature since SQL Server 2005 and allows Oracle 9i, or later, databases to act as a publisher for either snapshot or transactional replication to SQL Server. If you need this type of functionality, it is another reason why you need to have Enterprise Edition.

Microsoft's Matt Hollingsworth and Michael Blythe have written a good white paper called *Replication Quick Start Guide for Oracle* which is available on TechNet, at HTTP://TECHNET.MICROSOFT.COM/EN-US/LIBRARY/CC966428.ASPX.

Peer-to-peer replication

Peer-to-peer replication was first introduced in SQL Server 2005 Enterprise Edition as a scale-out and high availability solution. It is built on transactional replication, but allows you to maintain multiple writeable copies of your data, on multiple server instances (often referred to as nodes), across widely geographically-dispersed database servers. It migrates transactionally-consistent changes across these servers, usually in seconds. This can enable applications that require scale-out of read operations to distribute the reads from clients across multiple databases located on multiple database servers. Data is maintained across multiple nodes, so peer-to-peer replication provides some data redundancy, which can increase the availability of your data.

Replication is done at the table level, and you can even select which columns in the table are replicated. This lets you be pretty selective about which data you want to replicate. We used traditional transactional replication with SQL Server 2005 at NewsGator for about a year, as part of our scale-out efforts. We had limited success with this strategy, since replication is (in my experience at least) relatively brittle, with fairly frequent issues with the log reader, which caused me quite a bit of lost sleep during that period.

MSDN has a walk-through on how to configure peer-to-peer transactional replication, which is available at HTTP://MSDN.MICROSOFT.COM/EN-US/LIBRARY/MS152536.ASPX.

SQL Server 2008 R2

SQL Server 2008 R2 adds two new, high-end editions to those available in SQL Server 2008, namely the **Datacenter** and **Parallel Warehouse** editions, and makes a few enhancements to and occasional detractions from, existing editions. We'll focus on those here.

SQL Server 2008 R2 Express Edition

The headline news for 2008 R2 Express is that the user database size limit has risen from 4 GB to 10 GB. Microsoft's aim, it appears, is to help you become more dependent on your free version of SQL Server, and increase the likelihood that you will eventually upgrade to a more capable, non-free edition, such as Standard Edition. Fortunately, your database and application code will function just the same in SQL Server Express Edition as it will in the higher-end SQL Server editions, so there is nothing much wrong with this strategy of starting small and then moving up, as necessary.

If you are using SQL Server Express Edition, it really makes sense to upgrade to SQL Server 2008 R2 Express Edition because of that increased database size limit. The 1 GB memory limit and the one-socket processor limit remain unchanged from SQL Server 2008.

SQL Server 2008 R2 Web Edition

A significant detraction with SQL Server 2008 R2 Web Edition is the imposition of a new license limit of 64 GB of RAM. This decrease in RAM capacity from operating system limit (up to 2 TB) down to 64 GB is pretty drastic and could severely limit the number of customer databases that you could accommodate in a web hosting scenario.

SQL Server 2008 R2 Standard Edition

The nicest enhancement of 2008 R2 Standard Edition is the addition of native backup compression. A significant detraction is, again, the imposition of a new RAM limit of 64 GB. This lowered limit may catch many people by surprise, since it is very easy to have much more than 64 GB of RAM, even in a two-socket server. You should keep this RAM limit in mind if you are buying a new server and you know that you will be using Standard Edition.

SQL Server 2008 R2 Enterprise Edition

SQL Server 2008 Enterprise Edition had no limit for the number of processor sockets, but was limited to 64 logical processors. SQL Server 2008 R2 Enterprise Edition imposes a new limit of eight physical processor sockets, but will theoretically let you use up to 256 logical processors (as long as you are running on Windows Server 2008 R2). However, this is not possible, currently, since it would require a processor with 32 logical cores. As of early 2011, the highest logical core count you can get in a single processor socket is 16.

Also, the RAM limit for R2 has changed from operating system limit, as it was in the 2008 release, to a hard limit of 2 TB.

These licensing changes mean that any customers using machines with more than 8 sockets will be forced to upgrade to SQL Server 2008 Datacenter Edition. This will be the case, even if you have Software Assurance.

One interesting new feature is Utility Control Point (UCP), which allows you to monitor disk space usage and CPU utilization for up to 25 instances of SQL Server, from a central repository.

SQL Server 2008 R2 Datacenter Edition

Datacenter Edition is the new top-of-the-line edition of SQL Server 2008 R2. It allows an unlimited number of processor sockets and an unlimited amount of RAM. You are basically forced into buying Datacenter Edition if you have a database server with more than eight processor sockets, or (in the future) you need more than 2 TB of RAM in your database server. It also allows you to have a Utility Control Point (UCP) that manages more than 25 SQL Server instances. Realistically, you would not want to manage more than about 200 SQL Server instances in a single UCP, due to resource limitations in the UCP instance.

SQL Server 2008 R2 Parallel Data Warehouse

SQL Server Parallel Data Warehouse (which was code-named Project Madison) is a special OEM-only edition of SQL Server 2008 R2 that is intended for large data warehouses. This means that you cannot buy SQL Server 2008 R2 Parallel Data Warehouse by itself. Instead, you must buy it packaged with hardware from a major hardware vendor like HP. It enables SQL Server data warehouses to grow into the hundreds of terabytes range, and to be spread across multiple servers (similar to offerings from other companies, such as Teradata).

SQL Server 2008 R2 new features

Here is a listing that briefly explains the new features that were added in SQL Server 2008 R2. I will describe them in more detail in the next sections.

- **PowerPivot for SharePoint** – shared services and infrastructure for loading, querying, and managing PowerPivot workbooks that you publish to a SharePoint 2010 server or farm.

- **PowerPivot for Excel** – an add-in to Excel 2010 that is used to assemble and create relationships in large amounts of data from different sources, and then use that data as the basis for PivotTables.

- **Utility Control Point** – monitor historical disk space usage and CPU utilization for multiple instances of SQL Server from a central repository.

- **Data Tier Applications** – a DAC defines all of the database engine schema and instance objects, such as tables, views, and logins, required to support an application.

- **Master Data Services** – define non-transactional lists of data, with the goal of compiling maintainable master lists that can be used by multiple applications.

- **Extended Protection** – uses service binding and channel binding to help prevent an authentication relay attack.

- **Connectivity to SQL Azure** – use SQL Server Management Studio (SSMS) to connect to SQL Azure.

PowerPivot for SharePoint

Microsoft SQL Server PowerPivot for SharePoint is marketed as "self-service BI collaboration," where end-users can use SharePoint 2010, Excel Services, and SQL Server 2008 R2 to share, store and manage PowerPivot workbooks that are published to SharePoint 2010. If your organization is using SharePoint 2010, it is very likely that you will end up having to install and maintain PowerPivot for SharePoint sooner or later.

On the hardware front, it is a good idea to make sure that your PowerPivot for Share-Point servers have lots of memory, since PowerPivot is an in-memory service and is very dependent on memory. This feature also requires Excel 2010 in order to function.

PowerPivot for Excel

Microsoft PowerPivot for Excel is a data analysis tool that allows your users to use Microsoft Excel 2010 to perform complex data analysis, using PivotTable and PivotChart views, without having to involve the IT department in every ad hoc request.

In my experience, users and managers tend to be pretty impressed whenever they see a demonstration of PowerPivot, so it's wise to at least start familiarizing yourself with it. Of course, you will need SQL Server 2008 R2, along with Office 2010 to use PowerPivot for Excel. Microsoft has a dedicated website for PowerPivot at WWW.POWERPIVOT.COM/.

Utility Control Point

This is an interesting and potentially useful feature for historical tracking, reporting and trend analysis (it is *not* for real-time monitoring and alerting). However, it does require SQL Server 2008 R2 Enterprise Edition for your UCP instance and, if you need to monitor more than 25 instances in your UCP, you will need SQL Server 2008 R2 Datacenter Edition.

Another limitation is that you can only monitor SQL Server instances that are SQL Server 2008 R2 or SQL Server 2008 SP2. Finally, much of the functionality in UCP is already available in tools like System Center Operations Manager (SCOM), or third-party monitoring tools, such as Red Gate SQL Monitor.

MSDN has a walk-through on how to create a UCP, which is available at HTTP://MSDN. MICROSOFT.COM/EN-US/LIBRARY/EE210579(SQL.105).ASPX.

Data Tier Applications

Data Tier Applications, which are abbreviated as DAC (just to confuse people), are intended to make it easier to configure and package a database and its dependencies for deployment. In other words, the DAC includes the database schema plus some server-level objects required in order to support the database, such as logins. A DAC defines all of the database engine schema and instance objects, such as tables, views, and logins, required to support an application.

This is a great concept, and I foresee it being valuable in the future, but the initial implementation in SQL Server 2008 R2 was deeply flawed and widely scorned by many DBAs. The biggest issue was how DACs handled incremental changes to your database. For example, if you made a very simple change, such as a modification to a stored procedure, and then generated a DACPAC to deploy that change, DAC would actually perform a side-by-side upgrade, creating a new database, and then copying all of the metadata and data from the old database to the new database, and then renaming the new database and deleting the old one. While this was going on, your database would be unavailable, and you would have issues such as broken log chains and full transaction logs that you would have to clean up later.

Another problem was the fact that you had to use Visual Studio 2010 to create or modify a DACPAC, which was an issue for many DBAs. One bright spot is that Visual Studio 2010 SP1 has a major change that means that DAC upgrades are now in-place, instead of side-by-side. This is a huge improvement that makes DAC worth a second look, in my opinion.

Master Data Services

Master Data Services (MDS) helps you standardize common reference data that is used across multiple databases and applications. With Master Data Services, your organization can centrally manage common data company-wide and across diverse systems. While this sounds quite impressive, MDS 1.0 is definitely rough around the edges according to many people who have tried to use it.

Microsoft's Roger Wolter and Kirk Haselden have written a white paper called *The What, Why, and How of Master Data Management* which does a good job of explaining the concepts behind MDS. It is available at HTTP://MSDN.MICROSOFT.COM/EN-US/LIBRARY/BB190163.ASPX.

Extended Protection

SQL Server supports Extended Protection (EP), beginning with SQL Server 2008 R2. Extended Protection for Authentication is a feature of the network components that are implemented by the operating system. These components use service binding and channel binding to help prevent an authentication relay attack.

In an authentication relay attack, a client that can perform NTLM authentication connects to an attacker. The attacker uses the client's credentials to masquerade as the client and authenticate to a service, such as the SQL Server Database Engine.

SQL Server is more secure when connections are made using EP, which is supported in Windows Server 2008 R2 and Windows 7. EP is only supported by the SQL Server Native Client in SQL Server 2008 R2. Support for EP for other SQL Server client providers (such as ADO.NET, OLE-DB and ODBC) is not currently available. There are patches available for older Microsoft server and client operating systems, which you can get from WWW.MICROSOFT.COM/TECHNET/SECURITY/ADVISORY/973811.MSPX.

If your organization is using Transparent Data Encryption (TDE) because of the sensitivity of your data, you will probably also be interested in using EP. Tim Cullen has a good walk-though of EP in a blog post, available at WWW.MSSQLTIPS.COM/TIP.ASP?TIP=2104.

Connectivity to SQL Azure

If you need to manage SQL Azure databases, you can do so using the SQL Server 2008 R2 version of SSMS. The management and development experience in SSMS is not quite as rich as with traditional on-premises SQL Server, since you lose features like IntelliSense and many of the wizards and designers that you may be used to in SSMS. Even so, SSMS makes it relatively easy to work with SQL Azure databases, especially compared with web-based management tools.

Even if you are not currently using SQL Azure, I would strongly advise you to make a serious effort to stay abreast of what Microsoft is doing with it, since it is pretty obvious that SQL Azure is not going to be a passing fad. I strongly suspect that many new features that show up in SQL Azure in the future will eventually end up in the traditional, on-premises version of SQL Server.

One time-saving technique that I have used is to create a regular, on-premises database first, and then use the SQL Azure scripting option in SSMS to generate SQL Azure compatible T-SQL DDL and DML commands to create my SQL Azure databases. You can also use the SSMS Express version that comes with SQL Server 2008 R2 Express Edition with Tools to manage SQL Azure databases.

Brent Ozar has a good blog post called *Playing Around with SQL Azure and SSMS*, available at WWW.BRENTOZAR.COM/ARCHIVE/2009/11/PLAYING-AROUND-WITH-SQL-AZURE-AND-SSMS/.

SQL Server 2008 R2 improved features

Here is a listing that briefly explains the features that were improved in SQL Server 2008 R2. Again, I will describe them in more detail in the next sections.

- **Support for 256 logical** processors – adds support for up to 256 logical processors (which requires Windows Server 2008 R2).

- **Unicode Data Compression** – data that is stored in `nvarchar(n)` and `nchar(n)` columns can be compressed by using an implementation of the Standard Compression Scheme for Unicode (SCSU) algorithm.

- **Backup Compression** – native backup compression is now available in the Standard Edition.

Support for 256 logical processors

One of the most important improvements in the relational database engine enables SQL Server 2008 R2, running on Windows Server 2008 R2, to support up 256 logical processors (compared to 64 logical processors in SQL Server 2008).

Back in 2008, 64 logical processors was enough for almost anybody, and even now it might seem hard to imagine needing, or being able to afford, a machine that had more than 64 logical processors. However, this will change quickly. As of April 2011, you will be able to purchase a four-socket machine that uses the Intel E7 Westmere-EX processor (which has 10 cores, plus hyper-threading), which gives you 20 logical cores per socket. With four sockets, you have a grand total of 80 logical cores, in a commodity level, four-socket machine.

Even if you are using much smaller machines, with far fewer logical cores, you will benefit from performance and scalability enhancements that are a direct result of the low-level optimizations that Microsoft made in order to support more than 64 cores, in Windows Server 2008 R2 and SQL Server 2008 R2. Depending on your workload, this is typically in the 5–10% range, based on my experience.

Only the SQL Server Relational Engine is G64-aware (meaning it can take advantage of more than 64 logical processors) in SQL Server 2008 R2. Microsoft's Madhan Arumugam and Fabricio Voznika did a very nice presentation in late 2009 that has more details about these improvements. This presentation is available for viewing at HTTP://BIT.LY/HP3N6M.

Unicode data compression

SQL Server uses a UCS-2 encoding scheme that takes two bytes of storage regardless of the locale. When you need to use Unicode-based data types in your databases, it can increase the storage requirements significantly.

With most European languages, when you store characters as Unicode data types (such as `nvarchar` or `nchar`), each character only needs 1 byte of storage but it is stored using 2 bytes, with the significant byte being 0. SQL Server data compression was improved in SQL Server 2008 R2 to also compress `nchar` and `nvarchar` data types so that they often only require 1 byte of storage per character instead of 2.

If you store Unicode data types, and use SQL Server data compression, then this probably represents one of the more compelling database engine improvements in the entire SQL Server 2008 R2 release, since it can reduce your storage requirements by up to 50% (depending on your data). I have used this feature to save hundreds of gigabytes of storage space at NewsGator, and have seen a significant reduction in I/O requirements.

If you are already using row- or page-level data compression in SQL Server 2008 Enterprise Edition, you will not get the full benefit of Unicode data compression until you rebuild your indexes, after you upgrade to SQL Server 2008 R2. You will get some benefit from Unicode data compression when a new row is inserted or an existing Unicode value is modified even if the corresponding compressed index or the table has not been rebuilt after the upgrade.

Native backup compression

SQL Server native backup compression was discussed earlier in this chapter. Nothing has changed about its implementation or effectiveness compared to SQL Server 2008, but it is now available in SQL Server 2008 R2 Standard Edition. There are still better third-party solutions available for backup compression if you need or want the extra functionality that they provide.

Summary

By now, you should have a much better idea about the real differences between the various versions and editions of SQL Server. We have covered most of the important improvements in SQL Server 2008 and SQL Server 2008 R2, which will help you design, build and maintain a scalable, high-performance data tier that is reliable and resilient.

The extra functionality in SQL Server Enterprise Edition gives you much more flexibility and many more options as you design a solution that meets your organization's Recovery Point Objective (RPO) and Recovery Time Objective (RTO), as part of your overall High Availability and Disaster Recovery strategy. For example, you have the choice of combining a three-node fail-over cluster in one datacenter that also uses asynchronous database mirroring to maintain a copy of your data in another, geographically distant datacenter.

You can take advantage of features like fast recovery and online index operations to directly reduce your overall down-time. You can use features like data compression, partitioning, resource governor, enhanced read ahead, and advanced scanning for reads, to help increase your performance and scalability and to have more predictable query performance.

As a DBA, you are much better off in so many ways if you are using Enterprise Edition instead of one of the less expensive SQL Server editions! Your databases will perform better, and you are very likely to have less down-time. As such, it will save your company money – in some businesses, avoiding one outage could more than pay for the extra cost of SQL Server Enterprise licenses – and it will make your working life as a DBA significantly easier. Of course, your boss may not be overly concerned about reducing your stress level, but your organization will get these benefits anyway.

Hopefully, this chapter and the rest of this book will help you make a strong case as to why you should be running your SQL Server workloads on modern, high-performance hardware, using Windows Server 2008 R2 and SQL Server 2008 R2. You also have the knowledge you need to properly evaluate, select, and size the correct hardware to serve your needs and minimize your hardware and SQL Server license costs.

In the final chapter of the book, we'll cover how to install and configure your chosen version and edition of SQL Server for optimum performance.

Chapter 7: SQL Server Installation and Configuration

Up to this point in the book, we have discussed how to evaluate and select different server hardware components based on our planned workload, how to decide which version and edition of Windows Server we should use for SQL Server, how to properly configure the operating system to work best with SQL Server, and how to select the proper version and edition of SQL Server based on our budget and business requirements.

The final step is to finally install SQL Server, and then configure it for optimal performance and to minimize the number of future management headaches. So, in this final chapter, we'll cover:

- mandatory preparation and pre-installation tasks
- a step-by-step walk-through of a SQL Server 2008 R2 installation
- Service Packs and hot-fixes
- dynamic Slipstream installations
- configuring SQL Server, including coverage of options such as backup compression, MAXDOP, Max Server memory and so on.

Preparation for SQL Server Installation

There are a number of tasks that you need to complete before you begin your SQL Server installation, many of which are hardware configuration and verification tasks that we've covered throughout this book. The amount of time and planning required for this stage will vary, depending on the size of your organization, and level of bureaucracy. In a small organization, you can probably do many of these tasks yourself in minutes, and the others you can plan and coordinate with relative ease. In a larger organization, you will need more patience; you might be delayed for days or weeks waiting for someone else to complete a requested task (such as creating a Windows domain account).

Nevertheless, it is very important that *all* of these tasks have been completed before you attempt to install SQL Server. If not, then you risk a failed install or, probably even worse, a successful install that has a number of issues that will cause later problems for you and your organization.

Pre-Installation Checklist for SQL Server

Following is the checklist I use to ensure that all necessary tasks are complete, before I attempt a new SQL Server install. While the exact order in which you perform these tasks is variable, I believe the order presented, starting with the hardware and moving up the stack, is logical, and it is the order that I follow. Each item in the checklist will be described in more detail in the sections that follow.

1. The main BIOS on your database server is up to date.

2. You have gone into the BIOS and chosen the appropriate settings for settings such as power management, hyper-threading, and so on.

3. All other firmware (for RAID controllers, HBAs, NICs, SAS Backplanes, and so on) is up to date.

4. All of the latest drivers for the motherboard chipset, NICs, video, RAID controllers, HBAs, and so on, have been loaded and are functioning properly. Use Device Manager to double-check this.

5. The Windows Operating System on your database server is fully patched, with no pending reboots. SQL Server will not install if there is a pending reboot.

6. The logical disk where the Windows binary files are installed has been defragmented.

7. You have decided, based on your business and licensing requirements, which SQL Server components will be installed on the database server.

8. Your database server has a static IP address and is part of a Windows Domain.

9. Normal Windows Domain accounts for all SQL Server services have been created.

10. You know the credentials for all of the Windows Domain accounts that will be used by SQL Server.

11. You have a standardized naming scheme for logical disks and directories.

12. All logical disks have been properly provisioned and presented to the host machine.

13. All logical disks are visible to Windows.

14. All logical disks have been partition-aligned.

15. You have done testing with SQLIO to validate that each logical drive is functioning correctly and will meet performance expectations.

16. For use of fail-over clustering, ensure your database server is part of a Windows fail-over cluster.

17. For use of AlwaysOn HADRON features in SQL Server Denali, ensure your database server is part of a Windows fail-over cluster.

18. The **Perform volume maintenance tasks** right has been granted to the SQL Server Service account (see *Chapter 5*).

19. You have considered whether to grant the **Lock pages in memory** right to the SQL Server Service account (see *Chapter 5*).

20. You have access to the SQL Server installation media and license keys.

21. You have downloaded the latest SQL Server Service Pack and/or Cumulative Update.

BIOS, firmware, and drivers

Since your database server is not yet in production, now is the time to go through and make sure the main BIOS and all other firmware and drivers are completely up to date. I always go to the system manufacturer's website and download all of the appropriate firmware updates and drivers ahead of time, usually to a file share on the network, since I may have multiple servers of that same model that need to be updated. By doing all the firmware and driver updates now, before you install SQL Server and bring it online, you avoid the need for a maintenance outage shortly after, since these types of updates almost always require a reboot.

Having updated your firmware and drivers, go into your main BIOS, usually by hitting the F2 or DEL key during the Power On Self-Test (POST) sequence, and make sure all of the appropriate settings have been applied, according to your established hardware and configuration choices.

- **Should hyper-threading be enabled?** As discussed in *Chapter 1*, I am an advocate of hyper-threading (HT), especially second-generation HT, and especially for OLTP workloads, although it is vital to test it thoroughly for your particular workload, in your own test environment.

- **Which power management setting should be used?** As discussed in *Chapter 5*, I generally prefer to have power management settings either under OS control or disabled. This means I can change the Windows Power Plan settings dynamically and have the hardware honor them.

- **Do I need to enable hardware virtualization?** As discussed in *Chapter 5*, if you intend to exploit Windows Hyper-V you'll need to have hardware virtualization enabled.

- **Should I disable memory testing during the POST sequence?** This step is quite time consuming (taking more time, the more memory there is to check), and it only checks your memory when you reboot your server, which does not happen that often. Using a system management tool, such as the Dell Open Management System Administrator (OMSA) that interrogates and monitors your hardware, is a better way to detect memory problems, in my opinion.

Having selected the appropriate options, you should always, as a final check, go into **Device Manager** in Windows, and confirm that all of your devices and drivers are present and working properly. You don't want to see any yellow caution icons, like the ones you see in Figure 7.1, indicating that a device is not working properly or that a device driver is not installed.

A common problem is that the Windows operating system DVD did not have a driver for your network adapter, which means that you will not have any network connectivity until you do something to correct the issue. If this happens, you should be able to go the system manufacturer's website (using another computer that has Internet connectivity) and download the correct driver setup program, which you can then copy to a USB thumb drive. Then you can plug the USB thumb drive into the new server and copy the setup program to a hard drive on the server, then run it to get the driver installed.

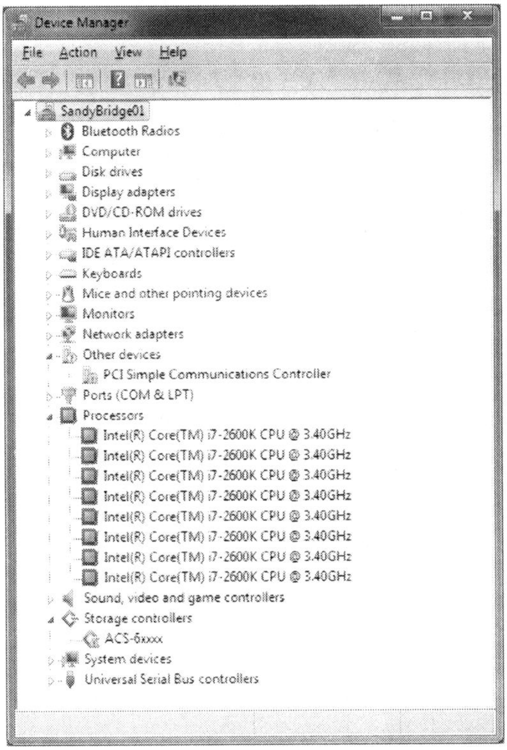

Figure 7.1: Windows Device Manager showing driver problems.

Windows OS

I always make sure that I install Microsoft Update on my database servers. Microsoft Update is an optional component, a superset of the functionality of Windows Update, which can, if you let it, automatically detect and install updates for components such as the .NET Framework and SQL Server.

For a Production SQL Server, I *don't* want Microsoft Update to automatically install updates and force an unexpected reboot on my database server. I therefore configure Microsoft Update just to download available updates and notify me that they are available. Many organizations have policies in place, and the required infrastructure to support them, which dictate that you use an internal Windows Server Update Services (WSUS) server to get your Windows and Microsoft Updates, instead of connecting directly to Microsoft's servers over the Internet.

Whichever way you get your Windows updates, it's vital that all "Important" updates are downloaded, tested in your test or development environment, and installed on your server, prior to installing SQL Server. Depending on your version of Windows and of SQL Server, you will need to make sure you have the appropriate version of the .NET Framework installed and fully patched before you install SQL Server, so that the SQL Server installation goes more quickly and smoothly.

If any of these updates require a reboot of the server, then you *must* reboot the server before you try to install SQL Server, since one of the first things the SQL Server setup program will check for is a pending reboot. If it finds a pending reboot, you will not be able to proceed with the SQL Server installation.

Installing and patching Windows will pretty heavily fragment a conventional magnetic disk drive so, once all of the patching and rebooting is done, I always manually run the built-in Windows **Disk Defragmenter** utility, shown in Figure 7.2, on the Windows system drive (usually the C: drive).

I also enable the built-in scheduler (by clicking on the **Configure Schedule** button shown in Figure 7.2) to automatically defragment that drive, using the default, once-a-week schedule. Keeping the system drive defragmented will help the system boot slightly faster, and will help programs load slightly faster.

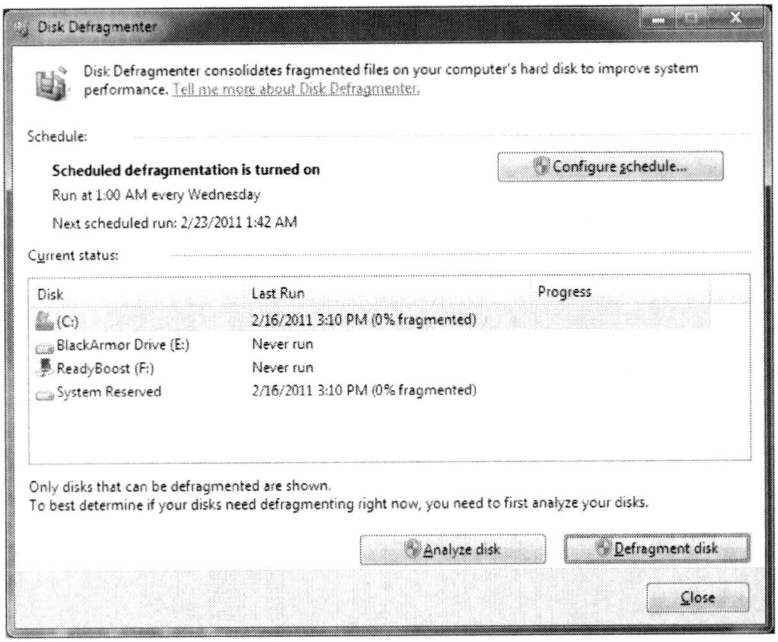

Figure 7.2:   Windows Disk Defragmenter utility.

SQL Server components

Hopefully, you will have done some planning and analysis, ahead of time, to determine which SQL Server components you need to install on your database server. This should take into account your business and technical requirements, along with licensing considerations. You should only install the components you actually need; never just install every available SQL Server component. Installing unnecessary components wastes resources and increases your attack surface. It also complicates and lengthens the process of making subsequent SQL Server updates, since more components need to be patched.

Network

I always make sure that my database server has a static IP address, in order to minimize the risk of DNS resolution problems, and that it has been added to the "proper" Windows Domain; when you first install Windows Server, your server will be in a Workgroup. Someone (possibly you in a small organization) will need to add the database server machine to the appropriate Windows Domain. This should be done before you attempt to install SQL Server. You should also be aware that this will require a reboot of the server.

If your motherboard (see *Chapter 1*) hosts multiple NICs, then you may want to consider using **NIC Teaming** to increase your bandwidth and redundancy. Another possibility is to have a second IP address, on a separate, dedicated NIC, so you can segregate network traffic for operations such as network backups and restores.

Accounts and privileges

Having decided which SQL Server components to install, you will have a better idea how many dedicated Windows Domain accounts are required (you need one for each SQL Server-related Service). In most cases, you will need at least two accounts, one for the main SQL Server Service and one for the SQL Server Agent Service, but you will need more if you need to install Full Text Search, SQL Server Integration Services (SSIS), SQL Server Reporting Services (SSRS), or SQL Server Analysis Services (SSAS).

Having a dedicated, separate Windows Domain account for each SQL Server service gives you more security and more reliability, since the other accounts will not be affected if one account is compromised by an attacker, or is simply locked out or disabled. Some DBAs will have a dedicated account for each SQL Service on each SQL Server instance to give themselves even more protection and reliability (at the cost of more administrative burden to manage what could be hundreds or thousands of Windows Domain accounts).

Each account should be a normal Windows Domain account, with no special rights. The SQL Server setup program will grant any special rights that these accounts need on the local machine, during the setup process. You will need to know the credentials of these accounts when you install SQL Server. Bear in mind that, depending on your organization, it may take some time to get these Domain accounts set up, so plan well ahead. Another factor to remember is that on a large network, with multiple sites, it may take some time for these new accounts to be replicated to your site and be available for you.

The SQL Server Service account may need to be granted some special rights or privileges, such as:

- **Perform volume maintenance tasks** – so that SQL Server can take advantage of Windows Instant File Initialization
- **Lock pages in memory (LPIM)** – to try to prevent the operating system from periodically paging out a large amount of memory from SQL Server's working set.

Both of these rights are discussed in detail in *Chapter 5*. The first one is clear-cut: Windows Instant File Initialization can greatly reduce the time it takes to create, grow, or restore database data files and this right should always be granted to the SQL Server Service account, so now is the time to go into Group Policy Editor and do so.

Use of LPIM for your SQL Server instance is more of a judgment call. If I was installing a new copy of SQL Server 2005 on top of Windows Server 2003 (which I hope you are not doing in 2011), I would definitely enable that feature. With SQL Server 2008 R2 running on Windows Server 2008 R2, I probably would not use LPIM.

Logical drives and directories

You should have a standardized naming convention for the logical drives and directories where you'll be locating the various SQL Server files. Maintaining multiple servers is *much* easier if the drives and directories are all set up in a consistent manner. This consistency is also very important if you ever have to add a data file to a database that is using database mirroring or SQL Server Denali AlwaysOn. If you have different drive letters or a different directory structure across machines, SQL Server will try to add the new SQL Server data file to the same relative location (i.e. `P:\SQLData`), that actually does not exist on the second server, which will cause your database mirror to go into a suspended state until you correct the issue.

Figure 7.3 shows the naming standards and directory structure that I like to use.

Purpose	Drive letter and directory
System drive	C:
SQL Server Backup drive	N:\SQLBackups
SQL Server Log drive	L:\SQLLogs
SQL Server Data drives	P:\SQLData
	Q:\SQLData
	R:\SQLData
	S:\SQLData
SQL Server TempDB	T:\TempDB
Optical Drive	Z:

Figure 7.3: Naming standards and structure for logical drives.

Depending on your workload, you may need multiple logical drives for SQL Server backup files and for SQL Server data files so that you can segregate the I/O workload across more controllers and a greater number of spindles. Having multiple drives for SQL Server backups will allow you to use striped backups to increase your backup and restore performance. A striped database backup is simply a backup with multiple backup files instead of a single backup file. If you have multiple logical drives (that represent dedicated physical disk arrays) that you can use for your backup files, using a striped backup can dramatically increase your backup and restore performance, since you will be spreading the I/O across more devices and spindles. You do have to be careful that all the files that are part of a striped backup are available when you want to restore. You can also use native backup compression or compression via a third-party tool (such as Red Gate's SQL Backup) to improve your backup and restore performance.

There is no performance advantage in having multiple SQL Server log files for a single database, as SQL Server writes to the log file sequentially and will always treat the log as a single logical file even if it comprises multiple physical files. However, if you have multiple user databases on the SQL server instance, it is a good idea to try to separate each log file onto its own logical drive.

You should have spent some time planning all of this, so that you know exactly what you need, and can communicate your requirements clearly and specifically to your SAN administrator or systems administrator. When requesting logical drives, don't make the mistake of just asking for a certain amount of space; instead, you need to indicate the type of workload that must be supported, including the read/write percentage, data volatility, and your best estimate of the required I/O performance (IOPS) and sequential throughput (MB/s).

One thing to keep in mind is that some SANs will spread their workload across all of the available spindles in the SAN. One example of this is 3PAR, which uses a technology called "disk chunklets" to spread the data for a LUN (logical disk) across every spindle in the SAN. If your SAN uses this type of technology, your request for separate logical drives (as outlined in Figure 7.3) may be pushed back by your SAN administrator. They may try to convince you, instead, to just have one large LUN where all of your SQL Server files will live. My advice is to stick to your guns, and get separate logical drives just like you would for DAS. That way, you will have more flexibility and more visibility about the performance of each LUN.

Again, depending on your organization, it may take some time to get your logical drives properly provisioned and presented to your database server. However, once this has been done, you should then check that the drives have been properly partition-aligned in order to get the best performance. This was a big issue with Windows Server 2003 and earlier operating systems, but less so with Windows Server 2008 and later (unless the drive was created with an older version of the operating system), which properly handles partition alignment for new volumes automatically. At any rate, you should always check the partition alignment.

Microsoft's Jimmy May and Denny Lee have written an excellent white paper, available at HTTP://MSDN.MICROSOFT.COM/EN-US/LIBRARY/DD758814(SQL.100).ASPX, which explains how to check and correct your disk partition alignment.

Functional and performance testing

After the drives have been provisioned and presented to your database server, you should spend at least a day doing functional and performance testing with tools such as SQLIO, SQLIOSim, CrystalDiskMark, and HDTune Pro, to validate that they are working correctly and are giving you the desired and expected performance that you require for your workload. These testing tools were described in much more detail in *Chapter 3*.

You should be careful about your disk testing and validation efforts if you are using storage (such as a SAN) that is shared by other systems that are already in production, since you will likely end up flooding and flushing the SAN cache, which would cause a negative performance impact for other systems that are using the SAN.

Fail-over clustering

In order to create a SQL Server fail-over cluster, using Windows Clustering, you need to make sure that your database server operating system is part of a traditional Windows fail-over cluster, which requires shared storage (usually meaning a SAN), before you attempt to install SQL Server. In Windows Server 2008 and above, you have to add the fail-over clustering feature (from Server Manager) to each node that will be part of the cluster. Then, you can use the Create Cluster Wizard to create and validate your Windows fail-over cluster.

Then, when you are ready to install SQL Server, you will also need to select the **New SQL Server fail-over cluster installation** option in the SQL Server setup program, in order to install a clustered SQL Server instance properly.

A full discussion of fail-over clustering is out of scope for this chapter, but I will make a couple of points. First, if you are using Windows Server 2008 or later, along with SQL Server 2008 or later, then you will find fail-over clustering much easier to install and manage than it was in the days of Windows Server 2003 and SQL Server 2005. Back then, you had to be much more careful about having identical hardware that was certified for clustering, and it was fairly tricky to get your cluster configured properly.

Second, I consider fail-over clustering to be verging on a legacy technology. It is mainly designed to protect against hardware failure in one of the nodes in the cluster, which is a relatively rare event with more reliable, modern server hardware. It also requires shared storage, usually meaning a SAN, which is an obvious single point of failure (since the entire SAN can fail), and it is a very significant hardware investment for many smaller organizations.

Personally, I tend to favor using SQL Server database mirroring instead of, or in addition to, fail-over clustering, as part of a high availability solution, for the following reasons:

- database mirroring works at the database level instead of the instance level

- it gives you two copies of your data instead of the one shared copy of the data that you get with fail-over clustering.

- you also get faster fail-overs with database mirroring compared to fail-over clustering, since you don't have to wait for disk resources to become available, and for the SQL instance to start up on the new node in the cluster.

If you are using SQL Server Denali, and want to take advantage of the SQL Server AlwaysOn/HADRON features, for High Availability and Disaster Recovery, your database server will also need to be part of a Windows Cluster. With SQL Server AlwaysOn, you have the choice of using shared storage for your Windows Cluster, or of creating a Windows Cluster with a number of stand-alone machines, with no shared storage. This gives you a lot more flexibility in how you design your AlwaysOn architecture.

When you are ready to install SQL Server, you will want to choose the regular **New installation or add features to an existing installation** option in the SQL Server setup program. You also have more flexibility with SQL Server AlwaysOn, in that you can create the Windows Cluster before or after you install SQL Server.

Installation media and Service Packs

Finally, you need to make sure that you have access to the SQL Server installation media, which could be on a DVD, an `.iso` file, or on a network file share, and that you have your license key.

You should also have downloaded the latest SQL Server Service Pack, making sure you have the correct version (x86, x64, or IA64). In some cases, there may not yet be a SQL

Server Service Pack available, but there may be a Cumulative Update. In other cases, there may be a Service Pack available for your version of SQL Server *and* a Cumulative Update for that Service Pack.

My general advice is always to install the latest Service Pack and Cumulative Update as part of your initial installation of SQL Server. Doing so will avoid a later maintenance outage in order to fix a problem that the SP and CU were designed to correct. Another option with SQL Server 2008 and later is to prepare a slipstreamed installation media, which we will cover later in this chapter.

SQL Server 2008 R2 Installation

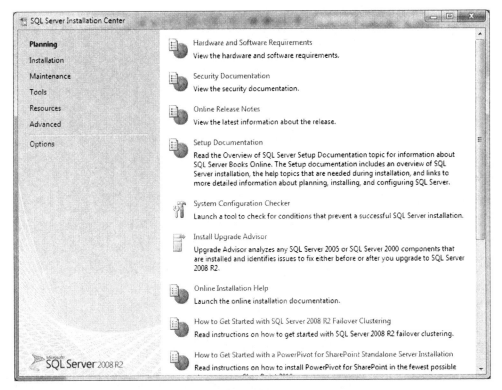

Figure 7.4:   Initial Installation Center screen for SQL Server 2008 R2.

After all the decisions and preparation, it is finally time to install SQL Server, and all your careful planning and information gathering will make the installation go much smoother. In this section, we'll walk through the process of installing an instance of SQL Server 2008 R2. So let's get started. Having started the SQL Server setup program, you will see the **SQL Server Installation Center** screen, shown in Figure 7.4.

In order to proceed, click on the **Installation** link, at the top of the left pane. This will open the Installation screen, shown in Figure 7.5.

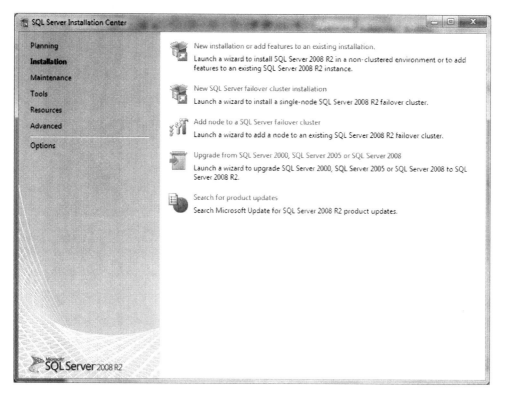

Figure 7.5:　Installation screen.

We'll be performing a regular, standalone installation of SQL Server 2008 R2, so click on the **New installation or add features to an existing installation** link on the top of the right pane. This will bring up the "Please wait..." screen, shown in Figure 7.6.

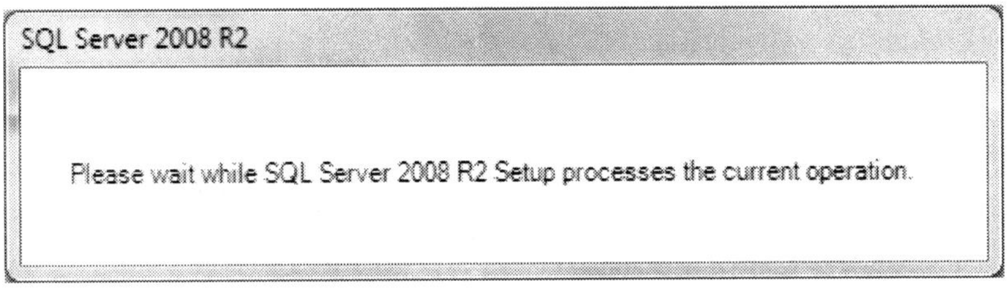

Figure 7.6:   "Please wait..." screen.

After a few seconds or minutes, depending on your hardware, the **Setup Support Rules** screen will appear, as shown in Figure 7.7. This portion of the setup is looking for conditions that will prevent the SQL Server setup program from installing the SQL Server Setup support files. This first set of checks is not comprehensive, and there are more checks later in the installation process that may stop you from proceeding.

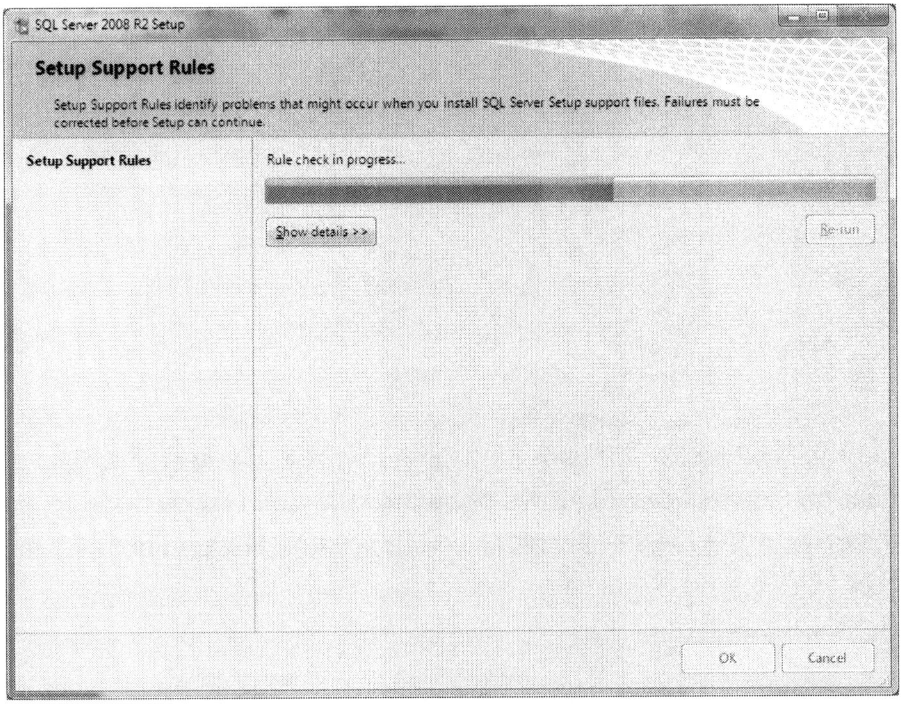

Figure 7.7:   Setup Support Rules check.

After a few more seconds, you should see the **Product Key** screen that is shown in Figure 7.8.

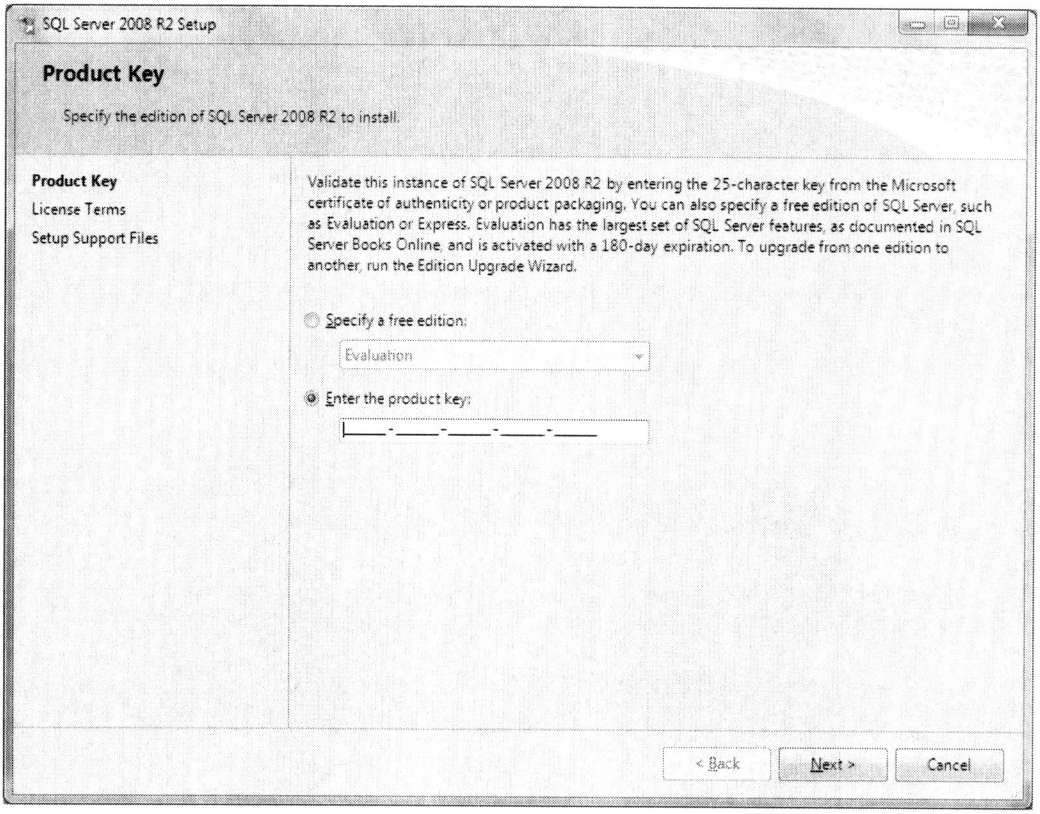

Figure 7.8:   Product Key and edition selection.

Here is where you enter the Product Key for your SQL Server license. If you are using a Volume License installer, the license key will be pre-populated for you. Having done so, click **Next** and you will arrive at the **License Terms** selection screen, shown in Figure 7.9.

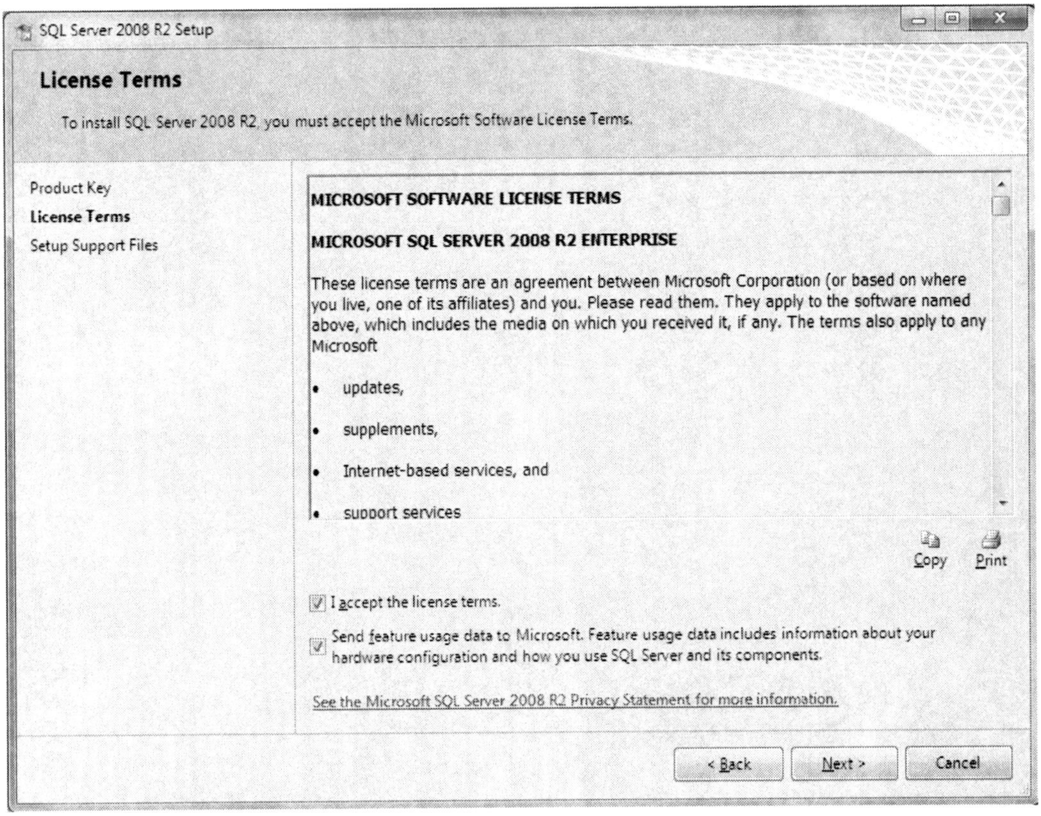

Figure 7.9: License Terms selection.

You must accept the license terms, or you won't be able to install SQL Server 2008 R2. Whether or not you decide to send feature usage data to Microsoft is up to you. I always check that second check box, since it provides telemetry data to Microsoft that they can use to improve SQL Server. If your database server does not have Internet access, there is no point in checking that second check box. After you make your choice, click **Next**. You will see the **Setup Support Files** screen shown in Figure 7.10.

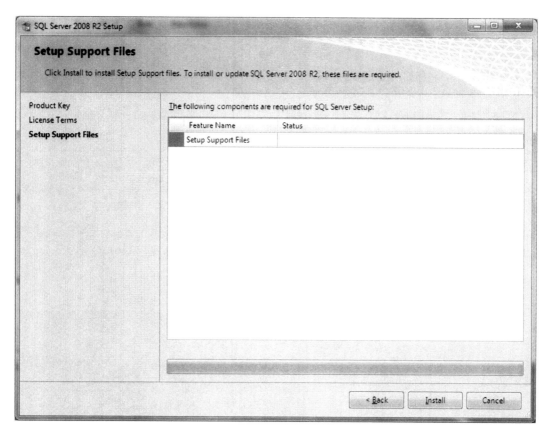

Figure 7.10: Setup Support Files ready to be installed.

Click the **Install** button to move past this screen. You will see the progress bar advance at the bottom of the screen, as shown in Figure 7.11.

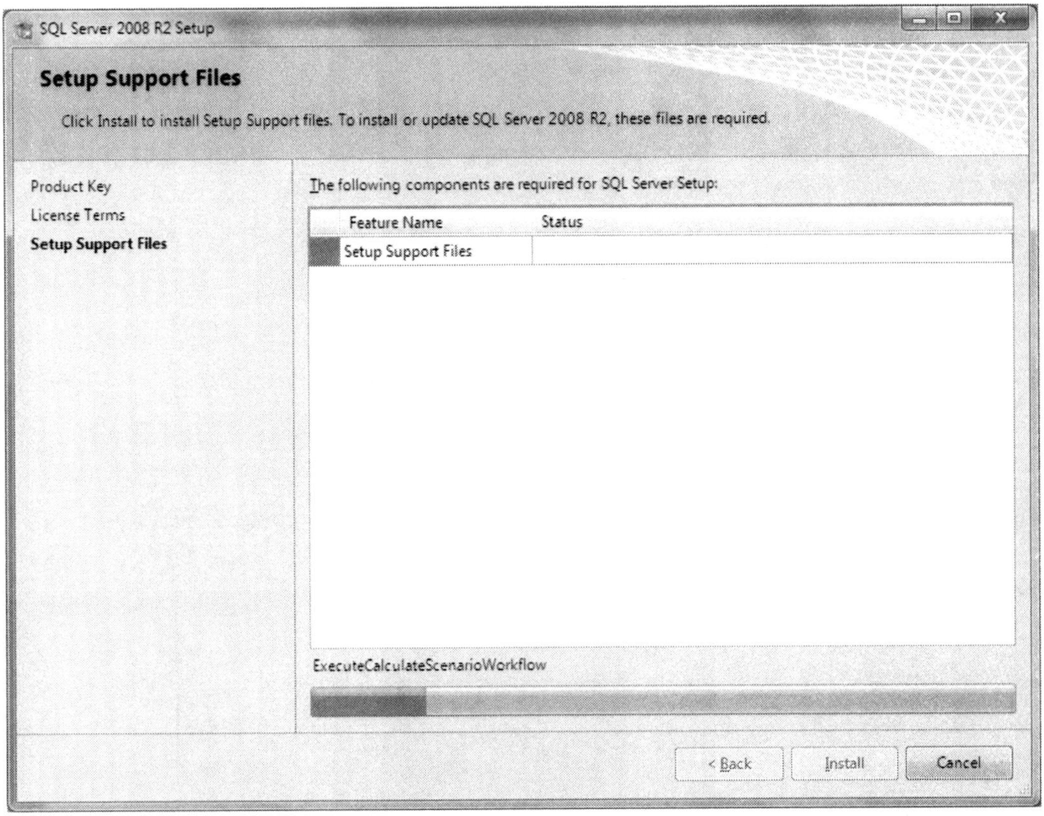

Figure 7.11: Setup Support Files installing.

How long this takes to complete depends on your hardware, but it is usually less than a minute. When all of the Setup Support files have been installed, you will see the **Setup Support Rules** screen shown in Figure 7.12.

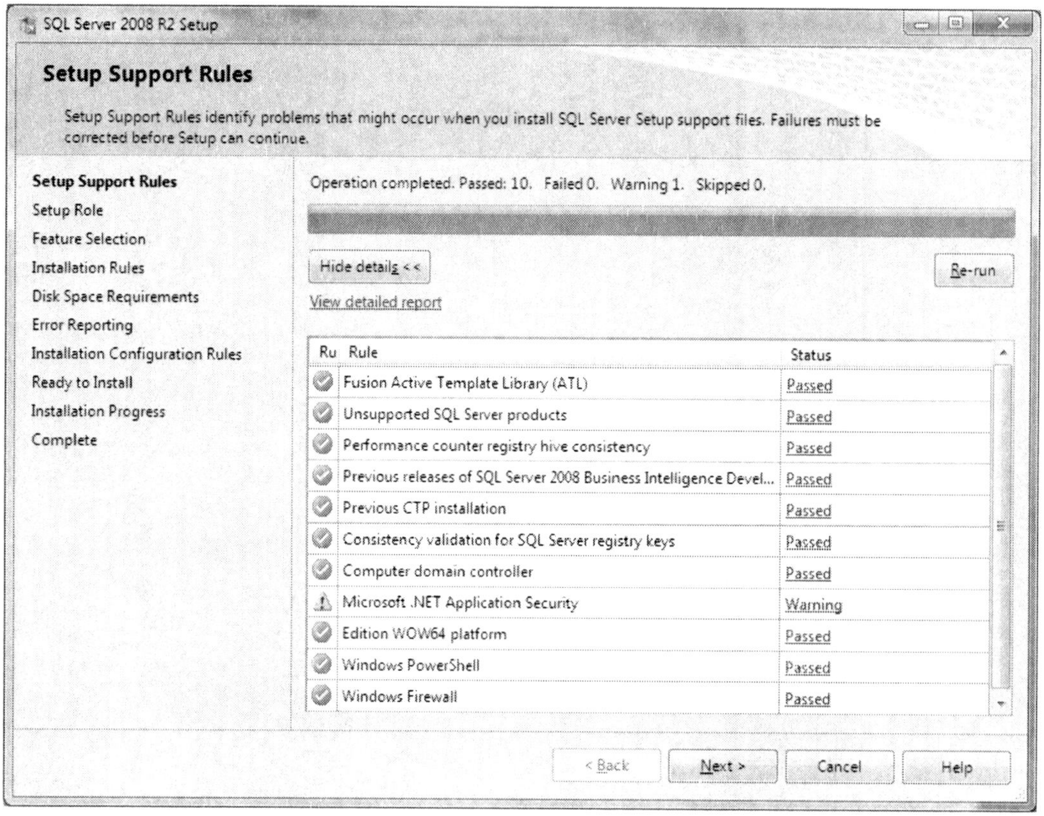

Figure 7.12: Setup Support Rules.

You can click on the blue links in the **Status** column to get more details about the rules that were checked. Warnings won't halt your progress, but you will have to correct any errors that show up in this list. Having a fresh, fully-patched copy of Windows Server 2008 R2 will minimize any problems. Click **Next** to continue to the **Setup Role** screen, shown in Figure 7.13.

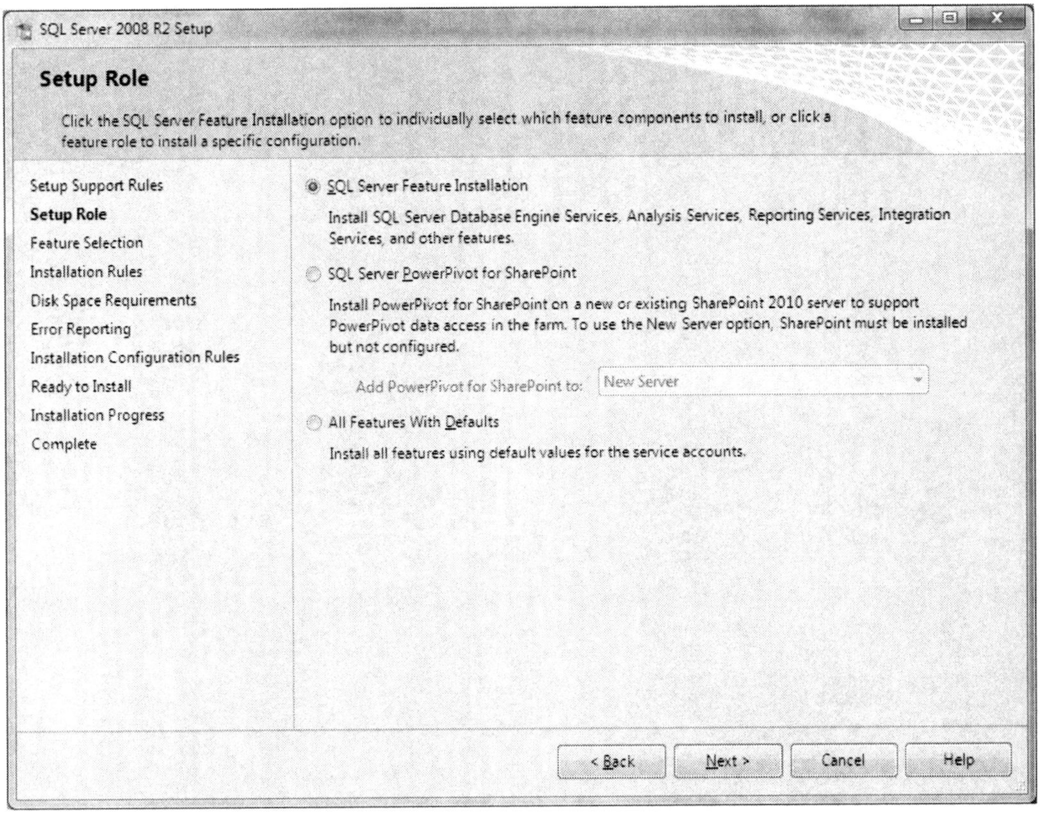

Figure 7.13: Setup Role screen.

In most cases, you should use the default **SQL Server Feature Installation** choice shown in Figure 7.13. This gives you much more flexibility and control over how SQL Server 2008 R2 is installed and configured. Click **Next** to continue to the **Feature Selection** screen, shown in Figure 7.14.

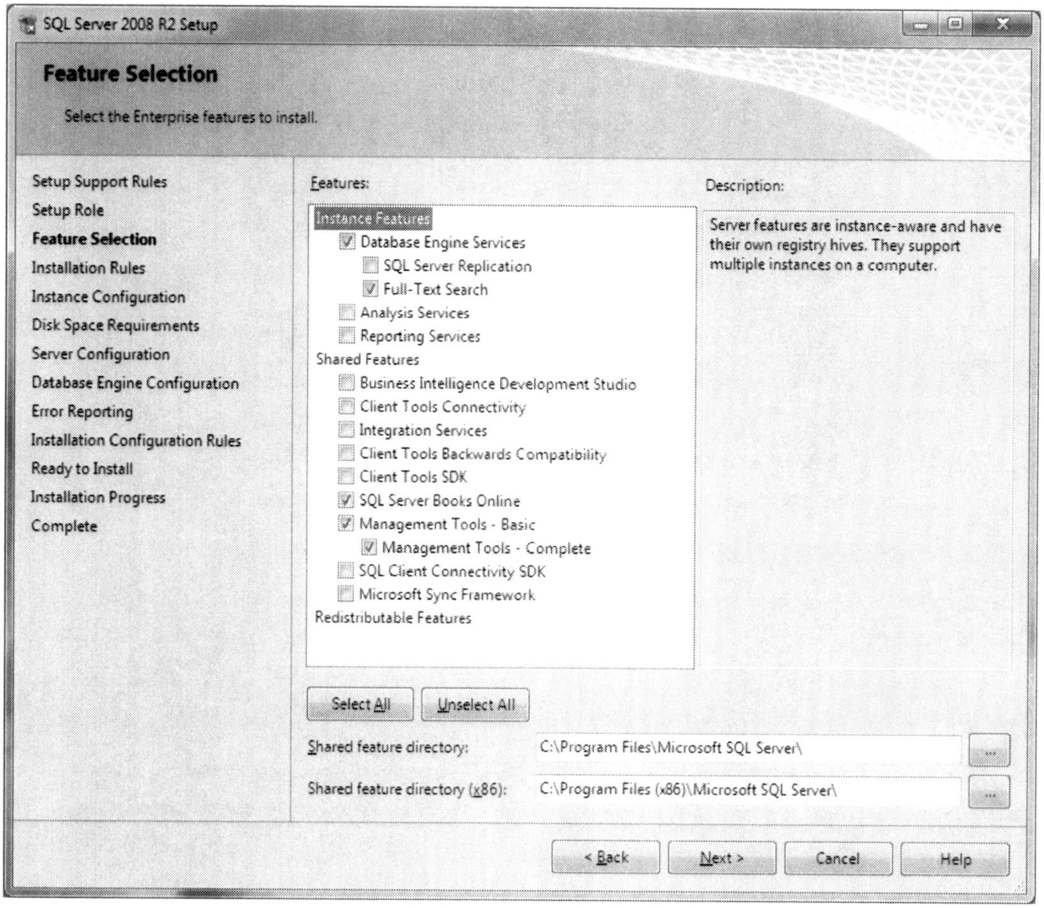

Figure 7.14: Feature Selection.

The **Feature Selection** screen is a very important screen. You should select *only* the SQL Server features and components that you will actually be using on this database server. Don't make the common mistake of just selecting every feature "just in case," or out of curiosity. As discussed, you should know ahead of time which features you need. Once you select the appropriate features, click **Next** to move on to the **Installation Rules** screen, shown in Figure 7.15.

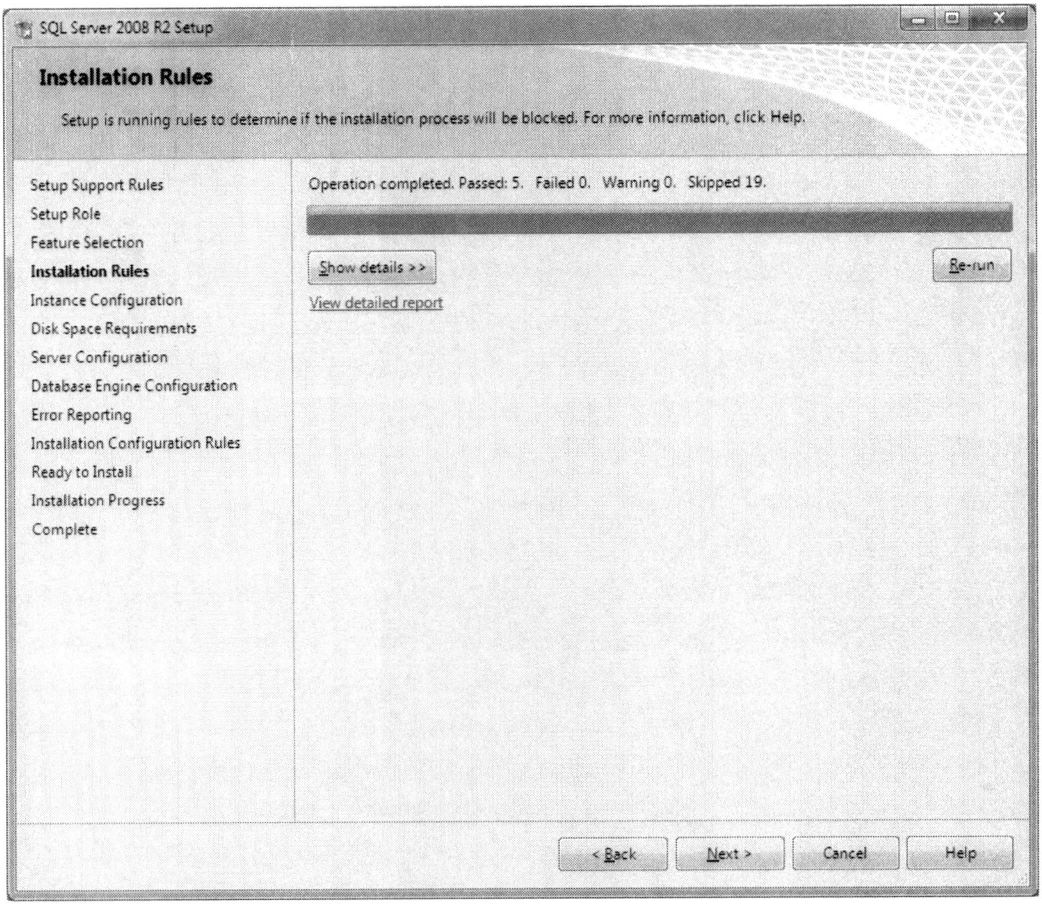

Figure 7.15:   Installation Rules.

Depending on which features you chose to install, different installation rules will be checked. You can click on the blue links in the **Status** column to get more details about the rules that were checked. Again, you can proceed despite any warnings, but you will have to correct any errors that show up in this list in order to continue with the installation. Once you are ready, click **Next to** continue to the **Instance Configuration** screen, shown in Figure 7.16.

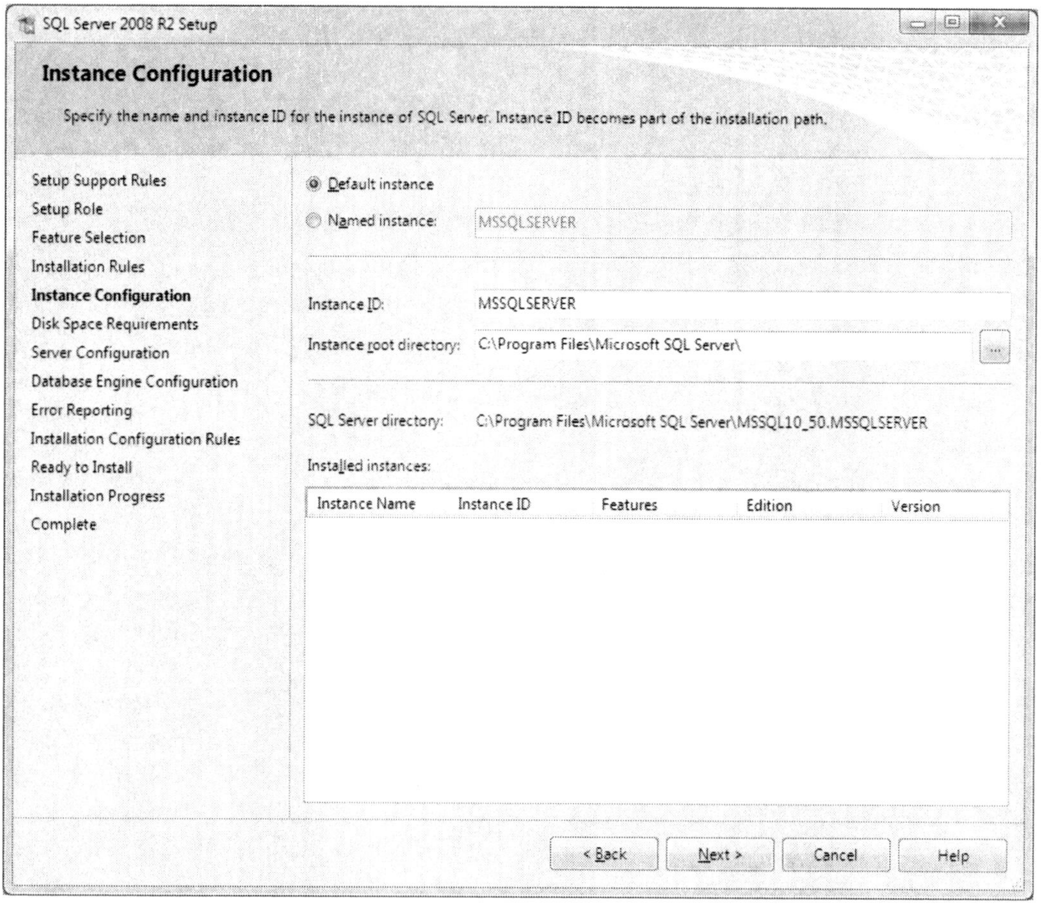

Figure 7.16: Instance Configuration.

This is where you determine whether you are installing a Default instance or a Named instance of SQL Server 2008 R2. The first instance of SQL Server that is usually installed on a server is called the default instance, and it has the same name as the server itself. You can only have one default instance of SQL Server on a machine.

If you have an existing default instance that is a recent, older version of SQL Server, you can upgrade in-place by installing a new default instance over the top of the old default instance. While this is officially supported by Microsoft, I would *never* do it myself as it will wipe out your old instance and upgrade all of your user databases to the new version of SQL Server, which I just think is too risky. You are much better off installing a fresh copy of SQL Server as the default instance, on top of a fresh copy of the operating system, preferably on a new server.

An alternative is to install a named instance, which leaves the old default instance intact (although it will upgrade shared components, such as SSMS, to the new version). I don't like to install additional named instances on a production server, due to resource limits on the server. However, named instances are great for development and testing machines as you can install multiple named instances on the same machine at no additional cost.

Once you make your selections, click **Next**, and you will see the **Disk Space Requirements** screen, shown in Figure 7.17.

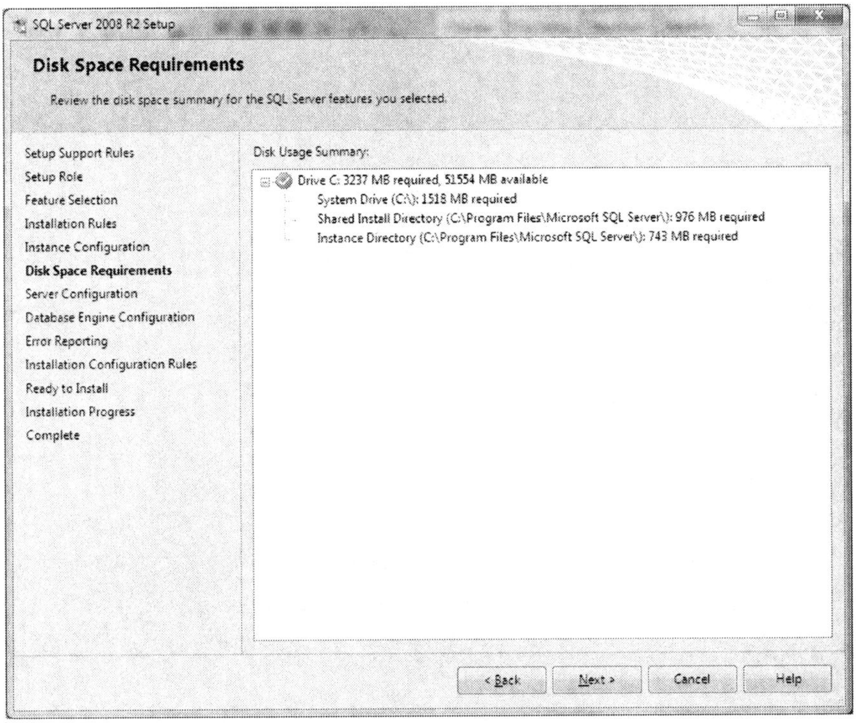

Figure 7.17: Disk Space Requirements.

After you make sure you will have enough disk space to install SQL Server with some extra space left over, there is not much to do here but click **Next** to move on to the **Server Configuration** screen, shown in Figure 7.18.

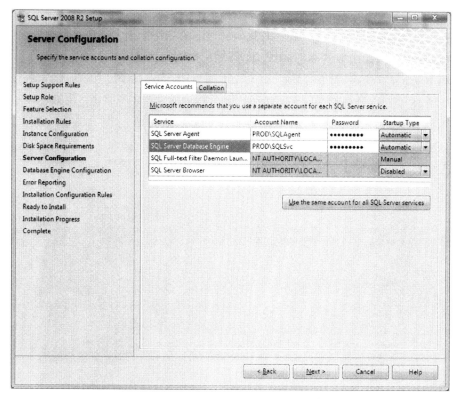

Figure 7.18: Server Configuration.

This is where you choose what accounts to use for each SQL Server-related service that you are going to install. Ideally, from a security perspective, you will have a dedicated Windows Domain account for each service. If you use a single Windows Domain account for each SQL Server-related service across all of your SQL Server instances, and that account is compromised by an attacker, your entire SQL Server related infrastructure will be affected.

From a reliability perspective, you may want a dedicated account for each SQL Server-related service, on each instance of SQL Server, since if you have a single shared service account, any problems with that account will affect all your SQL Server instances. However, bear in mind the administrative burden of managing larger numbers of Windows accounts for multiple machines and instances.

You also need to select the **Startup Type** for the service, which should be **Automatic** in most cases. After you enter the required information and make your choices, click **Next** to go to the **Database Engine Configuration** screen, shown in Figure 7.19.

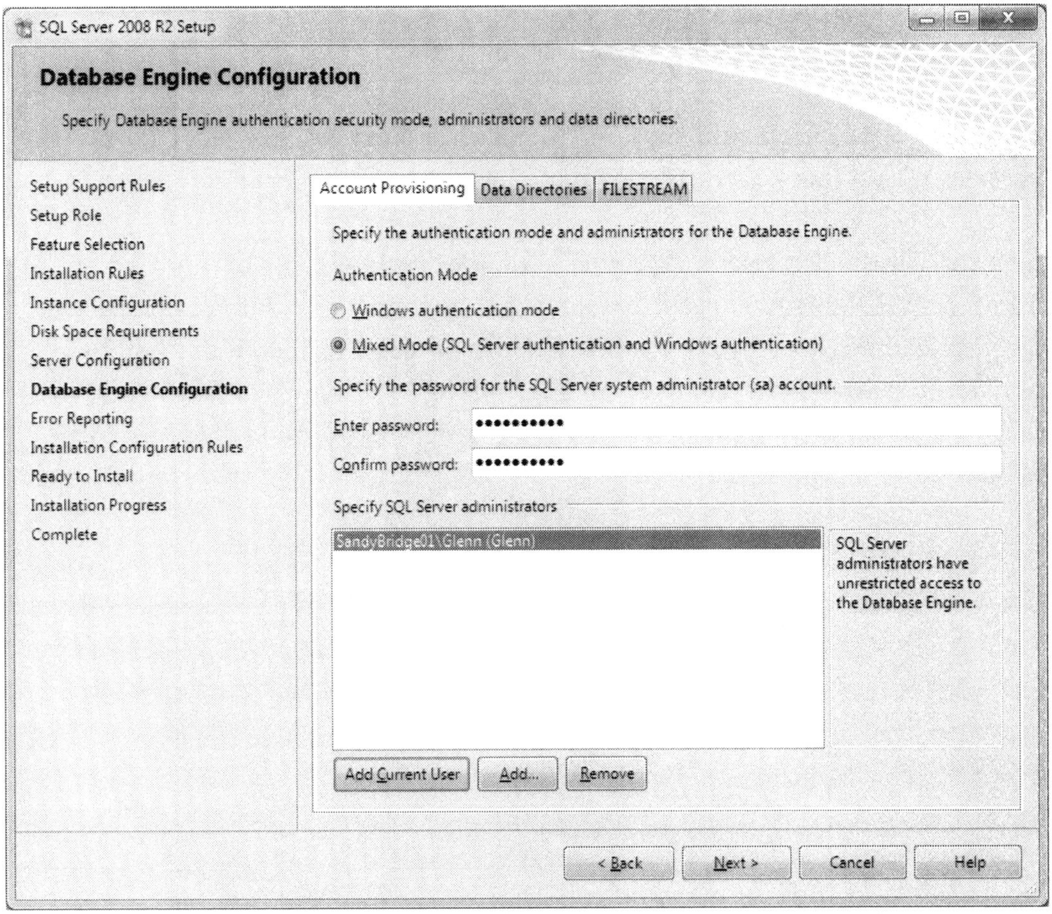

Figure 7.19: Database Engine Configuration.

The Database Engine Configuration screen is where you select the **Authentication Mode** for this instance of SQL Server. Ideally, you would always choose **Windows authentication mode**, but many legacy applications still use SQL Server authentication. If you choose **Mixed Mode** authentication, you will need to enter a password for the system administrator (**sa**) account. You should choose a "strong" password, with a combination of uppercase and lowercase letters, along with numbers and symbols. Do not choose a word that is found in the dictionary, since that will make the password vulnerable to what is known as a dictionary attack (where every word in the dictionary is tried in a brute force attack). You also want to make sure you remember the **sa** password!

When I am installing SQL Server, I always add myself as a SQL Server Administrator for the instance, by clicking on the **Add Current User** button.

Having entered the appropriate information, do **not** click **Next** yet. Instead, click on the **Data Directories** tab on this screen, as shown in Figure 7.20.

This is where you choose the default directories for your various types of SQL Server files. You can accept the default suggestions, and change them later, but I really like to set the appropriate directories during the initial setup process. That way, any databases or backups that are created later will go to an appropriate location, by default. You can still override these default locations when you create a database, or add data files to an existing database.

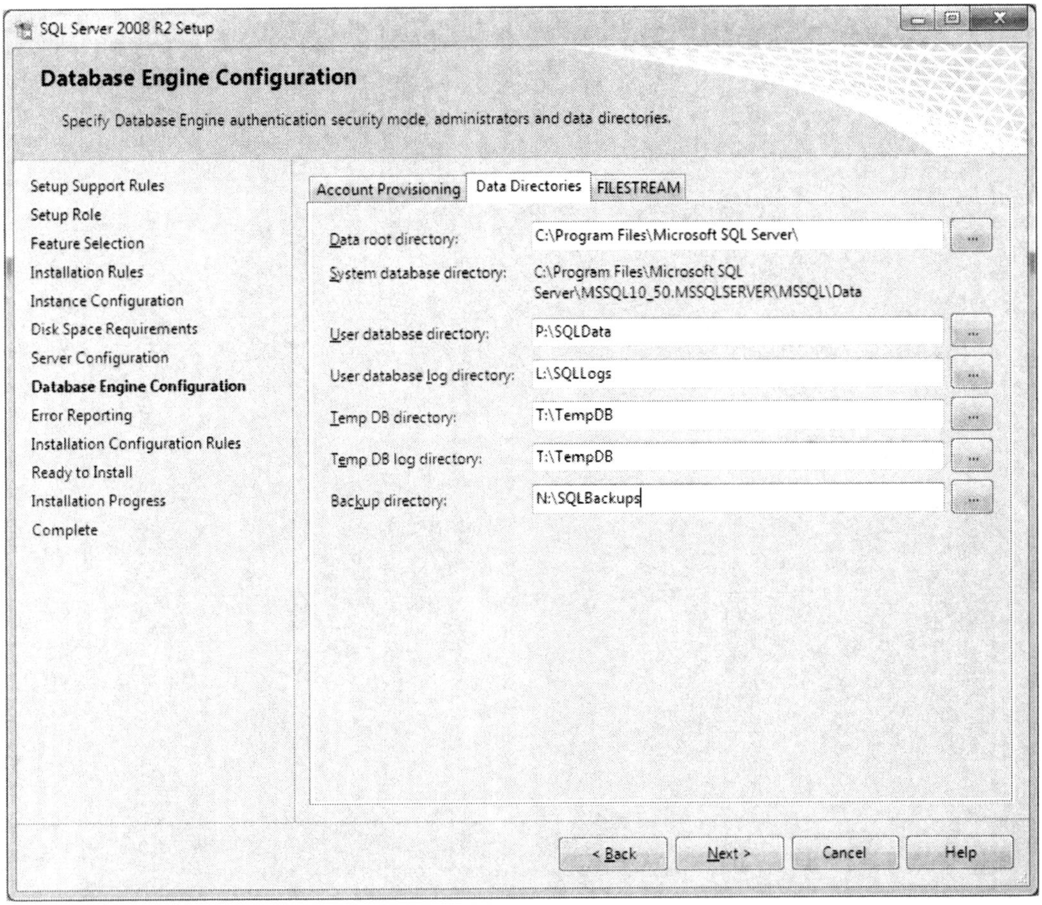

Figure 7.20: Database Engine Configuration, Data Directories.

Of course, in order for this to work as designed, you need to have all of your logical drives available, as you are installing SQL Server. You can either type the file path for each directory, or you can click on the ellipsis button to navigate around the file system, and create sub-directories if necessary. Once you have completed this screen, click **Next** to continue to the **Error Reporting** screen, shown in Figure 7.21.

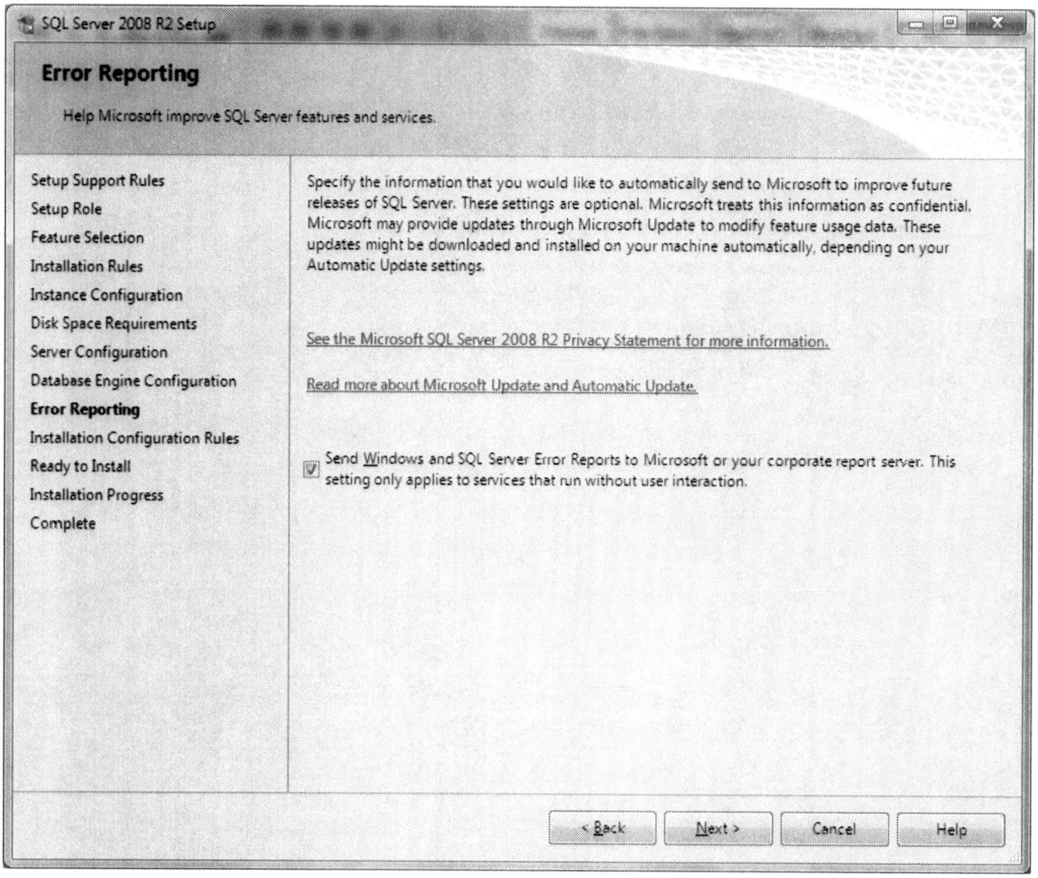

Figure 7.21: Error Reporting.

It is up to you whether or not you want to send Windows and SQL Server Error Reports to Microsoft. However, I will say that Microsoft pays very close attention to these reports and uses the information to detect and correct problems that are happening out in the field, so I always tick this check box. Once again, there is no reason to check the box if your database server does not have Internet access.

266

Having made your selection, click **Next** to continue to the **Installation Configuration Rules** screen, shown in Figure 7.22.

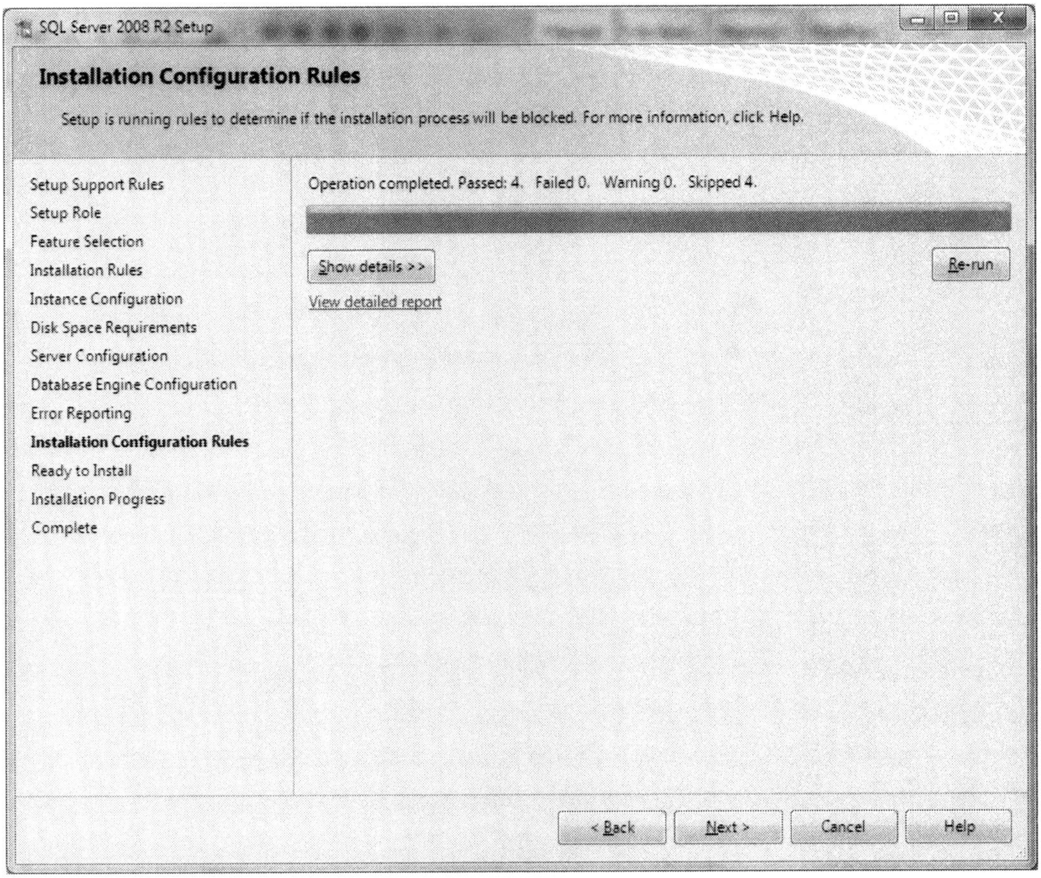

Figure 7.22: Installation Configuration Rules.

The Installation Configuration Rules screen shows the results of four checks that are run to make sure that the installation process will not be blocked. If each check passes, you will be able to click **Next** to continue to the **Ready to Install** screen, shown in Figure 7.23.

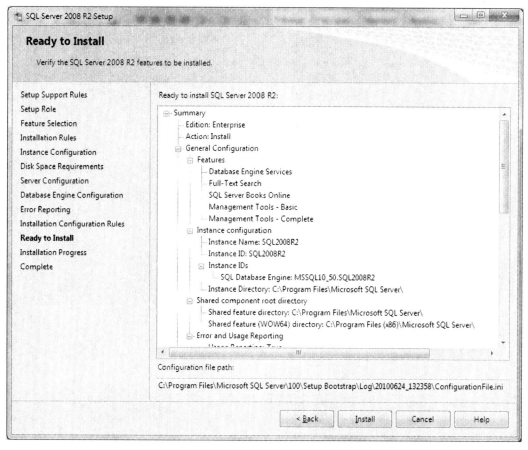

Figure 7.23: Ready to Install.

Here, you have a chance to review your choices before you click on the **Install** button to actually start the main installation process. When you're ready, take a deep breath and click on the **Install** button to continue.

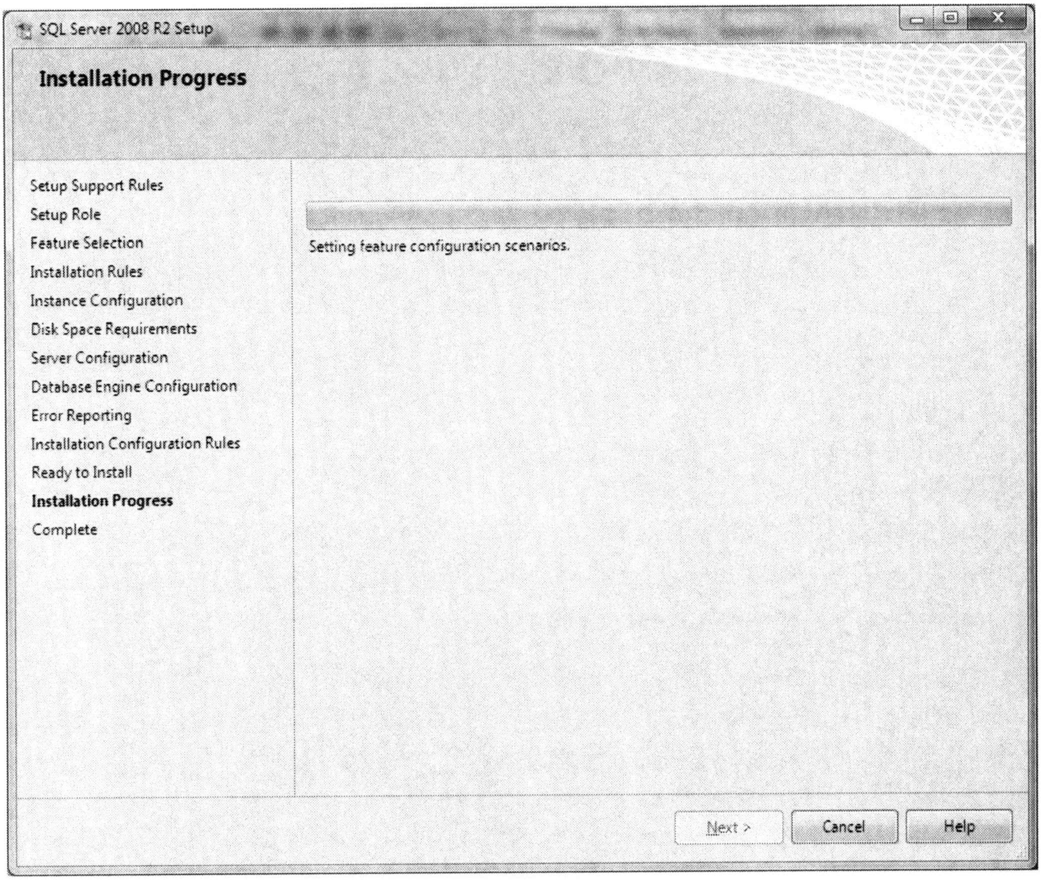

Figure 7.24: Installation Progress.

The Installation Progress screen shown in Figure 7.24 will update the progress bar as the installation continues. The length of time this takes will depend on your hardware and how many components you chose to install. If you are installing on a fast, modern SSD, the process should be pretty quick. All being well, you'll eventually see the **Complete** screen, indicating a successful installation, as shown in Figure 7.25.

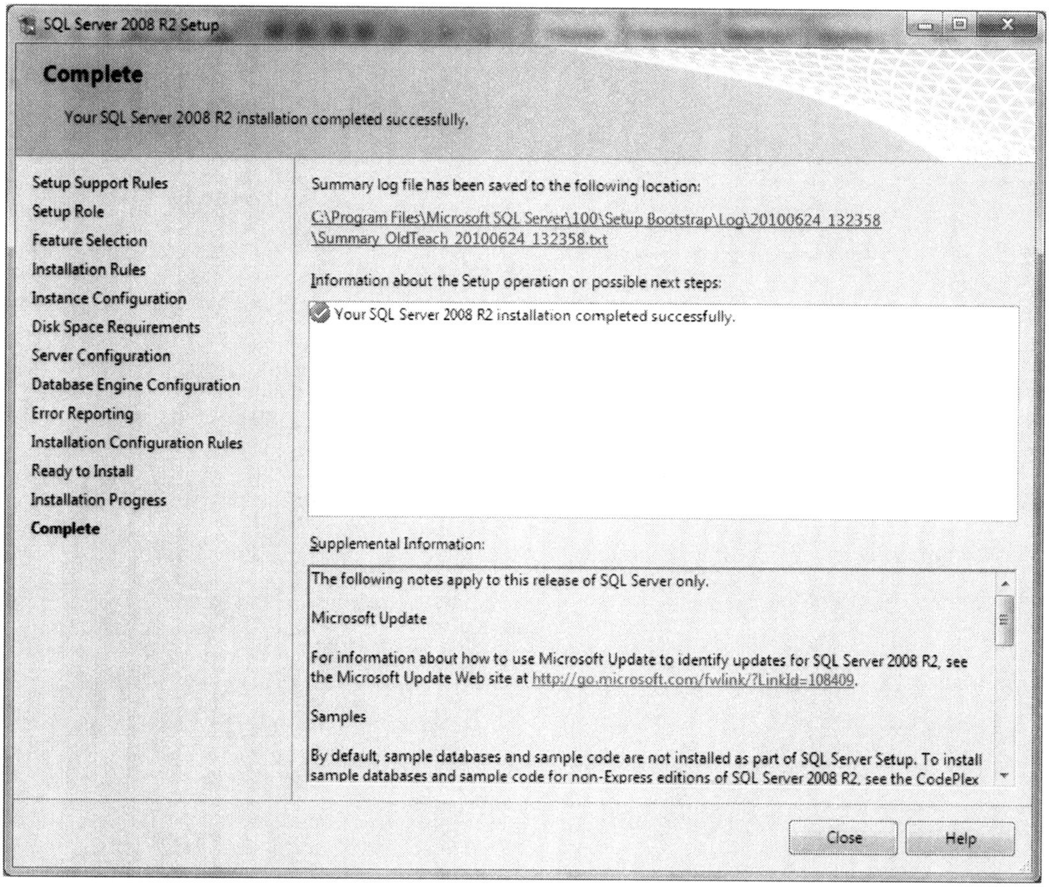

Figure 7.25: Installation Complete.

Job done! Make sure to click on the **Close** button before you remove the installation media.

SQL Server 2008 R2 Service Packs and Cumulative Updates

Having installed SQL Server 2008 R2, you need to install the latest Service Pack. At the time of writing (April 2011), there were no Service Packs available for SQL Server 2008 R2, but that will probably change sometime in late 2011. However, you still should apply the latest Cumulative Update for the SQL Server 2008 R2 RTM.

If you are in charge of one or more SQL Server instances, whether they are installed on a laptop or a large production datacenter, you need to be aware of how SQL Server updates and fixes are released, and how you can obtain them.

I find that there is some confusion around RTM releases, hot-fixes, CUs, SPs and so on, so I'll start with a few definitions.

- **RTM** means Release to Manufacturing. It is the original, released build for that version of the product, i.e. it is what you get on the DVD or when you download the .iso file from MSDN.

- A **hot-fix** is designed to fix a single issue, usually after a case has been escalated through Microsoft CSS to the SQL Server Product Team.

- A **Cumulative Update** is a cumulative package of hot-fixes (usually 20–40) that also includes all previous Cumulative Updates for the relevant Service Pack. Cumulative updates are not fully regression tested. They are released every eight weeks.

- A **Service Pack** is a much larger collection of hot-fixes that have been fully regression tested. Service Packs are only released every 12–18 months.

When you first install a shiny, new copy of SQL Server 2008 R2 (or 2005 or 2008) from the DVD that came with the box, what you have is the RTM build for that version of SQL Server. Depending on how long ago that major version of SQL Server was released, the build that you just installed could be years old.

I often encounter instances of SQL Server (outside my own place of work!) that are still running the RTM build of that version of SQL Server, which in my opinion is both lazy and irresponsible. If you don't do something about it, you could end up on an "Unsupported Service Pack," which means that you will only get limited troubleshooting support from Microsoft if you ever need to open a support case with Microsoft CSS. You are also more likely to run into issues that were fixed after the RTM release.

How often to patch?

Hot-fixes don't get added to SQL Server on a whim; the CSS and the Product Team first need to be convinced that the issue that is prompting the hot-fix is important enough to actually fix and release. When you look at the list of fixes for each Cumulative Update, you can determine whether they seem to address any issues that you have been experiencing in your environment. Then you can decide whether to go through the pain of getting the whole CU tested in your test environment and then installed in your production environment.

You can download Service Packs directly from Microsoft without making any special requests. Service Packs are cumulative, so you can go directly from RTM to SP4 without installing any intervening Service Packs. If you have Microsoft Update installed on your machine, it will offer up SQL Server Service Packs as updates, but I prefer to manually obtain and install them myself. The reason for this is that I need to plan the testing effort for the Service Pack, along with when and how I want to install it in my production environment.

Some organizations have a policy of only testing and deploying Service Packs, which Microsoft sometimes calls Public Cumulative Updates (PCU), deciding to ignore any regular Cumulative Updates that are released between the Service Packs. They argue that only Service Packs are fully regression tested by Microsoft, and that they don't have the resources to test and certify Cumulative Updates with their applications and environments. They also argue that third-party software vendors have not certified these

Cumulative Updates for use with their products. Personally, I am against this approach; I prefer to examine each CU individually and decide whether or not I need to install it.

Generally speaking, I am biased towards trying to stay current on my CUs and Service Packs, and anyone who follows my blog or Twitter feed (see *About the Author*) will know that I am pretty good about finding them, and announcing them to the world, as is my fellow SQL Server MVP, Aaron Bertrand, (blog at HTTP://SQLBLOG.COM/BLOGS/AARON_BERTRAND/ and handle on Twitter **@aaronbertrand**). You can also check the Microsoft SQL Server Release Services blog at HTTP://BLOGS.MSDN.COM/B/SQLRELEASESERVICES/, the SQL Server Solution Center at HTTP://SUPPORT.MICROSOFT.COM/PH/2855#TAB0 and the latest releases.

Downloading and installing CUs and SPs

Once you know that a CU for your version and Service Pack of SQL Server has been released, you need to find the accompanying Knowledge Base (KB) article that lists the fixes. For example, the KB for *SQL Server 2008 R2 RTM CU5* can be found at HTTP://SUPPORT.MICROSOFT.COM/KB/2438347/EN-US. In the top left portion of the KB page, you will see a **View and request hot-fix downloads** link.

Having followed that link, you need to click on the **Show hot-fixes for all platforms and languages** link in the center of the page. Otherwise, you will only see the hot-fixes for the platform (x86, x64, or IA64) on the computer where your browser is running, which is probably your laptop or workstation.

After you choose the correct packages, which can be confusing (see *Appendix B* for further help), provide a valid email address, and fill in the CAPTCHA information, and you will get an email with a link to download a zip file containing the CU, along with the Cumulative Update setup program. The zip file is password protected, so you will need the password that is included in the email to unzip it.

The password expires after seven days, so I always immediately unzip the file and save it in a directory structure similar to that shown in Figure 7.26 (with further subdirectories for x86 and x64).

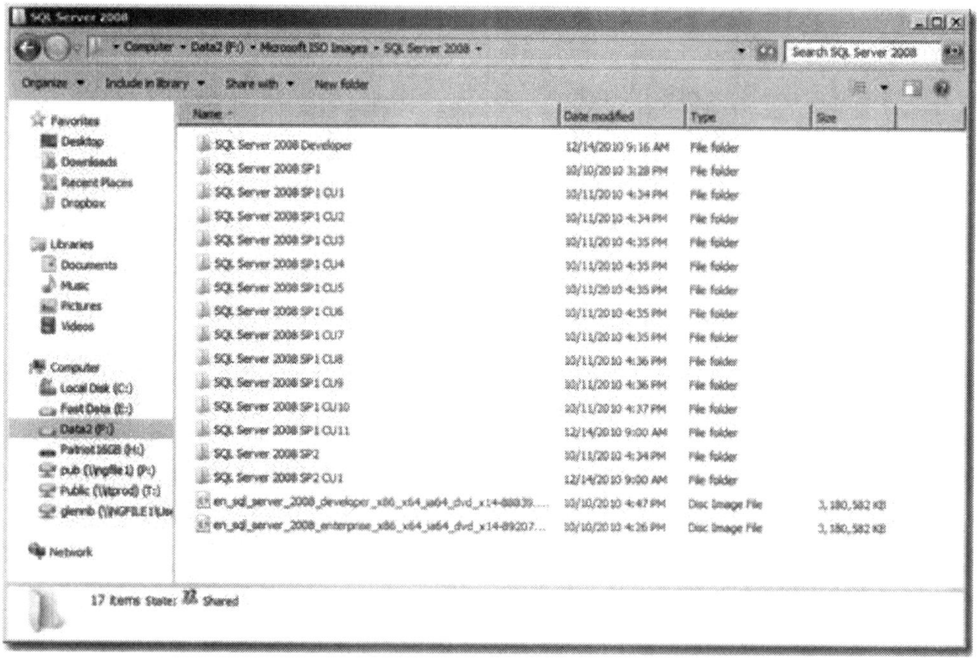

Figure 7.26: File system with multiple SQL Server Cumulative Updates.

Finally, after jumping through these small hoops, you are ready to install it on a test instance (which could be a virtual machine) just to make sure that the setup program works, and does not seem to break SQL Server. After this initial smoke test, you can do additional installs and further, more involved testing before you deploy it to your production environment.

The kind of testing that you do will depend on your time, development and QA resources. Ideally, you would want to do a full round of manual and automated regression testing on all of your applications that use that database server. In real life, that is often not possible with your available time and resources. I will say that, in the past five years, I have not run into a regression caused by a SQL Server Cumulative Update.

When it is time to deploy a CU in Production (see *Appendix B*), be prepared for some outage, even if only for a brief period. At a minimum, the CU setup program will stop and start the SQL Server Service, and it could be stopped for several minutes while the CU installation is running. Depending on what SQL Server components you are running, the CU setup program will sometimes insist on a reboot after it finishes.

If you don't have any high availability solution in place, such as database mirroring or fail-over clustering, this outage could last anywhere from 5 to 20 minutes, which is kind of bad. If you do have database mirroring or fail-over clustering, you can do a "rolling upgrade" where you upgrade the Witness, then the Mirror, and then the Principal (for mirroring) or each node in turn (with fail-over clustering), where you can install a CU with a couple of sub-minute outages. Using database mirroring, my outages are typically 10–12 seconds each for this type of maintenance (since I have eight databases that have to fail-over together).

SQL Server 2008 R2 Slipstream installation

With SQL Server 2008 and later, it is possible to create a "slipstream" installation that incorporates the updates from a Service Pack, or Cumulative Update, into the initial installation of SQL Server. This lets you avoid having to install a Service Pack or Cumulative Update separately, after installing from the original RTM installation media, so it could save you a significant amount of time if you need to install a large number of SQL Server instances.

SQL Server 2008 R2 lets you do a slipstream install dynamically, without having to create a full slipstream installation drop (which could then be reused for multiple servers). A dynamic slipstream installation allows you to simply run the SQL Server Setup program and specify where to find the extracted CU files, which it will then use to perform a slipstream install that includes the Cumulative Update.

The steps below are required for a Dynamic Slipstream install.

1. Download the Cumulative Update package (in this example, we are using the x64 Cumulative Update 6 for SQL Server 2008 R2) that you want to slipstream.

2. Extract the CU package to a folder, for example: C:\SQLCU.

3. Extract the package as follows (see Figure 7.27):

SQLServer2008R2-KB2489376-x64.exe /x:C:\SQLCU

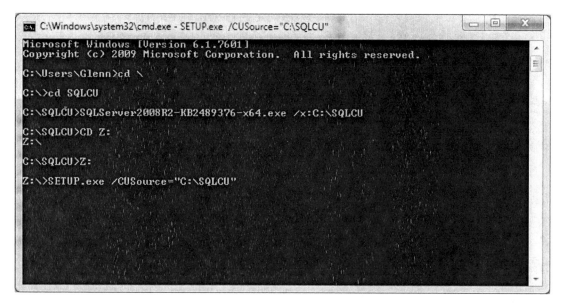

Figure 7.27: Command-line examples for a Dynamic Slipstream install in SQL Server 2008 R2.

4. Run Setup.exe from a command line with these switches:

Setup.exe /CUSource="C:\SQLCU"

5. You will see the normal SQL Server Setup program start to run.

6. Go through and make all your preferred selections.

7. You can verify you are using a slipstream, when you view the **Ready to Install** dialog. On this dialog, **(Slipstream)** will display after the **Action** as shown in Figure 7.28.

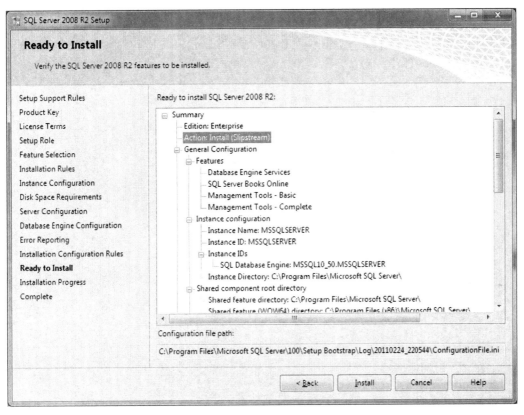

Figure 7.28: Ready to Install dialog, with Action: Install (Slipstream).

SQL Server 2008 R2 Instance Configuration Settings

Depending on your anticipated workload, and on the SQL Server components you have installed, there are a number of instance-level settings that you should consider changing from their default values. These include **max server memory, Optimize for ad hoc workloads**, **default backup compression**, **max degree of parallelism**, and the number of TempDB data files for the SQL Server instance.

Listing 7.1 shows some queries that let you check your current instance configuration settings, and some examples of how you might change them. These are example settings only; you need to use your own judgment for what values you choose. The sections that follow will discuss each of these settings in more detail.

```
-- Get configuration values for instance
SELECT   name ,
         value ,
         value_in_use ,
         [description]
FROM     sys.configurations
ORDER BY name ;
-- Set max server memory = 59000MB for the server
-- (example value only)
EXEC sp_configure 'max server memory (MB)', 59000 ;
GO
RECONFIGURE ;
GO
-- Some suggested Max Server Memory settings
-- Physical RAM    Max Server Memory Setting
--    4GB          3200
--    6GB          4800
--    8GB          6200
--   16GB          13000
--   24GB          20500
--   32GB          28000
--   48GB          44000
--   64GB          59000
```

```
--    72GB            67000
--    96GB            90000
-- Enable optimize for ad hoc workloads
-- (new in SQL Server 2008)
EXEC sp_configure 'optimize for ad hoc workloads', 1 ;
GO
RECONFIGURE ;
GO
-- Enable backup compression by default
-- (new in SQL Server 2008 Enterprise Edition)
-- (added to SQL Server 2008 R2 Standard Edition
EXEC sp_configure 'backup compression default', 1 ;
GO
RECONFIGURE ;
GO
-- Set MAXDOP = 1 for the server
-- Depends on workload and wait stats
EXEC sp_configure 'max degree of parallelism', 1 ;
GO
RECONFIGURE ;
GO
```

Listing 7.1: SQL Server Instance configuration setting queries.

max server memory

The **max server memory** option controls how much memory can be used by the SQL Server Buffer Pool, which is where cached data is held in memory after it is read off the disk subsystem. This is only for use by the relational database engine. This option has no effect on the memory available for other SQL Server components, such as SSIS, SSRS, or SSAS. It also does not affect other database engine components such as Full Text Search, the CLR, the procedure cache, connection memory, and so on.

By default, there is no limit on the amount of memory that SQL Server can allocate to the buffer pool. However, having some limit in place can reduce the number of situations where other SQL Server components, or the operating system, become starved of memory.

Listing 7.1 has some suggested starting values for a dedicated database server that is running only the Database Engine, and no other SQL Server components. If you do have other components installed, you should adjust the **max server memory** setting downward to account for them. The setting is dynamic, meaning that you can change it and it will take effect almost immediately, with no restart of SQL Server required.

The basic guideline is that you want the operating system to have 2–4 GB available while the system is operating under your normal workload. Listing 7.2 shows a DMV query that you can use to check how much memory is available to the operating system.

```
-- Good basic information about memory amounts and state
SELECT total_physical_memory_kb, available_physical_memory_kb,
       system_memory_state_desc
FROM sys.dm_os_sys_memory;
```

Listing 7.2: Checking available memory for the operating system.

You can also change the **max server memory** setting for a SQL Server instance in SSMS by right-clicking on the instance in Object Explorer, and selecting **Properties**. Then, you need to click on **Memory** in the left pane of the **Server Properties** dialog. You will see the dialog shown in Figure 7.29. You can make your desired changes and click **OK**.

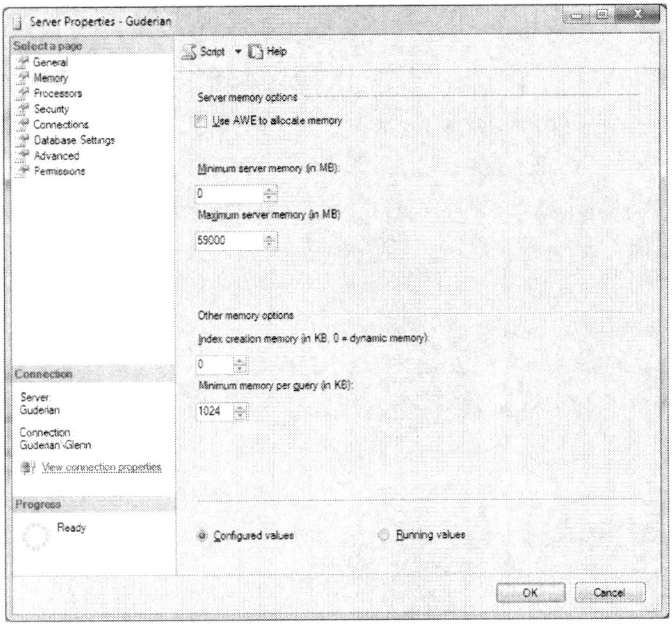

Figure 7.29: Server Properties, server memory options.

Optimize for ad hoc workloads

Optimize for ad hoc workloads is an instance-level option that was added in SQL Server 2008, and is designed to help control the amount of memory that is used by single-use, ad hoc query plans in the procedure cache. It allows SQL Server to store only a small stub of an ad hoc query plan in the procedure cache the first time the ad hoc plan is executed, which reduces the memory required by the plan in the procedure cache.

With SQL Server 2005, it was very common to see very large amounts of memory being used by single-use, ad hoc query plans (often in the 6–8 GB range). Later builds of SQL Server 2005 have code changes that are available as part of Cumulative Updates that reduced this problem somewhat by attempting to limit the size of the ad hoc cache, but it was still a big issue. Interestingly, one of the biggest offenders for generating ad hoc query plans in SQL Server 2005 was SQL Server Agent! Another was SharePoint.

This option is disabled by default but, in my opinion, should always be enabled on SQL Server 2008 and above. I really cannot think of a good reason not to do this.

You can also change the **optimize for ad hoc workloads** setting (and **max degree of parallelism** setting, discussed shortly) for a SQL Server instance, via SSMS. Simply right-click on the instance in Object Explorer, select **Properties**, and click on **Advanced** in the left pane of the **Server Properties** dialog, shown in Figure 7.30. You can make your desired changes and click **OK**.

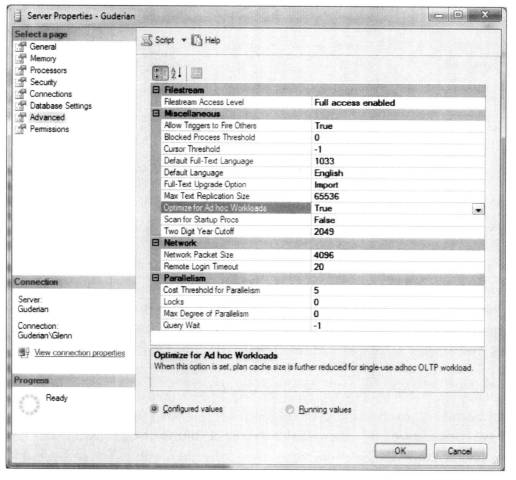

Figure 7.30: Server Properties, Advanced options.

Default backup compression

If you are not using a third-party backup tool, and have a version and edition of SQL Server that supports native backup compression, I recommend that you enable this setting, as shown in Listing 7.1. This simply means that all SQL Server backups will use native backup compression by default. Backup compression trades some extra CPU utilization (during the backup) in exchange for reducing the amount of data that needs to be written to your backup file(s). In most cases, this makes your backup (and restore) finish significantly faster, and it makes the backup file(s) much smaller.

You can always override this setting in your backup T-SQL command. SQL Server 2008 Enterprise Edition supports native backup compression, as does SQL Server 2008 R2 Standard Edition.

Max degree of parallelism

Max degree of parallelism is an instance-level configuration setting that can be used to control whether, and to what degree, the Query Optimizer will attempt to parallelize the execution of a complex or expensive query, i.e., to spread the execution load across multiple processor cores, which can be physical or logical cores.

The default setting is zero, which allows SQL Server to parallelize queries across as many cores as it sees fit. This default setting is usually the best choice for DW and reporting workloads, but it can often be problematic for OLTP workloads. There are additional costs associated with the initialization, synchronization, and termination of the parallel worker threads. For OLTP workloads, typically characterized by lots of short, simple transactions, these costs tend to outweigh the benefits of parallel execution. In "marginal" cases, sometimes the Query Optimizer will choose a parallel query plan when a non-parallel query plan would have actually have been less expensive.

In busy systems, this can cause a pressure point in the exchange iterator (which coordinates the execution of all the parallel queries), the outward sign of which is a high percentage of `CXPACKET` waits in your cumulative wait statistics for the instance (exposed via `sys.dm_os_wait_stats`).

At this point, many DBAs would advise you to immediately change your **max degree of parallelism** setting to a value of 1. Personally, I think you should look a little deeper to try to find the actual source of the problem, before you make that change. In my experience, it is quite common for the Query Optimizer to choose a parallel plan in an attempt to compensate a "missing index" that would have allowed that query to run much more efficiently. If SQL Server has to do a very large index or table scan, the Query Optimizer may think that it will be less expensive to parallelize the query.

As always, it is better to treat the cause of the problem by adding the missing index, than try to alleviate the symptoms by reducing parallelism. In any event, it is certainly worth some investigation.

One big exception to this advice is if you are working with SharePoint databases (either SharePoint 2007 or 2010). In that case, you should definitely set max degree of parallelism to 1 for the instance. Microsoft specifically recommends that you set max degree of parallelism to 1 for SharePoint workloads as a matter of course, and my own experience bears this out. Most SharePoint queries are very OLTP-like in nature. In addition, nearly every SharePoint database that I have ever seen has had a number of important "missing indexes" (according to the missing index DMV query). Unfortunately, you are not allowed to make any schema changes to SharePoint databases to correct such issues. This means your only recourse is to make instance-level configuration changes to try to minimize the problem.

One general rule of thumb that I have often used is that if you have **max degree of parallelism** set to 1, you will also want to make sure that you have hyper-threading enabled, if your processor supports it.

Number of TempDB data files

By default, SQL Server will create one rather small **TempDB** data file (and one log file), in the default location for **TempDB**, on your SQL Server instance. This is suboptimal on two counts.

Firstly, if you ignored my advice about default file locations, the **TempDB** files will be in a sub-directory on the same drive where your SQL Server binary files are located. This is likely to be the **C:** drive on your database server, which is not a good location! If your **TempDB** is on your **C:** drive, you need to move it someplace better – hopefully, a fast, dedicated logical drive.

Secondly, one small **TempDB** file is woefully inadequate for most OLTP workloads, where there can be considerable allocation contention on a single **TempDB** file, as objects are created and destroyed in **TempDB**.

You need to create some additional **TempDB** data files, which should all be the same size so that SQL Server will use all of them equally. You can check the number, location, and size of your **TempDB** files by using the query shown in Listing 7.3.

```
-- Get size and location of TempDB files
SELECT DB_NAME(database_id) AS [DatabaseName],
       physical_name, size, type_desc
FROM sys.master_files
WHERE DB_NAME(database_id) = N'tempdb';
```

Listing 7.3: Getting size and location of tempdb files.

The old guidance from Microsoft was to create one **TempDB** data file per physical processor core. Now, in the days of eight- and twelve-core processors, I think this is excessive. A general consensus seems to be forming that you should start out with perhaps four or eight **TempDB** data files (making them all the same size), and then look for signs of allocation contention before you consider creating any more **TempDB** data files.

One way to check for signs of page allocation contention is to query `sys.dm_os_wait_stats`, and look out for high levels of `PAGELATCH_xx` waits, where the `xx` suffix is often `UP`, i.e. `PAGELATCH_UP`, which is an update buffer page latch.

Steve Howard, from the Microsoft SQLCAT team wrote an excellent technical note, entitled *Table-Valued Functions and Tempdb Contention*, which outlines a number of techniques for detecting and resolving allocation contention in `TempDB`. This document is available at HTTP://SQLCAT.COM/TECHNICALNOTES/ARCHIVE/2011/01/25/TABLE-VALUED-FUNCTIONS-AND-TEMPDB-CONTENTION.ASPX.

Summary

We have covered a lot of material in this, the final chapter of the book. We started with a detailed pre-installation checklist that covered the steps necessary to have a smooth and successful stand-alone installation of SQL Server 2008 R2. Taking care of these steps ahead of time will save you a lot of headaches later. We then went into more detail about why these steps are necessary and important.

Then we stepped through an actual stand-alone installation of SQL Server 2008 R2, with important explanatory notes for each step of the installation. We covered how SQL Server Service Packs and Cumulative Updates work. Next, we showed how to do a dynamic slipstream installation of SQL Server 2008 R2 that also installed the updated components from a Cumulative Update. Finally, we discussed some important SQL Server Instance Configuration Settings.

With your hardware, operating system, and SQL Server carefully chosen, installed, and configured, you've given your applications the best possible chance of success. While it is true that poor database design or poor application design can eventually overwhelm even the best hardware, having this solid foundation will give you a much better chance to survive and resolve issues higher in the application stack. It also can afford you an extra margin of scalability and performance that can give you more time and more flexibility to make architecture and implementation changes as your workload changes and grows over time.

Having properly installed and configured both your operating system and SQL Server, you'll have a reliable and scalable foundation that will be easier to manage and maintain.

Overall, having the "best" version and edition of SQL Server running on new, high-performance hardware that is properly sized and configured, with the latest version of the operating system that has also been properly configured, gives you an excellent foundation to design, build, and maintain a scalable data tier that you can be proud of, which also will benefit your organization.

I sincerely hope that you have enjoyed this book as much as I have enjoyed writing it. I have a genuine passion for server hardware, and I have tried to do my best to spread as much knowledge about this subject as possible in this book!

Appendix A: Intel and AMD Processors and Chipsets

Processors

This section provides an overview of recent Intel and AMD processors.

Intel Xeon 3000 sequence

The Intel Xeon 3000 sequence is Intel's entry level server processor, designed for use in single-socket server motherboards. It is designed for single processor servers for small business, or entry level use. It includes processors based on the original 65 nm Core microarchitecture, the improved 45 nm Core microarchitecture, the 45 nm Nehalem microarchitecture, and the 32 nm Westmere microarchitecture. Quite often, Xeon 3000 series processors are nearly identical to the equivalent desktop Intel processor. This means that they are often somewhat limited in how much system memory they can support, so they are frequently not suitable for heavy SQL Server workloads. More details about the recent generations of this sequence are listed below.

The **Intel Xeon 3000** series (Conroe) is a dual-core processor used in single-socket servers starting in September 2006. It is based on the Core microarchitecture. The Core architecture was a huge improvement over the previous NetBurst microarchitecture. The Core architecture still relied on a shared front-side bus, so it does not support hardware NUMA. It was built on 65 nm process technology, and had clock speeds ranging from 1.86 GHz to 3.0 GHz with an L2 cache size ranging from 2 MB to 4 MB. Front-side bus speeds were 1066 MHz or 1333 MHz. It uses Socket LGA 775, and can use the Intel 3000, 3010, 3200 or 3210 chipset.

The **Intel Xeon 3100** series (Wolfdale) is a dual-core processor used in single-socket servers starting in November 2007. It is based on the Core microarchitecture. It is built on 45 nm process technology, and has clock speeds ranging from 3.0 GHz to 3.16 GHz with an L2 cache size of 6 MB. Front-side bus speed is 1333 MHz. It uses Socket LGA 775, and can use the Intel 3200 or 3210 chipset. The process shrink to 45 nm allowed Intel to increase the size of the L2 cache compared to the 3000 series, which is helpful for SQL Server workloads. The increased front-side bus speed of 1333 MHz also helped SQL Server workloads.

The **Intel Xeon 3200** series (Kentfield) is a quad-core processor used in single-socket servers starting in January 2007. It is based on the Core microarchitecture, and it uses two dual-core dies in a single CPU package. It is built on 65 nm process technology, and has clock speeds ranging from 2.13 GHz to 2.66 GHz with an L2 cache size of 8 MB (2x4). Front-side bus speed is 1066 MHz. It uses Socket LGA 775, and can use the Intel 3000, 3010, 3200 or 3210 chipset. This was the first generation Core microarchitecture, quad-core processor, and its performance was somewhat hampered by a relatively small L2 cache, along with a 1066 MHz front-side bus that was shared between four cores.

The **Intel Xeon 3300** series (Yorkfield) is a quad-core processor used in single-socket servers starting in March 2008. It is based on the Core microarchitecture, and it uses two dual-core dies in a single CPU package. It is built on 45 nm process technology, and has clock speeds ranging from 2.5 GHz to 3.16 GHz with an L2 cache size of 12 MB (2x6). Front-side bus speed is 1333 MHz. It uses Socket LGA 775, and can use the Intel 3200 or 3210 chipset. The process shrink to 45 nm allowed Intel to increase the size of the L2 cache compared to the 3200 series, and the faster 1333 MHz front-side bus was also very helpful for SQL Server workloads.

The **Intel Xeon 3400** series (Lynnfield) is a quad-core processor used in single-socket servers starting in September 2009. It was released later than the 3500 series, even though it has a lower model number in order to fill a cost gap in Intel's product line. It is based on the Nehalem microarchitecture, and it has both hyper-threading technology and Turbo Boost capability. It was built on 45 nm process technology, and has clock speeds ranging from 1.87 GHz to 2.93 GHz with an L3 cache size of 8 MB. QPI bandwidth ranged from 4.8

GT/s to 6.4 GT/s. It uses Socket LGA 1156 and can use the Intel 3400, 3420 or 3450 chipsets. Both the Xeon 3400 and 3500 series had **dramatically better** performance than the previous Xeon 3300 series with the move away from the old front-side bus architecture.

The **Intel Xeon 3500** series (Bloomfield) is a quad-core processor used in single-socket servers starting in March 2009. It is based on the Nehalem microarchitecture, and it has both hyper-threading technology and Turbo Boost capability. It is built on 45 nm process technology, and has clock speeds ranging from 2.4 GHz to 3.33 GHz with an L3 cache size of 4 MB or 8 MB. QPI bandwidth is 4.8 GT/s or 6.5 GT/s. It uses Socket LGA 1366, and uses the Intel X58 Express chipset. The main advantage of the Xeon 3500 series over the newer (but less expensive) Xeon 3400 series is the fact the Xeon 3500 has a triple channel memory controller, which gives slightly better performance and allows more memory slots to be used on the motherboard which also gives you a higher maximum memory capacity.

The **Intel Xeon 3600** series (Gulftown) is a four- or six-core processor used in single-socket servers starting in March 2010. It is based on the Westmere microarchitecture, and it has both hyper-threading technology and Turbo Boost capability. It is built on 32 nm process technology, and has clock speeds ranging from 1.87 GHz to 3.47 GHz with an L3 cache size of 12 MB. QPI bandwidth is 4.8 GT/s, 5.86 GT/s, or 6.5 GT/s. It uses Socket LGA 1366, and uses the Intel X58 Express chipset. Compared to the older Xeon 3400 and 3500 series, the Xeon 3600 series has more cores, a larger L3 cache size, and an improved memory controller, which combine to give significantly improved database server performance. As of late 2010, this is the best Intel processor for a single-socket database server, although it is limited to 24 GB of RAM. It is actually more common to see the Xeon 3600 series used in high-end workstations, rather than database servers.

Intel Xeon E3 sequence

The Intel Xeon E3-1200 series (Sandy Bridge) is a quad-core processor used in single-socket servers starting in April 2011. It is based on the Sandy Bridge microarchitecture, and it has both hyper-threading technology and improved Turbo Boost 2.0 capability. It is built on 32 nm process technology, and has base clock speeds ranging from 2.2 GHz to 3.5 GHz with an L3 cache size of 3 MB, 6 MB, or 8 MB. QPI bandwidth is 5.0 GT/s. The Xeon E3-1200 series is essentially the same as the Sandy Bridge desktop Core i7 processors that were released in January 2011.

Intel Xeon 5000 sequence

The Intel Xeon 5000 sequence is Intel's mid-level server processor, designed for use in dual-socket server motherboards. It is designed for two-processor general-purpose, standard high-volume servers, HPC systems, and workstations. It includes processors based on the old 65 nm NetBurst microarchitecture, the original 65 nm Core microarchitecture, the improved second-generation 45 nm Core microarchitecture, the 45 nm Nehalem microarchitecture, and the improved 32 nm Westmere microarchitecture. In my opinion, the Xeon 5000 series is the current "sweet spot" for many SQL Server workloads, since you get the best single-threaded performance, along with enough memory and I/O capacity to go along with it. More details about the recent generations of this sequence are listed below.

The **Intel Xeon 5000** series (Dempsey) is a dual-core processor used in two-socket servers starting in May 2006. It is based on the old NetBurst microarchitecture, and it has first-generation hyper-threading. It is built on 65 nm process technology, and has clock speeds ranging from 2.5 GHz to 3.73 GHz with an L2 cache size of 4 MB (2x2). Front-side bus speeds are 667 MHz or 1066 MHz. It uses Socket LGA 771, and uses the Intel 5000P, 5000V, 5000X, or 5000Z chipset. By modern standards, this is not a good processor to use for SQL Server workloads, and I would be pushing to retire any machines that I had running this processor for SQL Server.

The **Intel Xeon 5100** series (Woodcrest) is a dual-core processor used in two-socket servers starting in June 2006. It is based on the Core microarchitecture, and it was the first Tock release. It is built on 65 nm process technology, and has clock speeds ranging from 1.6 GHz to 3.0 GHz with an L2 cache size of 4 MB. Front-side bus speeds are 1066 MHz or 1333 MHz. It uses Socket LGA 771, and uses the Intel 5000P, 5000V, 5000X, 5000Z, 5100, or 5400 chipset. The Xeon 5100 series was a dramatic improvement over the Xeon 5000 series.

The **Intel Xeon 5200** series (Wolfdale-DP) is a dual-core processor used in two-socket servers starting in November 2007. It is based on the Core microarchitecture. It is built on 45 nm process technology, and has clock speeds ranging from 1.86 GHz to 3.5 GHz with an L2 cache size of 6 MB. Front-side bus speeds range from 1066 MHz to 1600 MHz. It uses Socket LGA 771, and uses the Intel 5400 chipset. The larger L2 cache and faster front-side bus were the main improvements over the older Xeon 5100 series. This was the best dual-core processor that Intel ever produced, but it has been supplanted by quad-core and six-core models.

The **Intel Xeon 5300** series (Clovertown) is a quad-core processor used in two-socket servers starting in November 2006. It is based on the Core microarchitecture, and it uses two dual-core dies in a single CPU package. It is built on 65 nm process technology, and has clock speeds ranging from 1.6 GHz to 3.0 GHz with an L2 cache size of 8 MB (2x4). Front-side bus speed is 1066 MHz or 1333 MHz. It uses Socket LGA 771, and uses the Intel 5000P, 5000V, 5000X, 5100, or 5400 chipset.

The **Intel Xeon 5400** series (Harpertown) is a quad-core processor used in two-socket servers starting in November 2007. It is based on the Core microarchitecture, and it uses two dual-core dies in a single CPU package. It is built on 45 nm process technology, and has clock speeds ranging from 2.0 GHz to 3.4 GHz with an L3 cache size of 12 MB. Front-side bus speed ranges from 1333 MHz to 1666 MHz. It uses Socket LGA 771, and uses the Intel 5000P, 5000X, 5100, or 5400 chipset. The larger L3 cache size and faster front-side bus are very important for SQL Server performance. This family of processors is still pretty useful for SQL Server workloads, and it was the best two-socket Intel processor available before the introduction of the Nehalem.

The **Intel Xeon 5500** series (Gainestown) is a quad-core processor used in two-socket servers starting in December 2008. It is based on the Nehalem microarchitecture, and it has both hyper-threading technology and Turbo Boost capability. It is built on 45 nm process technology, and has clock speeds ranging from 1.87 GHz to 3.33 GHz with an L3 cache size of 4 MB or 8 MB. QPI bandwidth ranges from 4.8 GT/s to 6.4 GT/s. It uses Socket LGA 1366, and uses the Intel 5500 or 5520 chipset. This processor has shown extremely good performance for SQL Server workloads, roughly doubling the performance of the previous Xeon 5400 series. It has even equaled and sometimes exceeded the performance of the six-core Xeon 7400 series on some benchmarks.

The **Intel Xeon 5600** series (Westmere-EP) is a four or six-core processor used in two-socket servers starting in April 2010. It is based on the Nehalem microarchitecture (with a process shrink to 32 nm), and it has both hyper-threading technology and Turbo Boost capability. It is built on 32 nm process technology, and has clock speeds ranging from 1.87 GHz to 3.46 GHz with an L3 cache size of 12 MB. QPI bandwidth ranges from 5.86 GT/s to 6.4 GT/s. It uses Socket LGA 1366, and uses the Intel 5500 or 5520 chipset. It has an improved memory controller and a larger L3 cache compared to the Xeon 5500 series. This is currently Intel's highest-performance processor for single-threaded workloads, which means that it is especially suited for OLTP performance. It is definitely the best Intel two-socket processor for SQL Server OLTP workloads in the 2010 to mid-2011 timeframe.

Intel Xeon 6000 sequence

The Intel Xeon 6000 sequence is a four-, six-, or eight-core processor that is used in one- and two-socket servers starting in April 2010. It is a lower-cost version of the Xeon 7500 series. It is built on 45 nm process technology, and has clock speeds ranging from 1.73 GHz to 2.0 GHz. It has hyper-threading technology and Turbo Boost technology and

12 MB or 18 MB of shared L3 cache. QPI bandwidth ranges from 4.8 GT/s to 6.4 GT/s. It uses Socket 1567. There are currently only three different specific processors in this family. The main reason you might consider this processor for a dual-socket system is that it supports a higher total memory capacity than a Xeon 5600 series processor. From a pure performance perspective, I would strongly prefer a Xeon 5600 series processor for a two-socket server, since it uses the newer 32 nm Westmere architecture, with a large L3 cache, improved memory controller, and faster clock speeds. This would give you much better single-threaded performance.

Intel Xeon 7000 sequence

The Intel Xeon 7000 sequence is Intel's high-end server processor, designed for use in 4- to 32-socket enterprise server motherboards. It includes processors based on the 90 nm and 65 nm NetBurst microarchitecture, the original 65 nm Core microarchitecture, the improved second-generation 45 nm Core microarchitecture, the 45 nm Nehalem microarchitecture, and the improved 32 nm Westmere microarchitecture. Traditionally, most large SQL Server workloads have run on four-socket servers or larger, but I argue that you may be able to move many SQL Server workloads to less expensive, but higher performance, two-socket servers. More details about the recent generations of this sequence are listed below.

The **Intel Xeon 7000** series (Paxville-MP) is a dual-core processor used in four-socket and above servers starting in November 2005. It is built on 90 nm process technology, it is based on the old NetBurst microarchitecture, with first generation hyper-threading technology, and clock speeds ranging from 2.66 GHz to 3.0 GHz, with an L2 cache size of 1 MB or 2 MB. It did not have an L3 cache. Front-side bus speeds are 667 MHz or 800 MHz. It uses Socket 604. This was a decent processor in its day, but it is quite obsolete in 2011. The relatively humble Intel Core i3 350M laptop that I am using to write this book on has about the same overall raw processor power as a quad-socket Xeon 7040 system!

The **Intel Xeon 7100** series (Tulsa) is a dual-core processor used in four-socket and above servers starting in August 2006. It is built on 65 nm process technology; it also has first generation hyper-threading technology, and has clock speeds ranging from 2.5 GHz to 3.4 GHz, with an L2 cache size ranging from 2 MB to 4 MB, and L3 cache sizes ranging from 4 MB to 16 MB. Front-side bus speeds are 667 MHz or 800 MHz. It uses Socket 604. The Tulsa had significantly better performance than the Paxville-MP for SQL Server workloads, due to its large L3 cache, which helped compensate for front-side bus contention in a four-socket server. At NewsGator, I saw a 40% performance improvement with our heavy OLTP workload when we simply replaced a Paxville-MP machine with an otherwise identical Tulsa machine. The Tulsa processor is also obsolete now, with a quad socket Tulsa machine being easily outclassed in terms of raw processor power by a single desktop Core i5 processor.

The **Intel Xeon 7200** series (Tigerton-DC) is a lower-cost, dual-core processor used primarily in four-socket and above servers starting in September 2007. It is based on the Core microarchitecture. It is built on 65 nm process technology, and has clock speeds ranging from 2.4 GHz to 2.93 GHz with an L2 cache size of 4 MB. Front-side bus speed is 1066 MHz. It uses Socket 604. I would not want to use this processor for a SQL Server workload, since it is only dual-core, and because of its relative age.

The **Intel Xeon 7300** series (Tigerton) is a quad-core processor that is used primarily in four-socket and above servers starting in September 2007. It is based on the Core micro-architecture. It is built on 65 nm process technology, and has clock speeds ranging from 1.6 GHz to 2.93 GHz with an L2 cache size of 8 MB. Front-side bus speed is 1066 MHz. It uses the Intel 7300 chipset, which supports a maximum of 256 GB of DDR2 FB-DIMM memory. It uses Socket 604.

The **Intel Xeon 7400** series (Dunnington) is a four- or six-core processor that is used primarily in four-socket and above servers starting in September 2008. It is based on the Core microarchitecture, using 45 nm process technology, and has clock speeds ranging from 2.13 GHz to 2.66 GHz with an L2 cache size of 6 MB, and an L3 cache size of 8 MB to 16 MB. Front-side bus speed is 1066 MHz. They were at the high end of the Intel processor performance spectrum until the introduction of the Xeon 5500 series. It uses the Intel 7300 chipset, which supports a maximum of 256 GB of DDR2 FB-DIMM memory. It uses Socket 604. When this processor was introduced, it was the best choice for many heavy duty SQL Server workloads, but you can now get much better performance from a Xeon X5680 equipped two-socket server. Any Intel four-socket server older than the Xeon 7500 series can easily be replaced by a Xeon X5680 equipped two-socket server (from a processor performance perspective). You could still be limited by the lower maximum RAM capacity or lower number of expansion slots in a two-socket server, but don't automatically assume you need a four-socket server.

The **Intel Xeon 7500** series (Nehalem-EX) is a six- or eight-core processor that is used in four-socket and above servers starting in April 2010. It is built on 45 nm process technology and has clock speeds ranging from 1.87 GHz to 2.67 GHz. It has second-generation hyper-threading technology and Turbo Boost technology, and 24 MB of shared L3 cache. QPI bandwidth ranges from 4.8 GT/s to 6.4 GT/s. It uses Socket 1567. Each processor has two integrated memory controllers, which allows it to support up to 16 memory slots per socket. This means you can have 1 TB of DDR3 RAM in a four-socket server, if you use 16 GB sticks of RAM. In the same four-socket server, you could have 256 GB of RAM with 4 GB sticks or 512 GB of RAM with 8 GB sticks of RAM. The Xeon 7500 series moves from the front-side bus to Intel Quick Path Interconnect, from FB-DIMM RAM to DDR3 RAM, and from PCIe 1.0 to PCIe 2.0. This means huge performance and scalability improvements with Nehalem-EX compared to the previous generation Xeon 7400 series. Intel claims a 9X increase in memory bandwidth, 3X increase in database performance, 1.7X increase in integer throughput, and a 2X increase in floating point throughput versus the Xeon 7400 series.

The **Intel Xeon E7-8800/4800/2800** series (Westmere-EX) is a six-, eight-, or ten-core processor (depending on the exact model) that can be used in two-, four-, or eight-socket and above servers starting in April 2011. The first digit in the model number tells you the allowed number of sockets that the processors supports, i.e. the 8800 series supports eight- or more socket servers, the 4800 series supports four-socket servers, and the 2800 series supports two-socket servers. It is built on 32 nm process technology and has clock speeds ranging from 1.73 GHz to 2.4 GHz. It has second-generation hyper-threading technology, second-generation Turbo Boost technology and between 18 MB and 30 MB of shared L3 cache. QPI bandwidth ranges from 4.8 GT/s to 6.4 GT/s. It uses Socket 1567, which means that it is socket-compatible with the previous Xeon 6500 and 7500 series processors. Each processor has two integrated memory controllers, which allows it to support up to 16 memory slots per socket. It uses the new Intel 7510 or 7512 chipsets, which allow it to use 32 GB sticks of RAM. This will allow you to have 2 TB of RAM in a four-socket server. Intel claims a 40% performance increase for the Xeon E7-4870 for some database workloads compared to the previous Xeon X7560.

Intel Itanium 9000 series

The **Intel Itanium 9000** (Montecito) is a dual-core processor, used in servers starting in July 2006. It was built on 90 nm process technology and had clock speeds ranging from 1.4 GHz to 1.6 GHz. Each core had a 256 K L2 data cache and a 1 MB LB instruction cache, with shared L3 cache sizes from 6 MB to 24 MB. Front-side bus speed was 400 MHz to 533 MHz. It used DDR2 SDRAM and Socket PAC611.

Intel Itanium 9100 series

The **Intel Itanium 9100** (Montvale) is a dual-core processor with hyper-threading, used in servers starting in November 2007. It was built on 90 nm process technology and had clock speeds ranging from 1.42 GHz to 1.66 GHz. Each core had a 256 K L2 data cache and a 1 MB LB instruction cache, with shared L3 cache sizes from 8 MB to 24 MB. Front-side bus speed was 400 MHz to 667 MHz. It also used DDR2 SDRAM and Socket PAC611.

Intel Itanium 9300 series

The **Intel Itanium 9300** (Tukwila) is a quad-core processor with hyper-threading and Turbo Boost, used in servers starting in February 2010. It is built on 65 nm process technology and has base clock speeds ranging from 1.33 GHz to 1.73 GHz. Each core has a 256 K L2 data cache and a 512 K L2 instruction cache. It has L3 cache sizes ranging from 10 MB to 24 MB. It uses QuickPath interconnect technology with a 4.8 GT/s transfer rate, and it has dual integrated memory controllers on each physical processor. It uses DDR3 SDRAM and Socket LGA 1248. It is somewhat ironic that the Itanium 9300 series (which performs substantially better than the previous Itanium 9100 series) was released just a few weeks before Microsoft announced that it was abandoning Itanium support in future releases of Windows Server and SQL Server.

AMD Opteron 1200 series

The **AMD Opteron 1200** (Santa Ana) is a dual-core processor used in one-socket servers starting in August of 2006. It was built on 90 nm process technology and had clock speeds ranging from 1.8 GHz to 3.2 GHz. Each core had a 1 MB L2 cache. It also used DDR2 SDRAM and Socket AM2.

AMD Opteron 2200 series

The **AMD Opteron 2200** (Santa Rosa) is a dual-core processor used in one- and two-socket servers starting in August of 2006. It was built on 90 nm process technology and had clock speeds ranging from 1.8 GHz to 3.2 GHz. Each core had a 1 MB L2 cache. It also used DDR2 SDRAM and Socket F.

AMD Opteron 1300 series

The **AMD Opteron 1300** (Budapest) is a quad-core processor used in one-socket servers starting in April of 2008. It was built on 65 nm process technology and had clock speeds ranging from 2.1 GHz to 2.3 GHz. Each core had a 512 K L2 cache, while there was a 2 MB shared L3 cache. It also used DDR2 SDRAM and Socket F.

The **AMD Opteron 1300** (Suzuka) is a quad-core processor used in one-socket servers starting in June of 2009. It was built on 45 nm process technology and had clock speeds of 2.2 GHz. Each core had a 512 K L2 cache, while there was a 6 MB shared L3 cache. It also used DDR2 SDRAM and Socket F.

AMD Opteron 2300 series

The **AMD Opteron 2300** (Barcelona) is a quad-core processor used in one- and two-socket servers starting in September of 2007. It was built on 65 nm process technology and had clock speeds ranging from 1.7 GHz to 2.5 GHz. Each core had a 512 K L2 cache, while there was a 2 MB shared L3 cache. It also used DDR2 SDRAM and Socket F.

The **AMD Opteron 2300** (Shanghai) is a quad-core processor used in one- and two-socket servers starting in November of 2008. It was built on 45 nm process technology and had clock speeds ranging from 2.1 GHz to 3.1 GHz. Each core had a 512 K L2 cache, while there was a 6 MB shared L3 cache. It also used DDR2 SDRAM and Socket F.

AMD Opteron 2400 series

The **AMD Opteron 2400** (Istanbul) is a six-core processor used in one- and two-socket servers starting in June of 2009. It was built on 45 nm process technology and had clock speeds ranging from 1.8 GHz to 2.8 GHz. Each core had a 512 K L2 cache, while there was a 6 MB shared L3 cache. It also used DDR2 SDRAM and Socket F.

AMD Opteron 8200 series

The **AMD Opteron 8200** (Santa Rosa) is a dual-core processor used in two-, four- and eight-socket servers starting in August of 2006. It was built on 90 nm process technology and had clock speeds ranging from 2.0 GHz to 2.6 GHz. Each core had a 1 MB L2 cache. It also used DDR2 SDRAM and Socket F.

AMD Opteron 8300 series

The **AMD Opteron 8300** (Barcelona) is a quad-core processor used in two-, four- and eight-socket servers starting in September of 2007. It was built on 65 nm process technology and had clock speeds ranging from 1.8 GHz to 2.5 GHz. Each core had a 512 K L2 cache, while there was a 2 MB shared L3 cache. It also used DDR2 SDRAM and Socket F.

The **AMD Opteron 8300** (Shanghai) is a quad-core processor used in two-, four- and eight-socket servers starting in November of 2008. It was built on 45 nm process technology and had clock speeds ranging from 2.2 GHz to 3.1 GHz. Each core had a 512 K L2 cache, while there was a 6 MB shared L3 cache. It also used DDR2 SDRAM and Socket F.

Amd Opteron 8400 Series

The **AMD Opteron 8400** (Shanghai) is a six-core processor used in two-, four- and eight-socket servers starting in June of 2009. It is built on 45 nm process technology and has clock speeds ranging from 2.1 GHz to 2.8 GHz. Each core has a 512 K L2 cache, while there is a 6 MB shared L3 cache. It also uses DDR2 SDRAM and Socket F.

AMD Opteron 4100 series

In the mainstream server space, AMD recently introduced the one- and two-socket San Marino platform, with four- and six-core Lisbon processors.

The **AMD Opteron 4100** (Lisbon) is a four- or six-core processor used in one- and two-socket servers starting in June of 2010. It is built on 45 nm process technology and has clock speeds ranging from 1.7 GHz to 2.8 GHz. Each core has a 512 K L2 cache, while there is a 6 MB shared L3 cache. It uses DDR3 SDRAM and Socket C32. The Lisbon is AMD's best-performing processor for single-socket servers, but the Magny Cours is a much better choice for two-socket servers.

AMD Opteron 6100 series

The **AMD Opteron 6100** (Magny Cours) is an eight- or twelve-core processor used in two- and four-socket servers starting in April of 2010. It is built on 45 nm process technology and has clock speeds ranging from 1.7 GHz to 2.5 GHz. Each core has a 512 K L2 cache; there is a 12 MB shared L3 cache. It uses DDR3 SDRAM and Socket G34. It is basically two six-core Istanbul processor dies combined in a single package, with improved, dual DDR3 memory controllers and improved hyper-transport (HT) connections between the processor dies. There are also eight-core versions of the Magny Cours. The AMD Opteron 6100 Magny Cours is part of the high-end Maranello platform, which supports both two-socket and four-socket configurations. Each processor die has its own memory controller, so there are four DDR3 memory channels on Magny Cours. The Magny Cours requires a new socket called Socket G34. The Magny Cours is AMD's best-performing processor in the 2010 to mid-2011 timeframe. The Magny Cours seems to perform better with multi-threaded workloads because of its high physical core count and overall design. This makes it better suited for non-OLTP usage (such as reporting and data warehouses).

Chipsets

This section provides an overview of recent Intel chipsets.

Intel 3000, 3010, 3200, 3210, 3400, 3420

The Intel 3000 and 3010 chipsets are designed for use with Intel Xeon 3000 Sequence, Intel Pentium 4 processor 600 Sequence, Intel Pentium D processor 800 Sequence and 900 Sequence, and Intel Celeron D, in the LGA775 package in entry-level, single-socket server platforms. The chipset contains two components: Memory Controller Hub (MCH) and Intel I/O Controller Hub 7 (ICH7). The MCH provides the interface to the processor, main memory, PCI Express, and the ICH7. The Intel 3000 chipset supports one PCI Express x8 port, while the Intel 3010 chipset supports two PCI Express x8 ports or one PCI Express x16 port. They both support 533, 800, and 1066 MHz system bus speeds.

The Intel 3200 and Intel 3210 chipsets are designed for use with Intel Xeon 3000 sequence processors, in the LGA775 package in single-socket server platforms. The chipset contains two components: Memory Controller Hub (MCH) and Intel I/O Controller Hub 9 (ICH9). The MCH provides the interface to the processor, main memory, PCI Express, and the ICH9. The Intel 3200 chipset supports one PCI Express x8 port for I/O. The Intel 3210 chipset supports two PCI Express x8 ports or one PCI Express x16 port for I/O. Both of these chipsets support 800, 1066, and 1333 MHz system bus speeds.

The Intel 3400 and Intel 3420 chipsets support the newer Intel Xeon 3400 processor series in the single-socket server platforms designed for use in small and medium businesses. The Intel 3400 chipset supports six flexible PCI Express x1 ports, configurable as x2 and x4, four SATA 3 Gb/s ports and eight USB 2.0 ports for I/O. The Intel 3420 chipset supports eight PCI Express x1 ports configurable as x2 and x4, six SATA 3 Gb/s ports, twelve USB 2.0 ports for I/O and Intel Matrix Storage Technology.

Intel 5000P, 5000V, 5500, and 5520 chipsets

The Intel 5000v chipset supports 1066 and 1333 MHz system bus speeds, one PCI Express x8 link (configurable as two x4 links), FBDIMM 533 and 667 technology, point-to-point connection for Intel 6321 ESB I/O Controller Hub at 2 GB/s, and an Intel 6700PXH 64-bit PCI hub.

The Intel 5000p chipset supports 1066 and 1333 MHz system bus speeds, three PCI Express x8 links (each configurable as two x4 links), FBDIMM 533 and 667 technology, point-to-point connection for Intel 6321 ESB I/O Controller Hub at 2 GB/s, and an Intel 6700PXH 64-bit PCI hub.

The Intel 5500 chipset supports the Intel Xeon 5500 series at 6.4 GT/s, 5.86 GT/s and 4.8 GT/s speeds via the Intel QuickPath Interconnect. This chipset has support for 24 lanes of PCI Express 2.0 I/O, and support for Intel ICH10, ICH10R and an Intel 6700PXH 64-bit PCI Hub.

The Intel 5520 chipset supports the Intel Xeon 5500 series and the Intel Xeon 5600 series at 6.4 GT/s, 5.86 GT/s and 4.8 GT/s speeds via the Intel QuickPath Interconnect. This chipset has support for 36 lanes of PCI Express 2.0 I/O, and support for Intel ICH10, ICH10R and an Intel 6700PXH 64-bit PCI Hub. It is currently the top of the line chipset for two-socket Intel Xeon 5500 and 5600 systems.

Intel 7300 and 7500 chipsets

The Intel 7300 chipset supports the Intel Xeon 7300 processor series and Intel Xeon 7200 processor series. The Intel 7300 chipsets incorporate four high-speed interconnects that move data at 1066 MT/s (mega transfers per second), FBDIMM support for up to 256 GB of memory capacity, and a 64 MB cached snoop filter for reduced traffic on the dedicated high-speed interconnects. Additionally, the Intel 7300 chipset has 28 lanes of PCI Express with support for third-party expanders for additional I/O.

The Intel 7500 chipset and Intel 7500 Scalable Memory Buffer support the Intel Xeon processor 7500/6500 series and Intel Itanium processor 9300 series. It supports Intel QuickPath Interconnects at 6.4 GT/s, 5.86 GT/s, and 4.8 GT/s speeds. Additionally, this chipset delivers up to dual x16 or quad x8 PCI Express 2.0 card support, and support for Solid-State Drives on ICH10 and ICH10R. The Intel 7500 Scalable Memory Buffer supports two DDR3 memory channels, each supporting up to 2 RDIMMs per channel, at speeds of 800 MHz, 978 MHz, or 1066 MHz. It also supports DIMM capacities up to 16 GB. The upcoming Westmere-EX processor will be able to use this chipset (with a BIOS update), upping the DIMM capacity to 32 GB.

Appendix B: Installing a SQL Server 2008 R2 Cumulative Update

As discussed in *Chapter 7*, a SQL Server Cumulative Update (CU) is a collection of individual hot-fixes for specific issues with SQL Server. These hot-fixes are collected and tested over time and, every eight weeks, a CU is released containing all of the hot-fixes for the relevant major version and Service Pack of SQL Server (including the RTM release). Each individual hot-fix is tested by Microsoft but a CU is not fully regression tested. Roughly every 12–18 months, Microsoft packages up a much larger collection of hot-fixes in a **Service Pack** release, which is fully regression tested.

For example, the RTM version of SQL Server 2008 R2 is released, and this is followed by a series of CUs relating to that release. So, SQL Server 2008 R2 RTM CU6 is the sixth Cumulative Update for the SQL Server 2008 R2 RTM, and it will contain all the hot-fixes from CU1 to CU5 plus any new CU6 hot-fixes. Around 12–18 months after the RTM release, Microsoft will package up all the hot-fixes into a Service Pack release (SP1). This is then followed by a series of CUs relating to the SP1 release, and so on. So, SQL Server 2008 SP2 CU3 is the third Cumulative Update for the SQL Server 2008 Service Pack 2 release.

If you're not fully concentrating, it's quite easy to confuse SQL Server 2008 SP2 with SQL Server 2008 R2, and to attempt to install a CU for SP2 on a R2 instance, or vice versa. It won't work, and you'll get a failed install. Don't make this mistake (I know a lot of people have, and the marketing "genius" at Microsoft who came up with the SQL Server 2008 R2 name should be very ashamed). **SQL Server 2008 SP2 and SQL Server 2008 R2 are completely different major releases**, each associated with a completely separate set of Service Packs and Cumulative Updates, and it is very important that you get the correct Cumulative Update for your version and Service Pack of SQL Server.

Microsoft describes this Incremental Servicing Model (ISM) in a Knowledge Base article at HTTP://SUPPORT.MICROSOFT.COM/KB/935897.

Also, a blog post from Microsoft's Matthias Berndt, called *A changed approach to Service Packs* (HTTP://BLOGS.MSDN.COM/B/SQLRELEASESERVICES/ARCHIVE/2008/04/27/A-CHANGED-APPROACH-TO-SERVICE-PACKS.ASPX) goes into much greater detail about how Microsoft intends to handle SQL Server servicing.

Obtaining a SQL Server 2008 R2 Cumulative Update

So, after all of this, how do you know when a Cumulative Update is released, and how can you get it from Microsoft? One of the most reliable ways to find out when a new SQL Server Cumulative Update is released is to check the Microsoft SQL Server Release Services Blog at HTTP://BLOGS.MSDN.COM/B/SQLRELEASESERVICES/. You can also check my blog, which is at HTTP://SQLSERVERPERFORMANCE.WORDPRESS.COM/.

Once you know that a Cumulative Update has been released, you need to go to the Microsoft Knowledge Base article for that Cumulative Update (as shown in Figure B.1). Once there, click on the **View and request hotfix downloads** link on the top left portion of the page.

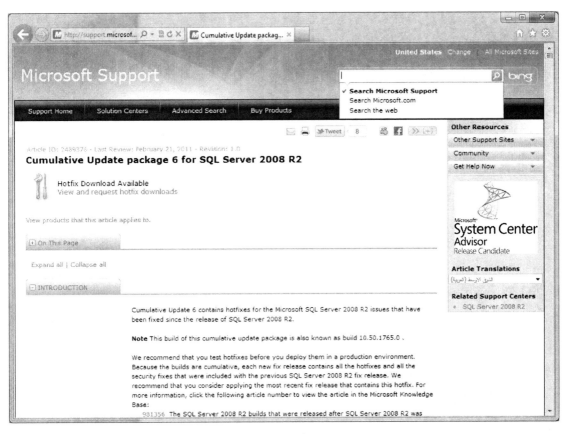

Figure B.1: Cumulative Update, Knowledge Base web page.

Next, click on the **Show hotfixes for all platforms and languages** link (shown in Figure B.2) so that all versions of the Cumulative Update are displayed (which means x86, x64, and IA64). If you don't do this, you will only see the version that matches the operating system version (x86, x64, or IA64) of your machine (which might be your laptop or workstation).

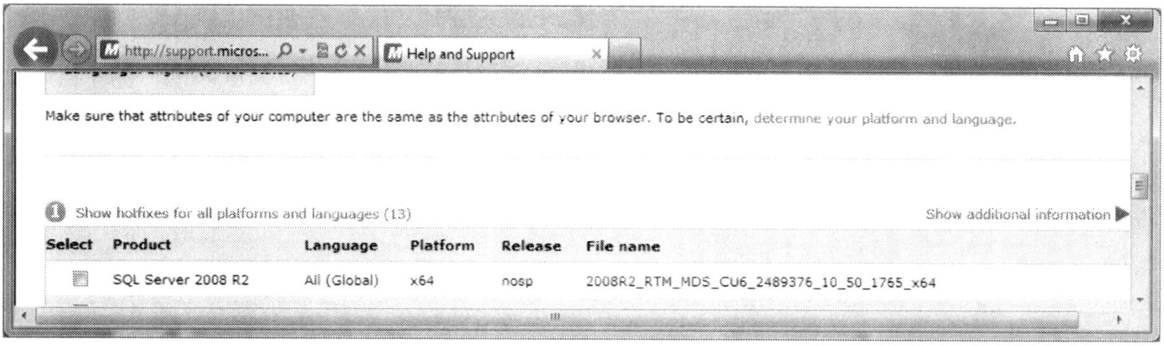

Figure B.2: Displaying all versions of the Cumulative Update package.

Next, you need to decipher the strange file names that Microsoft uses when it lists all of the available packages for that Cumulative Update, in order to choose the ones that you want, depending on what type and portion of your SQL Server installation you are trying to patch.

In most cases, you will want the complete Cumulative Update package, which will have a file name that looks like this:

```
SQLServer2008R2_RTM_CU6_2489376_10_50_1765_x64
```

This would be for the x64 version. You need to check the **Select** check box for each hot-fix package that you want, as I have done in Figure B.3. Next, supply a valid email address (so Microsoft can email to you the link to download the Cumulative Update), fill out the CAPTCHA symbols and, finally, click on the **Request hotfix** button.

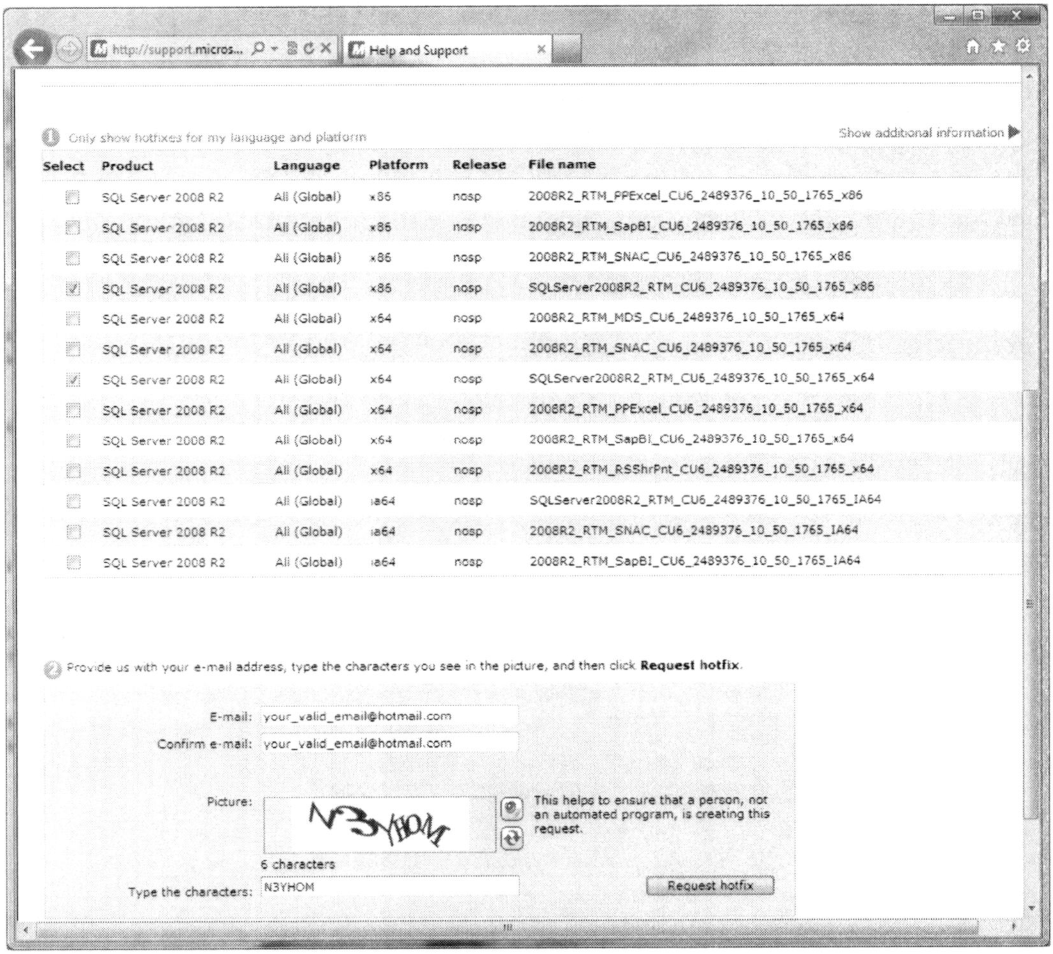

Figure B.3: Requesting the correct Cumulative Update package.

In a few minutes you should receive an email from Microsoft, with a link to download a password-protected zip file of the Cumulative Update setup program. The password will be included with the email. The password is only good for seven days, so it is best to just unzip it immediately and be done with it.

Installing a SQL Server 2008 R2 Cumulative Update

You should be aware that installing a Cumulative Update will cause a service outage for SQL Server, since the SQL Server Service must be stopped and restarted during the installation. In some cases, installing a Cumulative Update will require a reboot of the entire server. Installing a Cumulative Update typically takes five to ten minutes, depending on your hardware and what SQL Server components you have installed.

You can minimize your down-time if you have a high availability solution (such as fail-over clustering, Database Mirroring, or SQL Server Denali AlwaysOn), and you patch your idle node, mirror, or replica, in a rolling update process.

When you are ready to install your Cumulative Update, just double-click on it and, after a few seconds, you will see the screen shown in Figure B.4.

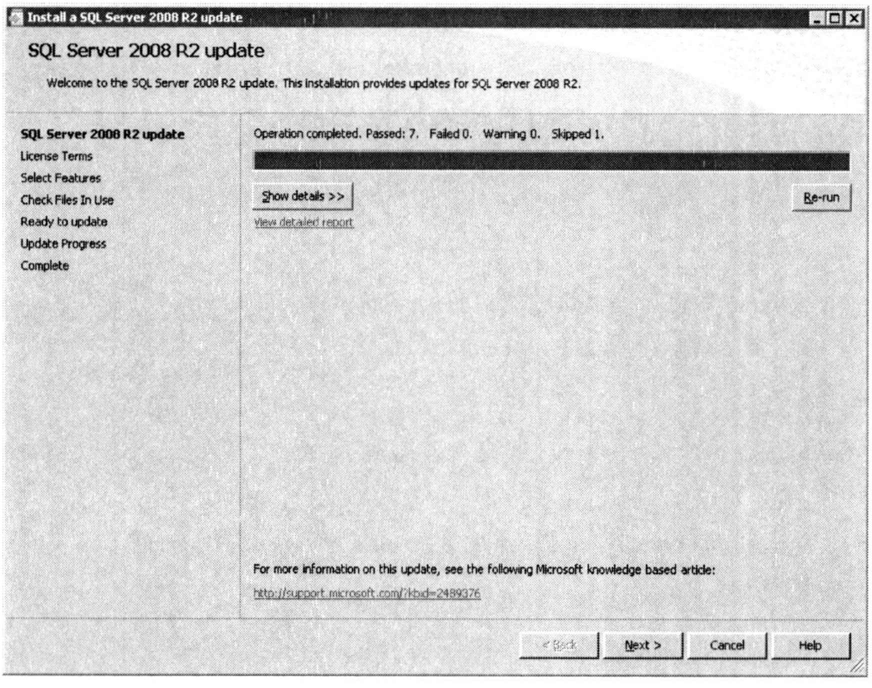

Figure B.4: Initial SQL Server 2008 R2 Cumulative Update screen.

After that, it is just a matter of clicking **Next** for pretty much every subsequent screen (Figures B.5 through B.10). You have to accept the license terms in order to proceed.

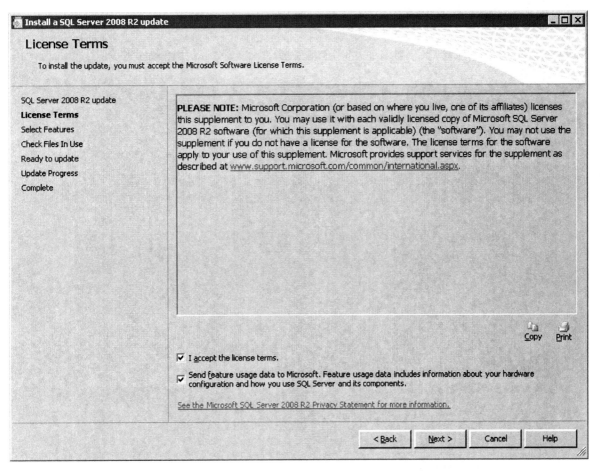

Figure B.5: SQL Server 2008 R2 Cumulative Update, License Terms screen.

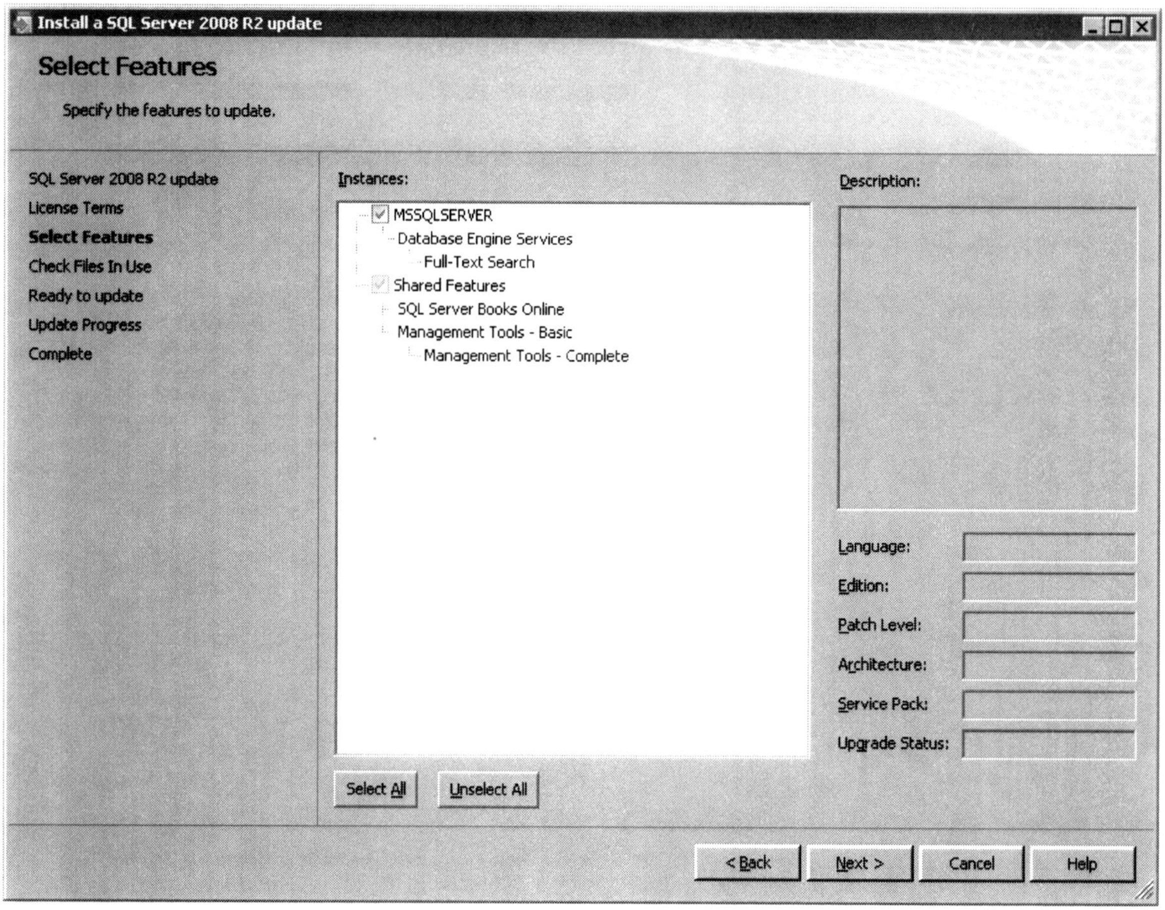

Figure B.6: SQL Server 2008 R2 Cumulative Update, Select Features screen.

You can minimize the chance of a restart by shutting down SSMS and any other SQL Server related services that you can.

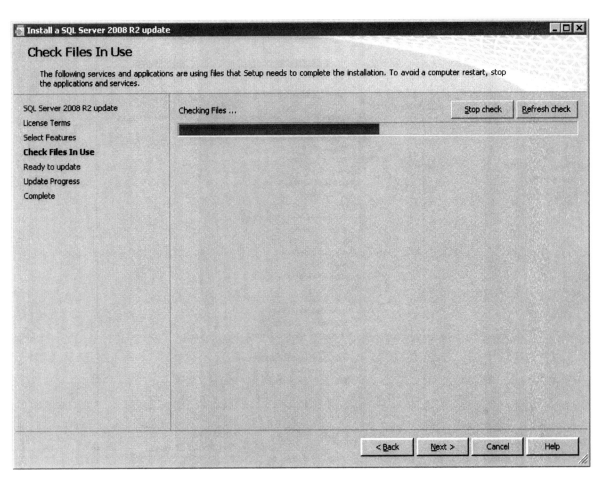

Figure B.7: SQL Server 2008 R2 Cumulative Update, Check Files In Use screen.

Click the **Update** button to start the installation.

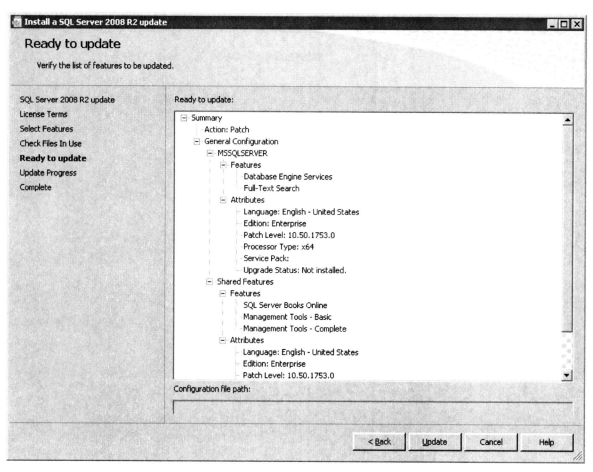

Figure B.8: SQL Server 2008 R2 Cumulative Update, Ready to update screen.

You'll sit at the Update Progress screen for a while.

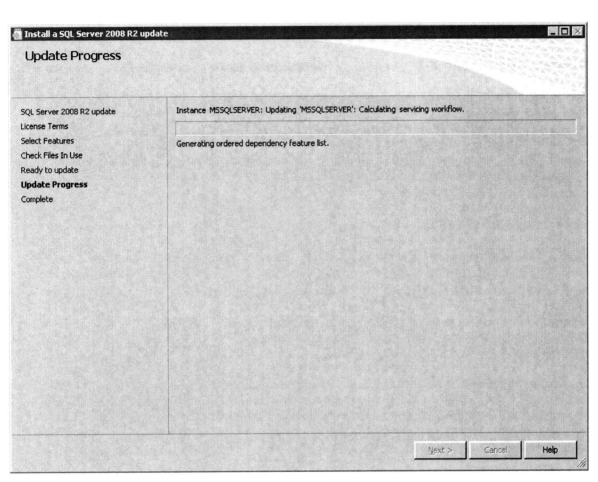

Figure B.9: SQL Server 2008 R2 Cumulative Update, Update Progress screen.

After perhaps five to ten minutes, the setup is done and you have installed the Cumulative Update.

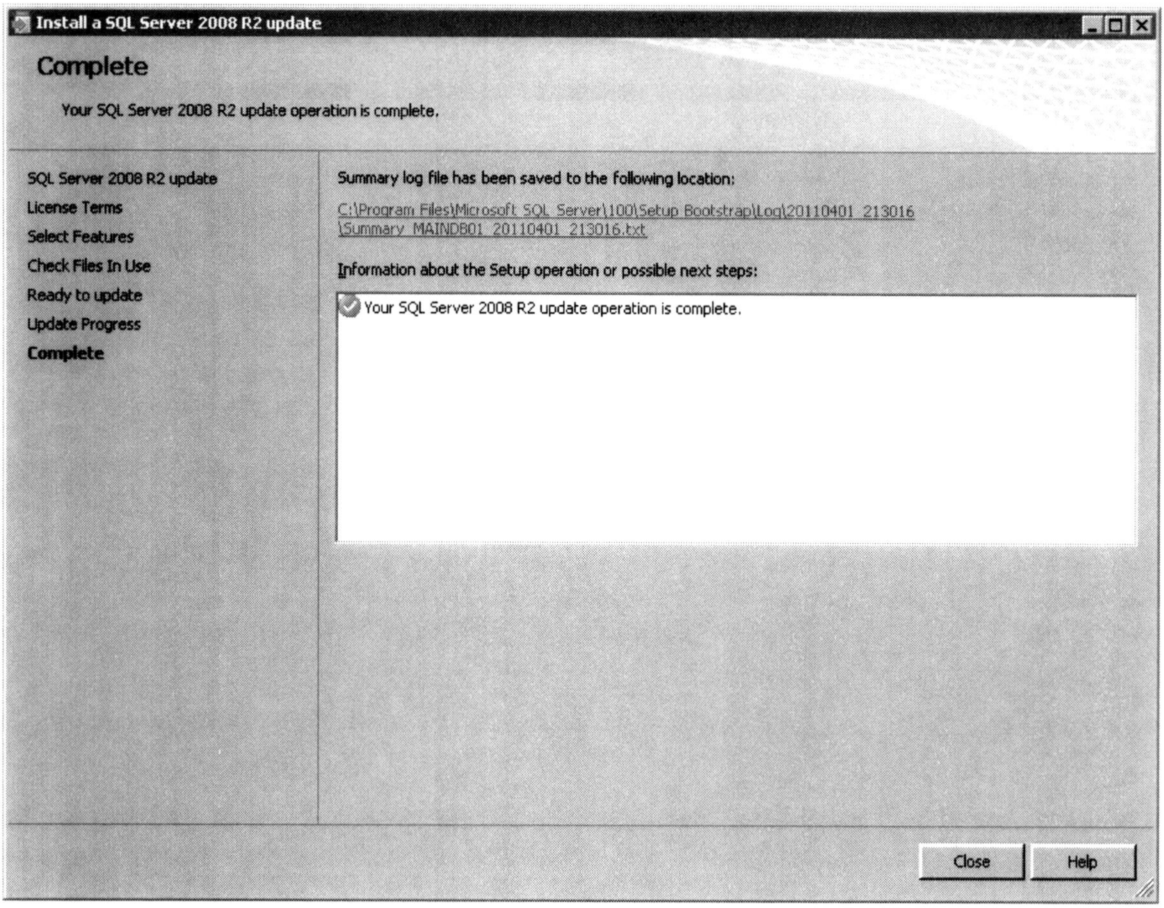

Figure B.10: SQL Server 2008 R2 Cumulative Update, Complete screen.

Appendix C: Abbreviations

AMB	Advanced Memory Buffer	DIMM	Dual In-Line Memory Modules
AMD	Advanced Micro Devices	DML	Data Manipulation Language
API	Application Programming Interface	DMV	Dynamic Management View
AWE	Address Windowing Extensions	DPV	Distributed Partitioned Views
BI	Business Intelligence	DRAM	Dynamic Random Access Memory
BIOS	Basic Input Output System	DSS	Decision Support System
CAL	Client Access License	DW	Data Warehouse
CDC	Change Data Capture	EE	Enterprise Edition
CIFS	Common Internet File System	EFD	Enterprise Flash Disks
CISC	Complex Instruction Set Computer	EIST	Enhanced Intel Speedstep Technology
CPI	Cost per Instruction	EP	Extended Protection
CSS	Customer Service and Support	EPIC	Explicitly Parallel Instruction Computing
CU	Cumulative Update	EPT	Extended Page Tables
DAC	Data Tier Application	FDR	Full Disclosure Report
DACPAC	Data Tier Application Package	HBA	Host Bus Adaptors
DAS	Direct Attached Storage	HT	Hyper-threading
DDL	Data Definition Language	IDE	Integrated Drive Electronics
DDR	Data Dependent Routing	ILP	Instruction Level Parallelism
DESC	(in T-SQL) Descending	IOP	Input Output Operation

IOPS	Input/Output Operations per Second		PK	Primary Key
ISM	Incremental Servicing Model		POST	Power On Self-Test
ISV	Independent Software Vendor		QPI	Quick Path Interconnect
LPIM	Lock Pages in Memory		RAID	Redundant Array of Independent Disk
LUN	Logical Unit Number		RAS	Reliability, Availability and Serviceability
MAXDOP	Max Degree of Parallelism		RDIMM	Registered Dual In-Line Memory Modules
MCH	Memory Controller Hub		RISC	Reduced Instruction Set Computer
MDS	Master Data Services		RPO	Recovery Point Objective
MLC	Multi Level Cell		RTM	Release to Manufacturing
MMC	Microsoft Management Console		RTO	Recovery Time Objective
MPIO	Multi Path Input Output		RVI	Rapid Virtualization Indexing
NIC	Network Interface Card		SAN	Storage Area Network
NTLM	NT Lan Manager		SAS	Serial Attached SCSI
NUMA	Non-Uniform Memory Architecture		SATA	Serial Advanced Technology Attachment
ODBC	Open Database Connectivity		SCOM	System Center Operations Manager
OEM	Original Equipment Manufacturer		SCSI	Small Computer System Interface
OLAP	Online Analytical Processing		SKU	Stock Keeping Unit
OLTP	Online Transaction Processing		SLAT	Second Level Address Translation
OMSA	OpenManage Server Administrator		SLC	Single Level Cell
PAE	Physical Address Extension		SMB	Server Message Block
PATA	Parallel Advanced Technology Attachment		SMP	Symmetrical Multiprocessing
PCU	Public Cumulative Update		SPD	Serial Presence Detect

SPEC	Standard Performance Evaluation Corporation
SQLCAT	SQL Server Customer Advisory Team
SQLIO	SQL IO, a disk benchmarking utility
SQLOS	SQL Server Operating System
SSAS	SQL Server Analysis Services
SSD	Solid-State Drives
SSMS	SQL Server Management Studio
SSRS	SQL Server Reporting Services
SUT	System Under Test
TAP	Technology Adoption Program
TDE	Transparent Data Encryption
TPC	Transaction Processing Performance Council
TpsE	Transactions per second for TPC-E benchmark
UCP	Utility Control Point
VAS	Virtual Address Space
VT	Virtual Technology
WSUS	Windows Server Update Services

Index

Symbols

A

B

C

D

.NET and
SQL Server Tools
from Red Gate Software

SQL Compare® Pro

$595

Compare and synchronize SQL Server database schemas

↗ Eliminate mistakes migrating database changes from dev, to test, to production

↗ Speed up the deployment of new databse schema updates

↗ Find and fix errors caused by differences between databases

↗ Compare and synchronize within SSMS

> **"Just purchased SQL Compare. With the productivity I'll get out of this tool, it's like buying time."**
>
> **Robert Sondles** Blueberry Island Media Ltd

SQL Data Compare Pro

$595

Compares and synchronizes SQL Server database contents

↗ Save time by automatically comparing and synchronizing your data

↗ Copy lookup data from development databases to staging or production

↗ Quickly fix problems by restoring damaged or missing data to a single row

↗ Compare and synchronize data within SSMS

> **"We use SQL Data Compare daily and it has become an indispensable part of delivering our service to our customers. It has also streamlined our daily update process and cut back literally a good solid hour per day."**
>
> **George Pantela** GPAnalysis.com

Visit **www.red-gate.com** for a 14-day, free trial

SQL Prompt Pro

$295

Write, edit, and explore SQL effortlessly

↗ Write SQL smoothly, with code-completion and SQL snippets

↗ Reformat SQL to a preferred style

↗ Keep databases tidy by finding invalid objects automatically

↗ Save time and effort with script summaries, smart object renaming and more

> **"SQL Prompt is hands-down one of the coolest applications I've used. Makes querying/developing so much easier and faster."**
> **Jorge Segarra** University Community Hospital

SQL Source Control

$295

Connect your existing source control system to SQL Server

↗ Bring all the benefits of source control to your database

↗ Source control schemas and data within SSMS, not with offline scripts

↗ Connect your databases to TFS, SVN, SourceGear Vault, Vault Pro, Mercurial, Perforce, Git, Bazaar, and any source control system with a capable command line

↗ Work with shared development databases, or individual copies

↗ Track changes to follow who changed what, when, and why

↗ Keep teams in sync with easy access to the latest database version

↗ View database development history for easy retrieval of specific versions

> **"After using SQL Source Control for several months, I wondered how I got by before. Highly recommended, it has paid for itself several times over"**
> **Ben Ashley** Fast Floor

Visit **www.red-gate.com** for a 28-day, free trial

SQL Monitor

SQL Server performance monitoring and alerting

↗ Intuitive overviews at global, cluster, machine, SQL Server,
and database levels for up-to-the-minute performance data

↗ Use SQL Monitor's web UI to keep an eye on server performance
in real time on desktop machines and mobile devices

↗ Intelligent SQL Server alerts via email and an alert inbox in the
UI, so you know about problems first

↗ Comprehensive historical data, so you can go back in time to
identify the source of a problem

↗ Generate reports via the UI or with Red Gate's free SSRS Reporting Pack

↗ View the top 10 expensive queries for an instance or database
based on CPU usage, duration and reads and writes

↗ PagerDuty integration for phone and SMS alerting

↗ Fast, simple installation and administration

> **"Being web based, SQL Monitor is readily
> available to you, wherever you may be on your
> network. You can check on your servers from
> almost any location, via most mobile devices
> that support a web browser."**
>
> **Jonathan Allen** Senior DBA, Careers South West Ltd

SQL Virtual Restore $495

Rapidly mount live, fully functional databases direct from backups

- ↗ Virtually restoring a backup requires significantly less time and space than a regular physical restore
- ↗ Databases mounted with SQL Virtual Restore are fully functional and support both read/write operations
- ↗ SQL Virtual Restore is ACID compliant and gives you access to full, transactionally consistent data, with all objects visible and available
- ↗ Use SQL Virtual Restore to recover objects, verify your backups with DBCC CHECKDB, create a storage-efficient copy of your production database, and more.

> **"We find occasions where someone has deleted data accidentally or dropped an index etc., and with SQL Virtual Restore we can mount last night's backup quickly and easily to get access to the data or the original schema. It even works with all our backups being encrypted. This takes any extra load off our production server. SQL Virtual Restore is a great product."**
>
> **Brent McCraken** Senior Database Administrator/Architect, Kiwibank Limited

SQL Storage Compress $1,595

Silent data compression to optimize SQL Server storage

- ↗ Reduce the storage footprint of live SQL Server databases by up to 90% to save on space and hardware costs
- ↗ Databases compressed with SQL Storage Compress are fully functional
- ↗ Prevent unauthorized access to your live databases with 256-bit AES encryption
- ↗ Integrates seamlessly with SQL Server and does not require any configuration changes

Visit **www.red-gate.com** for a 14-day, free trial

SQL Toolbelt

$1,995

The essential SQL Server tools for database professionals

You can buy our acclaimed SQL Server tools individually or bundled. Our most popular deal is the SQL Toolbelt: fourteen of our SQL Server tools in a single installer, with **a combined value of $5,930 but an actual price of $1,995**, a saving of 66%.

Fully compatible with SQL Server 2000, 2005, and 2008.

SQL Toolbelt contains:

↗ **SQL Compare Pro**

↗ **SQL Data Compare Pro**

↗ **SQL Source Control**

↗ **SQL Backup Pro**

↗ **SQL Monitor**

↗ **SQL Prompt Pro**

↗ **SQL Data Generator**

↗ **SQL Doc**

↗ **SQL Dependency Tracker**

↗ **SQL Packager**

↗ **SQL Multi Script Unlimited**

↗ **SQL Search**

↗ **SQL Comparison SDK**

↗ **SQL Object Level Recovery Native**

> **"The SQL Toolbelt provides tools that database developers, as well as DBAs, should not live without."**
>
> **William Van Orden** Senior Database Developer, Lockheed Martin

Visit **www.red-gate.com** for a 14-day, free trial

Performance Tuning with SQL Server
Dynamic Management Views

Louis Davidson and Tim Ford

This is the book that will de-mystify the process of using Dynamic Management Views to collect the information you need to troubleshoot SQL Server problems. It will highlight the core techniques and "patterns" that you need to master, and will provide a core set of scripts that you can use and adapt for your own requirements.

ISBN: 978-1-906434-47-2
Published: October 2010

Defensive Database Programming

Alex Kuznetsov

Inside this book, you will find dozens of practical, defensive programming techniques that will improve the quality of your T-SQL code and increase its resilience and robustness.

ISBN: 978-1-906434-49-6
Published: June 2010

Brad's Sure Guide to
SQL Server Maintenance Plans

Brad McGehee

Brad's Sure Guide to Maintenance Plans shows you how to use the Maintenance Plan Wizard and Designer to configure and schedule eleven core database maintenance tasks, ranging from integrity checks, to database backups, to index reorganizations and rebuilds.

ISBN: 78-1-906434-34-2
Published: December 2009

The Red Gate Guide to SQL Server
Team-based Development

Phil Factor, Grant Fritchey, Alex Kuznetsov, and Mladen Prajdić

This book shows how to use of mixture of home-grown scripts, native SQL Server tools, and tools from the Red Gate SQL Toolbelt, to successfully develop database applications in a team environment, and make database development as similar as possible to "normal" development.

ISBN: 978-1-906434-59-5
Published: November 2010

CPSIA information can be obtained at www.ICGtesting.com
Printed in the USA
LVOW110622140912

298769LV00001B/3/P

9 781906 434632